JONATHAN SWIFT:
THE CONTEMPORARY
BACKGROUND

CLIVE T. PROBYN

*Literature
in context*

Manchester
University Press

First published 1978
by Manchester University Press
Oxford Road, Manchester M13 9PL

British Library cataloguing in publication data

Probyn, Clive T
 Jonathan Swift, the contemporary background. —
 (Literature in context).
 1. Great Britain — Social conditions —
 Addresses, essays, lectures
 I. Title II. Series
 309.1'41'06   HN385.5

ISBN 0-7190-0697-X (cased)
ISBN 0-7190-0729-1 (paperback)

Computerised Phototypesetting
by G C Typeset Ltd., Bolton, Greater Manchester

Printed in Great Britain
by the Pitman Press, Bath

Contents

Illustrations

General editor's preface

One of the basic problems in reading literature is that of establishing a context for it. In the end the context of any work is infinite and unknowable. But if we approach the problem more simple-mindedly (and ignore questions posed by biography) we can say that a work's context is to a large extent definable by the ideas—theological, philosophical, political, and so on—current in the period in which it was written, and by the literary forms and genres that a period fosters and prefers. It is the ultimate aim of this series to try to help the student of English literature place works of all periods in their various contexts by providing volumes containing annotated selections of important background texts on the assumption that it is through contact with original texts only that true understanding may develop. Some of the volumes will be wide-ranging within a given period, containing a variety of texts (some in full, some extracts) illustrating dominant ideas and themes or forms; others will be more specialised, offering background material to the ideas and forms embodied in individual works of a particular author or concentrating on one or two thematic obsessions of a period. Although the emphasis is on English literature, much of the background material adduced will be of European origin. This will be presented in translation and, in appropriate cases (usually verse), the original will be printed with a translation on the facing page. The series should thus be of use to students pursuing comparative literature courses as well as interdisciplinary courses involving literature. In each volume there will be a substantial introduction, explanatory headnotes to the texts, and a bibliography of suggested further reading.

Douglas Brooks-Davies

For the Probyns
majores et pueri
and for Meg,
sine qua non

Introduction

For reasons that will, I hope, become clear in a moment, the nature of this book necessitates only a brief general introduction. My aim is a practical one: to understand Swift's work in its own time. This book is addressed to the reader who has already begun to ask questions about the society and the cultural context which first sustained Swift's work, and some knowledge of Swift's work is assumed. His major works, the *Tale of a Tub* volume, *A Modest Proposal,* the *Drapier's Letters*, *An Argument Against Abolishing Christianity*, and *Gulliver's Travels*, have provided the stimulus for and are the eventual focus of the following choice of passages. My selection has been based on two assumptions: that Swift's work is enriched when set into its contemporary context, and that such an approach makes Swift's work more rather than less relevant to us as readers today.

Even a cursory reading of Swift will show that we are dealing with a writer whose creativity was provoked by external events rather than by inner needs for self-expression: his work is generally a reply to an already existing situation rather than an opening, and his positive values emerge and are stated through conflict and counter-argument with others. It is untrue to say that Swift never wrote for the sheer pleasure of composition, but typically he wrote to fulfil a public purpose. This book is therefore designed to establish the public arena in which Swift was a key protagonist. It does so by providing *some* of the works of his opponents, antagonists, models, allies and sources.

Clearly, what follows should be regarded only as a primer, and not an exclusive choice of the possible material. But within the restrictive limits of a single volume I have attempted to work broadly within seven topic areas, each of which is introduced by a preliminary essay relating Swift's work to the passages chosen. All I shall attempt now is to indicate the process of this contextual dialogue by one or two examples.

Swift regarded his appointment to the Deanery of St Patrick's Dublin in 1713 as a sentence of exile imposed after the collapse of the Tory ministry of his friends Harley and St John. Fortunately, both for us and for Ireland at the time, he broke his vow never to meddle in Irish politics and the 1720s saw a stream of writings on Irish trade and political themes. In the fourth of his *Drapier's Letters* Swift's arguments involved the use of Locke's ideas on the social compact, consent and the rights of conquest. In short, Swift was taking steps to apply the most recent and influential political philosophy in Locke's *Second Treatise of Government* (1690) to the particular case of Ireland in order to vindicate Irish claims for equality under the crown of England. Swift was not the first to write on this vexed question. His most celebrated predecessor was William Molyneux, who had written what appeared to many to be the authoritative argument for the inclusion of Ireland within Locke's political theory. There are thus three states of this argument, each individually tailored to suit particular occasions and audiences. In chapter 16 of Locke's *Second Treatise* we find the 'source' formulation:–

Though Governments can originally have no other Rise than that before mentioned, nor *Polities* be founded on any thing but *the Consent of the People*; yet such has been the Disorders Ambition has fill'd the World with, that in the Noise of War, which makes so great a part of the History of Mankind, this *Consent* is little taken notice of: And therefore many have mistaken the force of Arms, for the Consent of the People; and reckon Conquest as one of the Originals of Government.

In the *Case of Ireland* (1698) Molyneux draws heavily on Locke's work and uses its authority to validate his own claims for Irish equality:

It may seem a strange Doctrine, that any one should have a Power over the Life of another Man, and not over his Estate; but this we find every Day, for tho' I may *kill* a Thief that sets on me in the High way, yet I may not take away his *Money*; for 'tis the Brutal Force the Aggressor has used, that gives his Adversary a Right to take away his Life, as a noxious Creature . . .

It must be confes'd that the Practice of the World is otherwise, and we commonly see the Conqueror (whether Just or Unjust) by the Force he has over the Conquer'd, compels them with a Sword at their Breast to stoop to his Conditions, and submit to such a Government as he pleases to afford them. But we enquire not now, what is the Practice, but what *Right there is to do so*. If it be said the Conquered submit by their own *Consent*; then this allows *Consent* necessary to give the Conqueror a Title to Rule over them.

Swift's Drapier, inheritor of Locke's political theory and disciple of Molyneux, puts the point thus:

It is true, that within the Memory of Man, the Parliaments of *England* have sometimes assumed the Power of binding this Kingdom, by Laws enacted there, wherein they were at first openly opposed (as far as *Truth, Reason*, and *Justice* are capable of opposing) by the famous Mr. Molineux, an *English* Gentleman born here; as well as by several of the greatest Patriots, and *best Whigs in England*; but the *Love and Torrent* of Power prevailed. Indeed, the Arguments on both Sides were invincible. For in *Reason*, all *Government* without the Consent of the *Governed*, is the very *Definition of Slavery*: But in *Fact, Eleven Men well armed, will certainly subdue one single Man in his Shirt*. But I have done. For those who have used *Power* to cramp *Liberty*, have gone so far as to resent even the Liberty of *Complaining*; although a Man upon the Rack, was never known to be refused the Liberty of roaring as loud as he thought fit.

The juxtaposition of these three passages shows several things. First, the explicit and implicit authorities marshalled behind the Drapier's position on Irish constitutional relationships with England (Molyneux is named, Locke's ideas and some phraseology are foregrounded); second, these passages together offer a clear line of development from a theoretical and detached political argument to the individual urgency of committed polemic; and third, their proximity in terms of shared ideas and contrasting tones and styles offers the material for a comparative analysis. In the first passage Locke halts in his sequential argument in order to point out the discrepancy which exists between a theoretical right and its neglect in political reality. Molyneux similarly chooses discursive argument (and elsewhere exhaustive lists of legal precedents) in order to make his point. The *Case* was directed at the Westminster politicians who were deliberating on further legislation to penalise Irish trade. Swift's Drapier, by contrast, makes a very different appeal though with the same material. He is weary of elaborating a point of constitutional theory which is already known, which has been stressed before, but which has proved ineffectual ('the Arguments ... were invincible'). Thus he combines a known, inoperative, theoretical point with a dramatic image of human anguish (the rack) and conveys his own desperation in a terse, almost throwaway style. His appeal is thus sharply focussed by the context: the government which acknowledges the wisdom of Locke's theories in general is the same government which turns a deaf ear to Irish self-assertion in particular. To political theory Swift adds a personal *cri de coeur* and an image of cruel torment: his essential appeal is to anyone with a sense of common humanity and minimal justice. Swift's own case for Ireland is thus an accumulation of disparate elements assumed as common knowledge in his contemporary audience (a reminder of their shameful inaction) with the unique injection of its results—a casual cruelty. Conscience and intellect are thus simultaneously invoked because the more objective writing of the political theorists has failed to bite.

The relationship between the fourth Drapier's letter and Molyneux' *Case of Ireland* is indicated by the Drapier's allusion: each is allied with the other in a common ideological cause, though each fights that battle with different weapons. Swift always exploited his sources in a fresh and creative way. His major satiric method is aggressive in a particular sense, however, and could be described as subversive imitation. The mood of parody in Swift's work is ever-present. It is the least autonomous of devices, a parasitic growth feeding off the errors imputed to a parent-model, and meaningless without some awareness in the reader of the parodied model. Swift was very much aware of this intrinsic limitation. In the Apology to *A Tale of a Tub* he asserted that the work 'seems calculated to live at least as long as our Language and Taste admit no great Alterations', but found it necessary to point out even to his contemporary audience the identity of two of the writers (Dryden and L'Estrange) thus attacked. Identification of the—parodied models is an important starting point, for Swift used parody not merely as a literary sleight of hand, nor because of any moral or artistic uncertainty of his own, but as a deliberate close-quarters technique of subverting an opponent's argument, rationality, dignity and reputation; exploding cant, hypocrisy, and theoretical constructs from within. Tactically, Swift as a satirist is a fifth-columnist, adopting his opponent's uniform in order to sabotage from within the fortress. Swift believed that the control-exercised by reason over the human personality was precarious, that it was 'a very light Rider, and easily shook off' (*Digression on Madness*). Rational appeals could make no progress where pride and self-interest were concerned. The effect of this on his literary techniques was crucial, for it led to the gradual abandonment of discursive methods of formal argument in favour of oblique attacks through satire and irony. A precise example is supplied by the evolution of the *Argument against Abolishing Christianity*, a *tour de force* of the Swiftian method. Here Swift's own positive convictions become puny negative values whilst the true objects of his attack are given all the best arguments (or so it seems). In fact Swift had begun a serious counter-argument to Tindal's *Rights of the Christian Church Asserted* (see section III, item 7 and notes below) but had given up the attempt. In his preferred ironic mode deists and freethinkers such as Tindal are revealed as even greater threats to Swift's established Church than they in fact were because the Anglican apologists are given patently ridiculous arguments in their campaign against them. Thus the Church is shown to be in greater peril from the merely nominal Christians who refuse to stand up in their own defence against the Tindals. In the mixed mode of satire friends and foes desert their ranks and are drawn into unexpected alliance by the puppet-master Swift, the master of the volte-face.

Tindal's rationalistic clothes are merely one item in Swift's occasional wardrobe. The uniform of the political arithmetician or economist is worn in *A Modest Proposal*. In 1729 this pamphlet was a bitter indictment of those responsible for Ireland's misery. Its particular attack was directed against the failure of the specialised economists, of whom Sir William Petty (see item 16 below) was the most important as far as Ireland was concerned. The immediate background of Swift's pamphlet reinforces Swift's own indignation, since the gap between Swift's fantasy of cannibalism and the barbarism of Petty's serious proposal is, in human terms, so narrow. The pamphlet remains a fierce protest against the exploitation of humanity in the mass by the detached, 'expert' theorist, and should remind us of the vile politics of mass deportation in our own more recent past. Conversely, the anti-Puritan passages in *A Tale of a Tub* may seem to anticipate 'modern' theories of sexual repression as the cause of compensatory obsessions (in this case the charge is that of a

5

physiologically-based religious mania), but their modernity is at least as old as the Commonwealth attacks of Henry More (see item 1 below). Inevitably, in such a case, questions are raised about Swift's satirical timing, about his envisaged audience, and their cultural assumptions.

Sometimes no parodic or imitative intention is present, but close reference is maintained to texts which directly influenced the formulation and presentation of ideas, plots, and satirical situations. The *Essay upon Ancient and Modern Learning* (item 3 below) by Swift's sometime mentor and employer Sir William Temple, supplied the plot and working basis for Swift's loyalties in *The Battle of the Books*. The political journalism of Swift's friend — Bolingbroke (items 14 and 15) is similarly a complement rather than an alternative to Swift's various devices of attacking Walpole's government in *Gulliver's Travels* and in the *Contests and Dissensions*. The section which I have termed *The nature of man* clearly moves into more abstract territory, but this is a part of the intellectual topography of the most complex satire in the English language (items 21, 22).

The territory of Swift's mind and imagination is not limited to the years of his life (1667–1745), peculiarly eventful though they were. This platitude should not conceal the fact that Swift was writing in a context of post-Renaissance European Christianity steeped in classical learning. For his satire the consequences are that both targets and weapons often turn out to be cultural 'constants', i.e. conventional in many of their features, and not limited to Swift's own time. When Swift attacked the Lagadian scientists for their preposterous scientific experiments in the third voyage of *Gulliver's Travels*, and for their manic obsession with mathematics, Swift no doubt had his eye on the Royal Society of his day (see items 18, 19, 20 below), yet the Lagadian approach to the universe is in its comic essence a burlesque of a long and distinguished tradition of drawing analogies between mathematics and the physical creation, found in Pythagoras' speculations on musical, astronomical and mathematical harmony in the fifth century B.C., in the work of Robert Fludd (1574–1637), in Joseph Kepler's *Harmonice Mundi* (1619), in Renaissance architectural theories, and in Shaftesbury's speculations in Swift's own period (see, for example, Rudolf Wittkower's *Architectural Principles in the Age of Humanism*, Tiranti, London, 1971, part four). Similarly, elements of the conceptual framework of Gulliver's fourth voyage are Aristotelian in their provenance, a fact which reminds us that for men of Swift's generation the classical tradition of philosophy and literature was not so much dead history as the current affairs of civilised discourse (as well as the materials of a traditional educational syllabus). It should not surprise us that Swift writes about an inherited intellectual world, however original his genius, for we in turn interpret *his* work in the context of our own contemporary awarenesses. Swift's insight is not something we can do without. He is the chameleon of literary style, a master of situations who habitually wears the masks of the satirist's office. What now follows could be regarded as a selection of the ready-made materials from which Swift fashioned his unique satirical garments.

TEXTUAL NOTE

Obvious errors and possibly misleading punctuation have been silently corrected, and extensive passages of italicised text have been generally downgraded. Contractions have been expanded where necessary, and a series of dots (. . .) or a space on the page indicate editorial cuts made for the present book. In all other respects the texts are reproduced as in the editions cited in the notes. In four cases I have preferred reliable modern editions. The following abbreviations are used throughout:

Prose The Prose Works of Jonathan Swift, ed. Herbert Davis and others, 14 vols. (Blackwell, Oxford, 1939–68).

Correspondence The Correspondence of Jonathan Swift, ed. Harold Williams, 5 vols. (Oxford, Clarendon Press, 1963–5).

Poems The Poems of Jonathan Swift, ed. Harold Williams, 3 vols. (second edition, Clarendon Press, Oxford, 1958).

Tale A Tale of a Tub, to which is added The Battle of the Books and the Mechanical Operation of the Spirit, ed. A. C. Guthkelch and D. Nichol Smith (second edition, Clarendon Press, Oxford, 1958).

Ehrenpreis, *Swift* Irvin Ehrenpreis, *Swift, The Man, his Works and the Age*, 2 vols. (Methuen, London; I, 1962; II, 1967).

Thanks are due to Cambridge University Press for permission to reproduce extracts from *The Economic Writings of Sir William Petty*, ed. C. H. Hull, 2 vols. (Cambridge University Press, 1899).

SURVEY OF SWIFT'S LIFE AND WORKS

1667   Jonathan Swift born in Dublin, 30 November, of English parents

1673–81   Attends Kilkenny College

1682–89   Trinity College Dublin; B.A. in 1686

1689   Goes to Leicester after violence in Ireland following Revolution in England; secretary to Sir William Temple at Moor Park, Surrey; meets Esther Johnson ('Stella')

1690   Returns to Ireland

1691   Returns to his former employment at Moor Park

1692   M.A. from Oxford; *Ode to the Athenian Society*

1694   Returns to Ireland and is ordained in the Anglican Church

1695   Appointed prebendary of Kilroot

1696–99   *A Tale of a Tub*, etc. written; Temple dies in January 1699; chaplain to Berkeley, Lord Justice of Ireland

1700   Vicar of Laracor

1701   Writes *Contests and Dissensions* (the *Tale* was to be dedicated to one of the Whig lords, Somers, defended in this tract)

1702   Doctor of Divinity degree from Trinity College

1702–4   Resident in England, but resident in Ireland in October 1702 to November 1703; *Tale* published in 1704

1707–9   Represented Irish clergy seeking remission of the clerical taxes ('first fruits'), rejected by Whig government

1708   *Sentiments of a Church of England Man* written, published 1711

1710–13   *Miscellanies in Verse and Prose*; *Argument Against Abolishing Christianity* (published in 1711); returns to London for four years, shifting allegiance from Whigs to Tories; *The Examiner* papers; *The Conduct of the Allies*; friendship with Harley and Bolingbroke

1713   Dean of St. Patrick's Cathedral, Dublin; *Cadenus and Vanessa* (Esther Vanhomrigh)

1714   Swift and others form the Scriblerus Club; returns to permanent residence in Ireland after the death of Queen Anne and fall of the Tory government; *The Publick Spirit of the Whigs*

1720   Begins to write Irish tracts; *A Proposal for the Universal Use of Irish Manufacture*

1721   Begins to write *Gulliver's Travels*

1724   *Drapier's Letters*, I–V

1726   *Gulliver's Travels* published, October 28, Swift having visited England, left the manuscript with the London bookseller Motte, and returned to Dublin

1727   Last trip to England, April

1729   *A Modest Proposal*

1730   Swift given the Freedom of the City of Dublin

1731   *Verses on the Death of Dr Swift* (published 1739)

1735   Collected edition of Swift's works, in four volumes, published by George Faulkner, Dublin
1742   His health failing, Swift was committed to the care of guardians
1745   October 19, Swift dies; buried in St. Patrick's Cathedral
1758   *History of the Four Last years of the Queen* published.

HISTORICAL EVENTS AND SOME LEGISLATION

1660   Restoration of Charles II; foundation of Royal Society (chartered in 1662)
1666   Irish Cattle Act: penal legislation prohibiting importation of cattle into England (as 'a public and common nuisance'); Woollen and Navigation Acts of the same period and nature
1667   War with Holland
1668   Sir William Temple negotiates the Triple Alliance of England, Holland and Sweden to curb the power of France
1678   The 'Popish Plot'
1679–81   The 'Exclusion Crisis': attempts to exclude James, Charles II's Catholic brother from the throne
1685   Charles II dies
1687   James II issues Declaration of Indulgence, suspending tests and granting liberty of worship to Protestant and Catholic dissenters
1688–9   Attainder Act: James provides for largely Catholic re-settlement of Ireland
    War of the League of Augsburg (1689–97) and War of the Spanish Succession
    James II's religious and political policies culminate in the 'Glorious Revolution'; William of Orange lands at Torbay on November 5; James flees to France.
1689   William summons Convention parliament: Bill of Rights defines the limits of royal power under the Parliament
    Toleration Act; limited toleration extended to Catholics and dissenters in England
    Catholic revolt in Ireland (as in 1641); siege of Londonderry; William's victory at the Battle of the Boyne
1694   Queen Mary dies
    Establishment of the Bank of England
1695   Expiry of the Licensing Act, lifting censorship of the press
1697   Treaty of Ryswick confirms William's power and ensures no help for England's enemies from France
1698   English House of Commons reject Ireland's claim for independence, condemning Molyneux' *Case* as 'bold and pernicious'
1701   Act of Settlement fixed Protestant succession in the House of Hanover

9

1702 William III dies (March); accession of Queen Anne
Declaration of War on France and Spain
1704 Sacramental Test extended to Ireland; Anne surrenders first fruits
and tenths to English clergy
1707 Act of Union with Scotland: 'Great Britain'
1709–10 Sacheverell affair
Fall of the Whigs; Tory victory (ministry of Harley with St John; Swift
as Tory pamphleteer)
1711 Occasional Conformity Bill prohibits dissenters taking occasional
Anglican communion in order to qualify for public office
1713 Peace treaties between England and France signed at Utrecht,
ending War of Spanish Succession; France abandons Pretender and
recognises House of Hanover
1714 Quarrel between Harley and St John; Queen Anne dies; Elector of
Hanover proclaimed George I; George dismisses all Tories; Harley
imprisoned in Tower, Bolingbroke flees to France. Whig ministries until
the end of the century
1715 Invasion of Scotland by 'Old Pretender'
1719 Declaratory Act enforces dependence of Ireland, denies Irish
Lords any power to alter judgements made in England
Toleration Acts extended to Irish protestant dissenters; thereafter Test
modified until its removal in 1780.
1720 English Parliament abolishes right of the Irish House of Lords to
act as Court of Appeal
'South Sea Year'; the climax of speculation; collapse of scheme in
1721. Walpole becomes 'prime minister' for next twenty-two years.
1723 Bolingbroke returns from France and establishes extra-
parliamentary opposition to Walpole
1727 Death of George I; succeeded by son George II
1739 War declared on Spain; unsuccessfully prosecuted by Walpole
1741 Motions in Parliament to remove Walpole; resigns in 1742
1745 Invasion of England by Charles Edward, the 'Young Pretender';
routed at Culloden in 1746 by Duke of Cumberland, George II's son.

I

Satire on
dissent and enthusiasm

The religious satire in *A Tale of a Tub* is largely indebted for its techniques to a long tradition of seventeenth-century Anglican apologetics. The *Tale's* intellectual comedy, allusiveness and verbal wit compose a satiric image of a certain type of religious writing which to many seemed to overemphasise symbolic meaning, allegorical interpretation and the mysterious sides of religion. Whether in fact or by prejudice, such qualities were associated with the non-conformist sects, with the Puritans, Quakers, Anabaptists, and also with the earlier mystical writers such as Paracelsus[1] and Thomas Vaughan. Enthusiasm, of which they all stood accused, was a key word in the pejorative vocabulary of the Age of Reason. In *An Essay Concerning Human Understanding*, book IV, xix (1690), Locke defined it as being founded neither on reason nor revelation but arising from the conceits 'of a warmed and overweening Brain'. In Johnson's *Dictionary* (1755), it is defined as 'a vain belief of private revelation; a vain confidence of divine favour or communication'. The enthusiasm of self-righteous Puritans was often related as a cause of the Civil War.

In his satire on modern learning in the *Tale*, Swift gave currency and continuity to anti-enthusiastic writings by associating religious enthusiasm with Modern textual critics and scholars such as Bentley.[2] As the first of the following extracts shows, there was a distinguished history behind Swift's technique of reducing both spiritual claims and intellectual schemes to their physical causes. More's tract is complementary in its method to Swift's *Tale*, though a generation earlier than it. Edwards's *The Preacher* is contemporary with the *Tale* and attacks the same targets from a non-satirical point of view.

The tradition of regarding enthusiasm as the result of physical maladjustment was begun by Meric Casaubon (the tutor of Henry Wotton, William's father), in his tediously argued *Treatise Concerning Enthusiasme: As it is an Effect of Nature: but is mistaken by many for either Divine Inspiration, or Diabolical Possession* (1655). Henry More, the Cambridge Platonist, refers to the method of this work in his *Enthusiasmus Triumphatus* (1656), but the immediate cause of his satirical exposure of enthusiasm was the work of the Rosicrucian Thomas Vaughan. Swift refers to Vaughan a dozen times in the *Tale*, and in particular to his *Anima Magica Abscondita* and *Anthroposophia Theomagica*, described as 'a Piece of the most unintelligible Fustian, that, perhaps, was ever publish'd in any Language'. Like Swift after him, More lumped together religious enthusiasts and occultists like Vaughan in order to ridicule their abstruse nonsense. Their intellectual pretensions are scathingly undercut by a depiction of their alleged physical causes, such as melancholy and, as in Swift's *Tale*, sexual repression. More's sketches are not restricted to the realm of religious enthusiasm, and he includes political and philosophical branches, both of which reappear in a more generalised and contemporary application in the *Tale*. In the 'Digression upon Madness' the fountains of enthusiasm are seen to infect all those who create systems and achieve conquests, in short all those whose conviction of personal superiority over their fellows leads them to systematise life and impose their own will on others. In this distinguished company of lunatic individualists may be found experimental philosophers, great heroes, and founders of religious sects: Descartes, Alexander the Great, and the Anabaptist leader Jack of Leyden. *The Mechanical Operation of the Spirit*, a logical elaboration of the satire on enthusiasm begun in the *Tale*, goes on to list the more or less futile or chimerical activities which have nourished the grain of enthusiasm, such as the search for the 'Philosopher's Stone; The Grand Elixir; The Planetary Worlds; The Squaring of the Circle; The Summum Bonum; Utopian Commonwealths'. For the narrator of the *Tale* the 'parent of all those mighty Revolutions, that have happened in Empire, in Philosophy, and in *Religion*' has been enthusiasm, now equated with madness. But this universal explanation of everyone else's ills becomes the hobby-horse, or 'humor', of Swift's narrator. Later on, at the end of the Digression, he himself is revealed as an enthusiast and a self-confessed madman.

More's tract was designed not to enter serious debate with Vaughan but to ridicule him and his methods, hence the weird and wonderful catalogue of enthusiasts with which More begins: of the man who believed he was made of glass; of the baker of Ferrara who thought he was made of butter; of the man who thought he was breeding frogs in his stomach. All these, says More, are examples of what happens when we allow the Imagination to get the better of Reason, a moral which Swift draws constantly.

Less humorous is John Edwards's *The Preacher* (1705–7). This was composed specifically for the use of the Anglican ministry, to demonstrate 'in this Giddy and Apostate Age' the need for continuing watchfulness against sectarian enthusiasts. This serious and self-appointedly authoritative work relies for its account of enthusiasm on the theory of (maladjusted) bodily humours, a diagnosis which More had applied in jest and Swift's narrator had applied with confident fervour. For Edwards nonconformist enthusiasm is due not to spiritual possession but to an over-active spleen, a 'Melancholick Flatus' or a 'Rumbling in the Hypochondria'—to anything physical, in short.[3] Edwards states quite uncompromisingly, and of course without satire, the enthusiasts' serious religious and political challenge to the position of the established church. Now though the *style* of Swift's religious satire in the *Tale* was clearly as old-fashioned as More's Commonwealth tract and therefore perhaps inappropriate for 1704, there is no doubt that its timing and motives were very firmly corroborated by the politico-religious climate of the time. Edwards makes the urgency of his rallying cry quite clear: the Church was in

Danger. More recent commentators reinforced the point: 1705 was a climax for establishment fervour and anti-dissent, when some thought that a Whig government would see the decease of the Church of England.[4] By 1709–10, Sacheverell's year, concern over the Church's safety from the attacks of dissenters, freethinkers, Low Church bishops and Whigs had led to a national furore.

In common with all the Anglican apologists both Edwards and Swift attack claims to special grace, inspiration, private convictions and mystical interpretations of scripture texts. As the positive alternatives to enthusiasm and fanaticism Swift and his fellow apologists were offering 'right reason', the 'grounds of Scripture' and an acknowledgement of the Church's irrefutable authority on spiritual orthodoxy. But whereas More and Edwards include in their attacks the *positive* alternatives to enthusiasm, what Swift gives us is a precise example of the methods, style and idiom of the object attacked. But the parody overflows, the exuberant sophistry, symbolism and mysticism of the Aeolists in section VIII of *A Tale of a Tub* feeds on every other spiritual symbolism, including the one Swift is professionally obligated to defend: if all enthusiasts have sublimated a physical malady into a religious ecstasy, how, if all religious experience is described in physical metaphors (light, inspiration, breath) can one tell the true from the false? Swift's radical distrust of rational efforts to understand religion was based on the realisation that reason can refute error, and if pursued further will also attack truths.

Without an antagonist values such as reason, moderation, common sense and social norms are difficult to dramatise effectively. For this reason the Augustan defending his values preferred to defend by satirical attack. The arguments used against the enthusiast, regarded as a political, religious, sexual and psychological deviant, reveal to us the core values of the eighteenth-century rational consensus. Experiences validated by and repeated in common life are esteemed more than the esoteric or the intellectual; a workable moderation and compromise are preferred above loyalties which depend upon factional interest for their viability (true of politics as much as religion), and all theorems are to be tested by the humilities of actual living. It is for such reasons that the enthusiast's claim to an exclusive, disembodied state of special grace and favour was such a fundamental insult.

Fanatical enthusiasts were the un-persons in a society which based its values on what Shaftesbury called 'common sense' (*Sensus Communis: An Essay on the Freedom of Wit and Humour*, 1709) and Pope 'common int'rest' (*Essay on Man*, 1733–4, II, 254).

NOTES

1 Paracelsus (i.e. Theophrastus Bombastus von Hohenheim, 1493–1541), Swiss alchemist and physician. His name may mean 'surpassing Celsus', the great classical physician. Paracelsus' natural philosophy was based on a theory of 'invisible spirits', the life substances in objects which only the magical physician's powers can unlock. His name is associated with the prohibited arts of alchemy. Swift owned the 1658 edition of his complete works, and along with others Paracelsus is placed in the Academy of Modern Bedlam in *A Tale*. He opens the battle, against Galen, in *The Battle of the Books*.

2 See Philip Harth, *Swift and Anglican Rationalism* (University of Chicago Press, Chicago and London, 1961)

3 In *The Mechanical Operation of the Spirit* Swift enumerates these three causes of enthusiasm as having been abundantly treated, and then concentrates on a fourth, i.e. 'the Effect of Artifice and Mechanical Operation'. One year before the appearance of *Gulliver's Travels* melancholic zanies were still being celebrated in Sir Richard Blackmore's *A Treatise of the Spleen and Vapours: or, Hypocondriacal and Hysterical Affections* (1725), pp. 161–2. See further, M. K. Starkman, *Swift's Satire on Learning in 'A Tale of a Tub'* (Princeton University Press, Princeton, N. J., 1950).

4 See Geoffrey Holmes, *The Trial of Dr Sacheverell* (Methuen, London, 1973), p. 47. The whole of chapter two is a pertinent and concise account of the politico-ecclesiastical scene at this time. See section III below.

1   From
HENRY MORE
Enthusiasmus Triumphatus:
or A Brief Discourse of the Nature,
Causes, Kindes, and Cure of Enthusiasm
(1656)

The great Affinity and Correspondency
betwixt Enthusiasm *and* Atheism

Atheism and *Enthusiasm*, though they seem so extremely opposite one to another, yet in many things they do very nearly agree. For, to say nothing of their joynt conspiracy against the true knowledge of God and Religion, they are commonly entertain'd, though successively, in the same Complexion. For that Temper that disposes a man to listen to the Magisterial Dictates of an over-bearing *Phansy*, more then to the calm and cautious insinuations of free *Reason*, is a subject that by turns does very easily lodge and give harbour to these mischievous Guests.

For as *Dreams* are the *Fancies* of those that *sleep*, so *Fancies* are but the *Dreams* of men *awake*. And these *Fancies* by day, as those *Dreams* by night, will vary and change with the weather and present temper of the •Body: So those that have onely a fiery *Enthusiastick* acknowledgement of God; change of diet, feculent old age, or some present damps of *Melancholy*, will as confidently represent to their *Phansy* that there is no God, as ever it was represented that there is one. And then having lost the use of their more noble Faculties of *Reason* and *Understanding*, they must according to the course of Nature be as bold *Atheists* now, as they were before confident *Enthusiasts*.

Nor do these Two unruly Guests onely serve themselves by turns on the same party, but also send mutual supplies one to another, being lodg'd in several persons. For the *Atheist's* pretence to Wit and natural Reason (though the foulness of his Mind makes him fumble very dotingly in the use thereof) makes the *Enthusiast* secure that *Reason* is no guide to God: And the *Enthusiast*'s boldly dictating the careless ravings of his own tumultuous *Phansy* for undeniable Principles of Divine knowledge, confirms the *Atheist* that the whole business of Religion and Notion of a God is nothing but a troublesome fit of over-curious *Melancholy*.

Wherefore there being that *near alliance* and *mutuall correspondence* betwixt these two enormous distempers of the Mind, *Atheism* and *Enthusiasm*; I hold it very suitable and convenient, having treated of the former, to adde this brief Discourse of the *Nature*, *Causes*, *Kinds*, and *Cure* of this latter Disease.

What Inspiration *is*
and what Enthusiasm

The Etymologie and varietie of the significations of this word *Enthusiasme* I leave to *Criticks* and *Grammarians*; but what we mean by it here, you shall fully understand after we have defined what *Inspiration* is: For *Enthusiasme* is nothing else but a misconceit of being *inspired*. Now to be inspired is, *to be moved in an extraordinary manner by the power or Spirit of God to act, speak, or think what is holy, just and true*.

From hence it will be easily be understood what *Enthusiasm* is, viz. *A full, but false, perswasion in a man that he is inspired*. . .

The enormous strength of Imagination
the Cause of Enthusiasme

. . . To be short therefore, The Originall of such peremptory delusions as mankind are obnoxious to, is the enormous strength and vigour of the Imagination; which Faculty though it be in some sort in our power, as *Respiration* is, yet it will also work without our leave . . . and hence men become mad and fanaticall whether they will or no . . .

Sundry natural and corporeal
Causes that necessarily work on
the Imagination

Now what it is in us that thus captivates our *imagination*, and
carries it wide away out of the reach or hearing of that more
free and superiour Faculty of *Reason*, is hard particularly to
define. But that there are sundry *material* things that do most
certainly change our Mind or Phansy, experience doth
sufficiently witnesse.

For our *Imagination* alters as our Blood and Spirits are
altered . . . and indeed very small things will alter them even
when we are awake; the mere change of Weather and various
tempers of the Aire, a little reek or suffumigation, as in those
seeds *Pomponius Mela*[1] mentions, which the *Thracians*, who
knew not the use of wine, wont at their feasts to cast into the
fire, whereby they were intoxicated into as high a measure of
mirth as they that drink more freely of the blood of the
grape . . .

Melancholy *a pertinacious*
and religious complexion

For besides that which is most generall of all, that *Melacholy*
enclines a man very strongly and peremptorily to either
believe or misbelieve a thing (as is plain in that passion of
Suspicion and Jealousie, which upon little or no occasion will
winne so full assent of the Mind, that it will engage a man to
act as vigorously as if he were certain that his jealousies were
true) it is very well known that this Complexion is the most
Religious complexion that is, and will be as naturally
tampering with Divine matters . . . as Apes and Monkies will
be imitating the actions and manners of Men.

Neither is there any true spiritual *Grace* from God but this mere natural constitution, according to the several tempers and workings of it, will not only *resemble*, but sometimes seem to *outstrip*, by reason of the fury and excess of it, and that not onely in *Actions*, but very ordinarily in *Eloquence* and *Expressions*; as if here alone were to be had that lively sense and understanding of all holy things, or at least as if there were no other state to be parallel'd to it.

The event of which must be, if a very great measure of the true Grace of God does not intervene, that such a *Melancholist* as this must be very highly puffed up, and not onely fancy himself *inspired*, but believe himself such a special piece of *Light* and *Holiness* that God has sent into the world, that he will take upon him to *reform*, or rather *annull*, the very *Law* and *Religion* he is born under, and make himself not at all the inferiour to either *Moses* or *Christ*, though he have neither any sound *Reason* nor visible *Miracle* to extort belief.

That men are prone to suspect some special presence of God
or
of a Supernatural power in whatever is Great *or* Vehement

But this is still too general, we shall yet more particularly point out the *Causes* of this Imposture. Things that are *great* or *vehement*, People are subject to suspect they rise from some *Supernatural* cause; insomuch that the Wind cannot be more then ordinarily high, but they are prone to imagine the Devil raised it, nor any sore Plague or Disease, but God in an extraordinary manner to be the Authour of it.

So rude Antiquity conceiv'd a kind of Divinity in almost any thing that was extraordinarily *great*. Whence some have worshipped very tall Trees, others large Rivers, some a great Stone or Rock, other some high and vast Mountains; whence the Greeks confound *great* and *holy* in that one word ['ieros'],[2] that signifies both; and the Hebrews by the *Cedars of God, the mountains of God, the Spirit of God*, and the like,

19

understand *high Cedars*, *great Mountains*, and *a mighty Spirit* or *Wind*.[3] We may adde also what is more familiar, how old Women and Nurses use to tell little Children when they ask concerning the *Moon*, pointing at it with their little fingers, that it is *God's Candle*, because it is so great a Light in the night. All which are arguments or intimations, that mans nature is very prone to suspect some special presence of God in any thing that is *great* or *vehement*.

Whence it is a strong temptation with a *Melancholist* when he feels a storm of devotion or zeal come upon him like a mighty wind, his heart being full of affection, his head pregnant with clear and sensible representations, and his mouth flowing and streaming with fit and powerfull expressions, such as would astonish an ordinary Auditorie to hear, it is, I say, a shrewd temptation to him to think that it is the very *Spirit of God* that *then moves* supernaturally in him; whenas all that excess of zeal and affection and fluency of words is most palpably to be resolved into the power of *Melancholy*, which is a kind of *naturall inebriation*.

And that there is nothing better then *Nature* in it, it is evident both from the experience of good and discreet men, who have found themselves strangely vary in their zeal, devotion and elocution, as *Melancholy* has been more or lesse predominant in them: and also from what all may observe in those that have been wicked, mad and blasphemous, and yet have surpassed in this mistaken gift of *Prayer*; as is notorious in *Hacket*, who was so besotted with a conceit of his own zeal and eloquence, that he fancied himself the *Holy Ghost* . . .

The *Spirit* then that wings the *Enthusiast* in such a wonderful manner, is nothing else but that *Flatulency* which is in the *Melancholy* complexion, and rises out of the *Hypochondriacal* humour upon some occasional heat, as *Winde* out of an *Aeolipia*[4] applied to the fire. Which fume mounting into the Head, being first actuated and spirited and somewhat refined by the warmth of the Heart, fills the Mind with variety of *Imaginations*, and so quickens and inlarges

Invention, that it makes the *Enthusiast* to admiration *fluent* and *eloquent*, he being as it were drunk with new wine drawn from that Cellar of his own that lies in the lowest region of his Body, though he be not aware of it, but takes it to be pure Nectar, and those waters of life that spring from above. *Aristotle*[5] makes a long Parallelism betwixt the nature and effects of *Wine* and *Melancholy*, to which both *Fernelius* and *Sennertus* do referre.

That Melancholy *partakes much of the*
Nature of Wine,
and from what complexion Poets *and* Enthusiasts *arise,*
and what the difference is betwixt them

But now that Melancholy partakes much of the nature of *Wine*, he evinces from that it is so *spiritous;* and that it is so *spiritous*, from that it is so *spumeous*: and that *Melancholy* is *flatuous* or *spiritous*, he appeals to the Physicians . . .

Now besides this *Flatulencie* that solicits to lust, there may be such a due dash of *Sanguine* in the *Melancholy*, that the Complexion may prove stupendiously ravishing. For that more sluggish *Dulcor* of the blood will be sometime so quickned and actuated by the fiercenesse and sharpnesse of the *Melancholy* humour[6] (as the fulsomnesse of Sugar is by the acrimony of Limons) that it will afford farre more sensible pleasure; and all the imaginations of *Love*, of what kind soever, will be farre more lively and vigorous, more piercing and rapturous, then they can be in pure *Sanguine* it self.

From this Complexion are *Poets*, and the more highly-pretending *Enthusiasts*: Betwixt whom this is the great difference, That a *Poet* is an *Enthusiast in jest*, and an *Enthusiast* is a *Poet in good earnest*; Melancholy prevailing so much with him, that he takes his no better then *Poeticall* fits and figments for divine Inspiration and reall Truth.

That a certain Dosis of Sanguine *mixt with* Melancholy
is the Spirit that usually inspires Enthusiasts,
made good by a large Induction of Examples

But that it is a mere naturall *flatuous* and *spirituous* temper
with a proportionable *Dosis* of *Sanguine* added to their
Melancholy, not the pure *Spirit of God*, that thus inacts them,
is plainly to be discovered not onely in their language, which
is very sweet and melting, as if sugar-plums lay under their
tongue, but from notorious circumstances of their lives. And
in my apprehension it will be a sufficient pledge of this Truth,
if we set before our eyes those that have the most highly
pretended to the Spirit, and that have had the greatest power
to delude the people.

For that that *Pride* and tumour of mind whereby they are
so confidently carried out to profess, as well as to conceive, so
highly of themselves, that no lesse Title must serve their turns
then that of *God, the Holy Ghost* or *Paraclet, the Messias, the
last and chiefest Prophet, the Judge of the quick and the dead*,
and the like; that all this comes from *Melancholy* is manifest
by a lower kind of working of that Complexion.

For to begin with the first of these Impostours, *Simon
Magus*,[7] who gave out that he was *God the Father*, he prov'd
himself to be but a wretched lecherous man by that
inseparable companion of his, *Helena*, whom he called
Selene, and affirmed to be one of the *Divine powers*, when she
was no better then a lewd Strumpet.

There was also one *Menander*[8] a *Samaritan*, that vaunted
himself to be the *Saviour of the world*, a maintainer of that
same licentious and impure opinions with *Simon* . . .

Mahomet, more successfull then any, the last and chiefest
Prophet that ever came into the world, (if you will believe
him) that he was *Melancholick* his *Epileptical* fits are one
argument; and his permission of plurality of wives and
concubines, his lascivious descriptions of the joyes of Heaven
or Paradise, another . . .

But men of a purer blood and finer spirits are not so obnoxious to this distemper: For this is the most natural feat of sublimer Reason; whenas that more Mechanical kind of *Genius* that loves to be tumbling of and trying tricks with the *Matter* (which they call *making Experiments*) when *desire of knowledge* has so heated it that it takes upon it to become *Architectonical* and fly above its sphere, it commits the wildest hallucinations imaginable, that material or corporeal fancie egregiously fumbling in more subtile and spiritual speculations.

This is that that commonly makes the *Chymist* so pitiful a *Philosopher*, who from the narrow inspection of some few toys in his own art, conceives himself able to give a reason of all things in *Divinity* and *Nature*; as ridiculous a project, in my judgement, as that of his, that finding a piece of a broken Oar on the sand, busied his brains above all measure to contrive it into an entire Ship.

The Cure of Enthusiasm by
Temperance, Humility, *and* Reason

We have spoken of the *Kinds of Enthusiasm* so far as we held it serviceable for our design, we shall now touch upon the *Cure of this Disease*. Where waving all pretence to the knowledge of *Physick* or acquaintance with the *Apothecarie*'s shop, we shall set down onely such things as fall under a *Moral* or *Theological* consideration, giving onely instructions for the guidance of a mans life in reference to this grand errour of *Enthusiasm*: which a sober man cannot well determine whether it be more ridiculous, or deplorable and mischievous.

Now the *most soveraign Medicine* that I know against it is this *Diatrion*, or *Composition* of *Three* excellent *Ingredients*, to wit, *Temperance, Humility*, and *Reason*; which as I do not despair but that it may recover those that are somewhat farre gone in this *Enthusiastick* distemper, so I am confident that it will not fail to prevent it in them that are not as yet considerably smitten.

What is meant by Temperance

By *Temperance* I understand a measurable Abstinence from all hot or heightening meats or drinks, as also from all venerous pleasures and tactuall delights of the Body, from all softness and effeminacy; a constant and peremptory adhesion to the perfectest degree of *Chastity* in the single life, and of *Continency* in wedlock, that can be attain'd to. For it is plain in sundry examples of *Enthusiasm* above named, that the more hidden and lurking fumes of *Lust* had tainted the Phansies of those Pretenders to *Prophecy* and *Inspiration* . . .

What is meant by Humility, *and the great advantage thereof for Wisdome and Knowledge*

By *Humility* I understand an entire Submission to the will of God in all things, a Deadness to all self-excellency and preeminency before others, a perfect Privation of all desire of singularity or attracting of the eyes of men upon a mans own person, as little to relish a mans own praise or glory in the world as if he had never been born into it; but to be wholly contented with this one thing, that his Will is a subduing to the Will of God, and that with thankfulness and reverence he doth receive whatever Divine Providence brings upon him, be it sweet or sour, with the hair or against it, it is all one to him, for what he cannot avoid, it is the gift of God to the world in order to a greater good . . .

What is meant by Reason, *and what the danger of leaving that Guide*

By *Reason* I understand so settled and cautious a Composure of Mind as will suspect every high-flown & forward Fancy that endeavours to carry away the assent before deliberate examination; she not enduring to be gulled by the vigour or garishnesse of the representation, nor at all to be born down by the weight or strength of it; but patiently to trie it by the known Faculties of the Soul, which are either the *Common notions* that all men in their wits agree upon, or the *Evidence of outward Sense,* or else a *clear and distinct Deduction from these.*

Whatever is not agreeable to these three, is *Fancy*, which testifies nothing of the *Truth* or *Existence* of any thing, and therefore ought not, nor cannot be assented to by any but mad men or fools.

2
JOHN EDWARDS
The Preacher
(*1705–7*)

This Age calls upon us to beware of all *Enthusiastick Delusions and Impostures*, and to warn our People against them. The Advice is as Seasonable in these days as that other preceding one which I have so amply insisted upon. And truly there is too great an Affinity between these two, *Popery* and *Enthusiasm*; they have often met together in the same Persons, and it might easily be evinced that this latter is very Serviceable towards the promoting and advancing the former. I wish there were not some ground to think that we have Instances of this in the deluded People called *Quakers*, and in some of those who have lately pretended to an Extraordinary and Prophetick Spirit. So far as I have enquired into the Conduct of both these sorts of Persons, I am enclined to believe that there are among them some that are downright Cheats and Impostors, and have nothing but Mischief at their Hearts, designing to Impose on the World, and foster Error and Falsehood, and particularly to Advance the *Roman Cause* in the sequel of all. These are the First Movers, and are Active and Intentive on the Design they have formed. But then, there are others (and who are far the greatest numbers) that may be said to be Passive, in Comparison of the former; they have no direct designs of Mischief, but mean well: only 'tis their unhappiness to be of that peculiar nature and disposition which makes them apt to take evil Impressions from others: Fancy and Imagination have the Ascendent over them, and Reason runs low with them: they Affect new discoveries in Religion, and Perswade themselves that a Divine and Extraordinary Spirit moves and actuates them, and powerfully influences upon them: and they wholly give themselves up to the Conduct of it, tho' in things very Unreasonable and Unjustifiable. This is the Pernicious Spirit of *Enthusiasm* which possesses the minds of many, and doth a great deal of Hurt in Religion: and therefore those who by their Office are the Publick Instructers of Mankind are Obliged to warn them against this Great Evil.

I would not here be misunderstood: *Enthusiasm*, as Tully well observes, is taken both in a good and a bad sense, namely, Either for a Divine Afflation and Inspiration, or for a Pretence to it.[1] The first is the Proper Signification of the Word, which Imports the Presence of *God in us*, the Divine and Holy Spirit moving and actuating us: The *True Enthusiasm* is when the Soul of Man is wholly and Entirely Enlightned, and set on work by God. So the Patriarchs, Prophets and Apostles of old were right *Enthusiasts*: and such are all Holy Men in some measure, especially at that time when Christ is formed in them by the New Birth . . .

But this word which is Good in it self hath by the fault of some men been depraved, and distorted to a Bad meaning. This *Enthusiasm* which is taken in the worst sense, is only a Pretence of being acted by the Spirit, when indeed the persons have experience of no such thing. They have a false conceit of Inspiration, and Dream they feel a Divine *Impetus* when it is

26

only the Height of their Pulse. Or the Vapours that fly from an Obstructed Spleen are fansied to be Sacred Inspiring. A *Melancholick Flatus* is taken for the Strong Breathings of the Spirit. A Rumbling in the *Hypochondria* passes for a Voice Celestial. Or, sometimes the Impure and Diabolical Spirit actuates their fancies, and yet is taken for a Divine Guest: some who are little better than Possessed, imagine themselves Inspired. This is the Root of this *Mistaken Enthusiasm*. Now let us see its Branches, let us view it in its Fruits. That *Enthusiasm* which is deservedly blamed by all sober men is known by these Effects,

1. A Wild and Raging Behaviour, which yet these Persons think fit to Entitle the Holy *Spirit*. Thus, whatever the *Right of Zealots* among the *Jews*, whereby private Persons by Extraordinary Impulse might do Strange Acts and not be question'd, was at first, it is certain that it was turned at last into Sedition, Rapine, and the most Bloody Outrages: the Pretenders to it were rather Assassines and Cut-Throats, than men Sacredly Inspired. This is the right meaning of *Fanatick*, which Imports a mans being Inspired with an *Enthusiastick* Fury. Such were the *Pagan Priests* oftentimes, who were first dispossessed of themselves, their Reason and Sense, before they were possessed by a Deity: they were said to be Inspired when they Raged, and were really Mad. We are told that the *Indians* take Mundungo to Stupify their Brains, and confound their Senses, that they may comprehend and entertain their *Gods*. So among the *Turks* not only Fools and Idiots, but Mad Men are in great Esteem, and are thought to be *Inspired* Persons. It is Deplorable to add that it is thus sometimes among those who Profess *Christianity*; when they do the most Uncomely and Unchristian Actions, they conceit they are Inspired, as the *Anabaptists* of *Munster* about the beginning of the 16th Century. When they shew most of the Devilish and Hellish Spirit, they think they have most of God in them. We have known some of our Modern *Enthusiasts* turn *Libertines* and *Ranters*, one Excess making way for the

27

other; pretending to too great heights in Divinity, they sunk at last below Humanity. Or,

Secondly, If they run not so high, their *Enthusiasm* is pretending to *Extraordinary* and *Immediate Revelations*, such as the Prophets had who were before or under the Law, such as some Holy Men had in the days of our Saviour and his Apostles, which are since ceased. Many Impostors of this rank have appeared in the World, of whom Ecclesiastical History will give us an Account; but none hath been more Eminent for the Mischief done by him than he who gave Name to the *Mahometan Sect*. This wild and Frantick Enthusiast, by professing himself to be the Last and Greatest Prophet whom God would send into the World, and by feigning that he had Extraordinary Visions and Discoveries from Heaven, Cheated an Incredible Number of Men into the belief of his absurd Doctrines. The *Romanists* have been noted for this sort of *Enthusiasm*: many of them have pretended to Immediate Revelation; especially their most Celebrated Women have been Eminent for this, as *Machildis*, *Gertrude*, *Juliana*, *Briget*, *Catharine*, *Donna Maria d'Escobar*: and who hath not heard of the Rapturous and High-flown *Teresa*?[2] The deluded Quakers among our selves Bragged at their setting up that they dealt in Visions and Revelations, and held Immediate Converse with God, and by this Artifice gained many Proselytes to their Impious Errors and Unchristian Practices.

Thirdly, Another Ingredient of *Enthusiasm* is a preferring of these Revelations (which they would Perswade us they commonly have) before or above the *Holy Scriptures*, or even against them. They have not been ashamed to oppose the Written Word of God, when they knew it spoke not in their behalf, and Instead of those Written Oracles they have alledged the *Dictates of the Spirit* (so they called them) and made these Confront the other. Of this sort in *Luther*'s time were those heady and rash Enthusiasts *Nicolas Stork*, *Thomas Muntzer*, Anabaptists; *Islebius* the Ringleader of the

Antinomians, Caspar Swenkfeld, and several other bold Sectaries, of whom *Luther* Complains.[3] With whom may be reckoned *John* of *Leyden*, and *David George* of *Delph*,[4] with others who pretended to the Spirit in an Extraordinary manner, and by their ill Practices Eclipsed and Defamed the happy *Reformation*.

Fourthly, It is an Instance of *Enthusiastick* folly not only to pretend Revelations in Opposition to the Written Word of God, but also to Despise and Reject this Word as a *dead Letter*, and to prize only the *Mystical* part of it. This some, who boast of a sublime and Seraphick Genius, are known to do. They proudly vilify the Literal Sense of Scripture, they scorn to take notice of so Low and Mean a thing as they Imagine that to be. The Historical part of the Bible, yea, of the New Testament, and that concerning the Incarnation, Passion, Death, and Resurrection of our Blessed Saviour, are Disregarded by them, as a Mean and Contemptible thing in their Eye, and is mentioned by them as such. And all the other Great things which the Scripture Testifies were done by our Saviour, are poor and sorry things with them, and whether they were done or no is no Great Matter, they think. They mind not the *History*, they tell us, but their way is to resolve all into *Mystery* and *Allegories*. Of this sort was *Henry Nicholas* and his Followers who called themselves the *Family of Love*, and some *Quakers* (as I shall shew anon.)[5]

Fifthly, Another part of this *Enthusiasm* is to make it their care to serve God *Invisibly*. All their Religion lies within, and is confined to their own Breasts. As for the Outward Worship and Service of God, they are stiled by them External Forms, and the Rudiments and Elements of Children. Several have affected this *Spiritual way*, as they call it: and it hath been lately revived by some *Quakers*, and by *Molinos*[6] and his Disciples. Inward and Mental Prayer is all the Devotion of the *Quietists:* for Religion they say, consists in the mind and Spirit alone, Contemplation, is the only Devotion. This Questionless is a Limb of *Enthusiasm*, and is Repugnant to the true Spirit of Religion, which is Constituted both of the Inward and the outward Man.

Sixthly, It Excludes the Exercise of the *Rational faculty*. Those that have drunk deep of the *Enthusiastick* Spirit bid Defiance to *Reason* as an Utter Enemy to Religion. They hate to *Discourse* and *Argue*: they are exceedingly taken with *Allusions* and *Metaphors*: a *Similitude* is more powerful than a *Syllogism*: they love Canting and Gibberish; they are pleased with Non-sense, and mere Raving sometimes. This is rank Enthusiasm . . .

Our greatest fear and danger is from another Quarter, I mean that Sect which hath in a manner Distinguished itself from all others by Pretensions to *a Light within them*, and by perpetually inculcating this in all their Discourses and Writings. They are by their great Sedulity and Boldness grown up into a Formidable Body of Men, and are Busy and Zealous in Asserting and Vindicating their Opinions, and decoying of the unwary Souls to their Societies . . . And it is Absolutely Requisite that all should guard themselves, in this Giddy and Apostate Age, against the Suggestions of these Professed Hereticks and Deceivers . . .

As for their *Revelations*, their *Immediate Impulses* and *Inspirations* which they boast of, it is thought by very Wise Men that what they call Inspiration depends upon their Humours and Blood: they owe it and their particular Religion to their *Spleen* and *Hypochondria*. Yea, I fear that the Inspiration of some of them, (for I am not so severe as to lay it to the charge of them all) is no other than a *Demoniack* Impression, accompanied with great disturbance of Body. I reckon it to be the same which the *Pagans* heretofore felt. The Devils us'd to enter their Priests, and forthwith to fill them with all Disorder of *Body* and *Mind*. Which of these two was greatest was hard to tell. Only the former was visible, and therefore the more Observable. When those impure Daemons took possession of their Bodies, it was to be seen and lamented how the poor Wretches foamed at the Mouth, how their Limbs were Distorted, how their Hair stood on end, how they Trembled and Quak'd, how their Eyes Roll'd, how their Hearts beat against their Breasts. These were the Symptoms of the Deities Inspiring them (as they call'd it), or rather of the Devils Possessing them. To be Inspired, was to be every way Distempered and Diseased: nay, to be Inspired was to Rave and run Mad. This was truly *Divinatio per Furorem*, as *Tully* calls That of the *Roman Priests:*[7] it was accompanied with Alienation of Mind, and horrible Disturbance of Body. This very thing was to be seen also among some of the deluded *Hereticks* in the *Christian Church*. *Epiphanius* tells us,[8] that the Disciples of *Simon* the *Sorcerer* (as well as the Heathen Priests) were seen to Foam, and Sweat and Quake extraordinarily: and when they felt these things, they said they were Inspired: and so they were, but by an Infernal Spirit. The *Gnosticks* pretended to Divine Revelation, and thence asserted things in defiance of what the Apostles had said and wrote. *Montanus* and his followers[9] held they were Divinely Inspired, and under pretence of that, vented their Blasphemies, and caus'd them to be entertain'd of many. The *Church of Rome* hath afforded many such Inspired Persons. *Ignatius Loyola*[10] lay in an Extasie, as a Person devoid of all Sense, Eight Days together . . .

This I fear is the Case of many *Quakers*, who are their Offspring: whilst they would make others believe (and they partly do so themselves,) that they are moved by the Spirit of God, they are acted by the Spirit of Darkness. It can't be denied that several Bodily Extravagancies and Agitations discovered a kind of Possession in them at first. They let Men see that they were extraordinarily disturbed both in Mind and Body. Like Possessed Persons they Foamed, they Trembled, they Acted, Spoke, and look'd Distractedly; they were Wild and Raving. Indeed now of late they do not Quake and Tremble, or shew any signs of Discomposure and Distraction. What the Devil did before, he can do now without all that great Stir: he now enters silently and stays the longer. To be brief, these Men, notwithstanding their Pretences to immediate Revelations and familiar Converse with the Spirit, Indulge themselves in Evil Habits of Vice, and in a Continual Practice of Ungodliness: Therefore their Revelations and Inspirations cannot be alledged as a Testimony of their Strictness and Holiness.

II

Ancients and Moderns

Swift's *Battle of the Books* is a comic drama enacting in simple terms the complexities of a serious and partisan chapter in the intellectual history of the seventeenth century. It is the clearest illustration of Swift's personal loyalty to Sir William Temple and to the cultural position of support for the Ancients which Temple represented. In addition, as a discussion of the respective merits of certain sorts of learning, the *Battle* may be read as a further digression from the *Tale* and as an exploratory anticipation of parts of *Gulliver's Travels*.

Though the Ancients and Moderns controversy had very wide implications, its debate in England largely excluded literary matters and concentrated on the evaluation of modern science and philosophy against the standard of ancient science and philosophy. The prime mover in the challenge to ancient authority had been Bacon, who attacked the 'contentious and thorny' philosophy of Aristotle in the *Advancement of Learning* (1605). It was here, in Bacon's work, that the notion of subservience to classical authority and established opinions was opposed by a demand for a fresh look at the physical universe. Bacon proposed a method of investigation which was to be based on the empirical observation of facts and on the accumilation of data established by experiment and recognised by the senses. Such accumulated data might eventually supply the bases for general laws, but would not be used specifically to support *a priori* theories. For Bacon the Moderns had nothing to lose by rejecting ancient authority but the chains of preconception and useless theory. His proposed intellectual revolution was supported by an optimistic and progressive estimate of human ability and by a confidence in the ultimate usefulness of scientific knowledge.

Bacon's challenge to ancient authority was reiterated in Sprat's *History of the Royal Society* (1667) and in Glanvill's *Plus Ultra* (1668). The publication of Sir William Temple's *Essay upon the Ancient and Modern Learning* (1690) fanned into flames the controversy which had been smouldering since, in Temple's words, 'the new philosophy had gotten ground' in the work of Descartes, the Royal Society, and the French Academy. It is Temple's version of the controversy which involved Swift, Wotton, Bentley and Boyle. The extracts from Temple's *Essay* and Wotton's *Reflections* on that *Essay* reproduced here reflect the first stage of the Ancients and Moderns debate most closely related to the *Battle of the Books*.

Though the literary, as opposed to the scientific aspects of the controversy had been given prominence in Dryden's *Essay of Dramatic Poesy* (1668) and were later to be taken up in Swift's *Battle*, the cause of the literary Moderns was vaunted mainly in France by Perrault and Fontenelle, the latter being one of the chief irritants which compelled Temple to rush to the defence of Ancient literature.

Temple's *Essay* compares ancient philosophers such as Plato, Aristotle and Epicurus with their modern counterparts Descartes and Hobbes; Hippocrates and Archimedes are favourably compared with the scientists of the newly founded Royal Society. A retrenched Ancient, Temple infused into his *Essay* a spirit utterly opposed to that of Bacon. Temple adopts a condescending attitude towards his contemporary culture, an attitude which has its roots not only in a scepticism of the ultimate value of the new science but also in his sense of permanent human limitations. At one point in his *Essay* he pronounces: 'We are born to grovel upon the Earth, and we would fain sore up to the Skies.' It is a response to the human condition which his pupil Swift shared: both conceal the potential values of modern science in their preference for its obvious futilities—the search for the Philosopher's Stone which would turn base metals into gold, and for the Universal Medicine which would bestow the gift of immortality (but which, without perpetual youth also, renders the Struldbruggs so despicable). In their own ways Temple and Swift assault the idea of progress and the efficacy of modern scientific discoveries. Temple sees the history of humanity as a series of cyclical progress and following decline. Swift is often stating a variation of the widely held belief among the upholders of the Ancients, that nature was decaying and the quality of life deteriorating. The Laputian scientists live in daily terror of impending calamities revealed by their astronomical knowledge.

In very marked contrast to Temple (and Swift), William Wotton, in his *Reflections* (1694), communicates confidence and exhilaration in the new science and its discoveries. He writes with vigour and conviction that the new science and the created world which it is revealing are each part of one pattern: Geometry and Arithmetic 'are general Instruments whereby we come to the Knowledge of many of the abstrusest Things in Nature,' and he approvingly quotes Plato's dictum that 'God always Geometrizes in all his Works'.[1] The *Reflections* returns to Bacon's emphasis on the *method* of the Moderns, opposing *a priori* rational assumptions with observation, experiment and a scepticism of ready conclusions. But to Swift the idea of a mechanistic universe was abhorrent, and his attacks on the speculating mathematicians—through the grotesque characters in the Academy of Lagado, at the Laputian court, and by means of the Spider's mathematical prowess in the *Battle*—were all calculated to assail the Moderns on the subject most confidently produced to demonstrate their superiority. Accordingly, the mathematicians in the *Travels* are mad, and Sprat's joyful metaphor for the new intellectual world, 'the Beautiful Bosom of Nature', is implicitly denied by the physically revolting bosom of the Brobdingnagian nursemaid, scrutinised as if with the device beloved by the Moderns, the microscope.

Swift's personal loyalties to Temple played a large part in the creation of the *Battle*, which is very closely modelled on Temple's *Essay*. The *Battle* vindicates Temple as 'the greatest Champion' of the Ancients among the Moderns, and avenges the attack not only of Wotton but also of Bentley, the prodigious classical scholar who introduced the second, literary critical stage of the controversy by a learned demonstration of the fact that Temple's admired examples of Ancient literature, the *Epistles of Phalaris*, were spurious. Thus, during Swift's mock-heroic combat of books, Homer slays Davenant, Perrault and Fontenelle; Dryden is simply overawed by Virgil; Lucan slays Blackmore; Pindar slays Oldham; and Bentley and Wotton are skewered together by the editor of the *Epistles*, Boyle. Probably in deference to Temple's designation of Bacon as one of the great modern wits, Swift allows the arrow meant by Aristotle for Bacon to strike his French counterpart Descartes by mistake.

Without question the strongest and most authoritative defence of the new philosophy and experimental science is found in Thomas Sprat's *History of the Royal Society*. Though it antedates both the Temple and Wotton extracts it is of less specific reference to Swift's *Battle* than these texts and is more closely relevant to Swift's attack on the abuses of science in Gulliver's second and third voyages. The first part of Sprat's *History* relates to ancient and modern philosophy and experimental knowledge, the second part to the Society, and the last part defends experimental philosophy against those who saw in its progress a threat to the religious and social establishment. Its importance, apart from its intrinsic merit, lies in the fact that Sprat was officially appointed to write the *History* by the members of the Royal Society and thus his statement of their aims and methods carries their official sanction. In addition to its descriptive and polemical functions Sprat's *History* was clearly designed to stimulate and dignify the new science: the English are 'the head of a Philosophical League, above all other countries in *Europe*', and even the climate contributes to make England 'a Land of *Experimental Knowledge*'. If this seems euphoric, Swift's image of the Academy of Lagado certainly shows how hostile Sprat's opposition could be, even in 1726. Yet Swift and Sprat *both* show experimenters attempting the impossible—the search for the Philosopher's stone or the elixir of life. Gulliver himself was 'a Sort of Projector' in his younger days and Swift endorses through him the style of the Brobdingnagians: 'clear, masculine, and smooth, but not Florid; for they avoid nothing more than multiplying unnecessary Words, or using various Expressions' (II,vii), a concept of style in accord with Sprat's own stated views. On the other hand Sprat's emotional advocacy of plain, denotative language which should relate to things rather than abstractions is dealt a sharp, satirical blow in Swift's School of Languages, where there is a project to 'shorten Discourse by cutting Polysyllables into one, and leaving out Verbs and Participles, because in Reality all things imaginable are but Nouns ... since Words are only Names for *Things*, it would be more convenient for all Men to carry about them, such *Things*, as were necessary to express the particular Business they are to discourse on'. Yet even here, Swift is not satirising the idea of plain, denotative speech, but the perversion of a sound idea by preposterous and extreme theorising. Such, indeed, was part of Sprat's own aim in attempting to separate the 'discreet, and sober flame' of the Royal Society men from the 'wild lightning of other Brains'. There is no doubt, however, that in his satirical reflection of scientific studies in the Academy of Lagado Swift has made it very difficult for us to separate a total antipathy towards all of the new experimental science from a patent contempt for its more perverse and foolish ambitions. To Swift, science proved its value by ameliorating the human condition, but he could never have been a true Baconian for as long as he denied the necessary freedom to experiment in areas where a utilitarian product was not demonstrably both the aim and the result.

Swift's personal loyalty to Temple meant that historically he would lose the argument. Intellectually also the dilettante Temple was no match at all for the precocious scholarship of the young Wotton (whose *Reflections* had been sponsored by the Royal Society and published at the age of twenty-eight)² and Bentley, unrivalled classical scholar as he was. Swift wisely chose ridicule; he would have been wasting his time to enter the argument seriously in support of Temple's shaky learning. But if the *Battle* makes poor intellectual history, it nevertheless makes good barbarian fun.

1 This is attributed to Plato, in Plutarch's *Symposium*, but not found in his works. A similar idea is found in Milton's *Paradise Lost*, book VIII, 224 and ff., and in Sir Thomas Browne's *Religio Medici* (I, xvi) and *Garden of Cyrus* (chapter 3).

2 See Henry Wotton, *An Essay on the Education of Children . . . with a Narrative of what Knowledge WILLIAM WOTTON, a Child six Years of Age, had attained unto . . . in the Latin, Greek and Hebrew Tongues* (1753).

3   From
SIR WILLIAM TEMPLE
An Essay upon the Ancient and Modern Learning
(1690)

. . . Two Pieces that have lately pleased me . . . are, one in *English* upon the *Antideluvian* World; and another in *French* upon the *Plurality of Worlds*; one writ by a Divine, and the other by a Gentleman, but both very finely in their several Kinds, and upon their several Subjects, which would have made very poor Work in common Hands:[1] I was so pleased with the last (I mean the Fashion of it, rather than the Matter, which is old and beaten) that I enquired for what else I could of the same Hand, till I met with a small Piece concerning Poesy, which gave me the same Exception to both these Authors, whom I should otherwise have been very partial to. For the first could not end his Learned Treatise without a Panegyrick of Modern Learning and Knowledge in comparison of the Ancient: And the other falls so grossly in the Censure of the old Poetry and Preference of the new, that I could not read either of these Strains, without some Indignation, which no Quality among Men is so apt to raise in me as Sufficiency, the worst Compostion out of the Pride and Ignorance of Mankind. But these two, being not the only

Persons of the Age that defend these Opinions, it may be worth examining how far either Reason or Experience can be allowed to plead or determine in their Favour.

The Force of all that I have met with upon this Subject, either in Talk or Writing is, first, as to Knowledge; that we must have more than the Ancients, because we have the Advantage both of theirs and our own, which is commonly illustrated by the Similitude of a Dwarf's standing upon a Gyant's Shoulders, and seeing more or farther than he. Next as to Wit or Genius, that Nature being still the same, these must be much at a Rate in all Ages, at least in the same Climates, as the Growth and Size of Plants and Animals commonly are; and if both these are allowed, they think the Cause is gained. But I cannot tell why we should conclude, that the Ancient Writers had not as much Advantage from the Knowledge of others, that were Ancient to them, as we have from those that are Ancient to us. The Invention of Printing has not perhaps multiplied Books, but only the Copies of them; and if we believe there were Six hundred thousand in the Library of *Ptolemy*,[2] we shall hardly pretend to equal it by any of ours, not, perhaps, by all put together; I mean so many Originals, that have lived any Time, and thereby given Testimony of their having been thought worth preserving. For the Scribblers are infinite, that like Mushrooms or Flies, are born and die in small Circles of Time; whereas Books, like Proverbs, receive their chief Value from the Stamp and Esteem of Ages through which they have passed. Besides the Account of this Library at *Alexandria*, and others very Voluminous in the lesser *Asia* and *Rome*, we have frequent mention of Ancient Writers in many of those Books which we now call Ancient, both Philosophers and Historians. 'Tis true, that besides what we have in Scripture concerning the Original and Progress of the *Jewish* Nation; all that passed in the rest of our World before the *Trojan* War, is either sunk in the Depths of Time, wrapt up in the Mysteries of Fables, or so maimed by the Want of

Testimonies and Loss of Authors, that it appears to us in too obscure a Shade, to make any Judgement on it . . .

But what are the Sciences wherein we pretend to excel? I know of no New Philosophers, that have made Entries upon that Noble Stage for fifteen hundred Years past, unless *Des Cartes* and *Hobbs* should pretend to it; of whom I shall make no Critick here, but only say, That by what appears of Learned Mens Opinions in this Age, they have by no means eclipsed the Lustre of *Plato*, *Aristotle*, *Epicurus*, or others of the Ancients. For Grammar or Rhetorick, no Man ever disputed it with them; nor for Poetry, that ever I heard of, besides the New *French* Author I have mentioned; and against whose Opinion there could, I think, never have been given stronger Evidence, than by his own Poems, printed together with that Treatise.

There is nothing new in *Astronomy*, to vie with the Ancients, unless it be the *Copernican* System; nor in *Physick*, unless *Harvey*'s Circulation of the Blood.[3] But whether either of these be modern Discoveries, or derived from old Fountains, is disputed: Nay, it is so too, whether they are true or no; for though Reason may seem to favour them more than the contrary Opinions, yet Sense can very hardly allow them; and to satisfie Mankind, both these must concur. But if they are true, yet these two great Discoveries have made no Change in the Conclusions of *Astronomy*, nor in the Practice of *Physick*, and so have been of little Use to the World, though perhaps of much Honour to the Authors . . .

. . . we are lame still in Geography itself, which we might have expected to run up to so much greater Perfection by the Use of the Compass, and it seems to have been little advanced these last hundred Years. So far have we been from improving upon those Advantages we have received from the Knowledge of the Ancients, that since the late Restoration of Learning and Arts among us, our Flights seem to have been the highest, and a sudden Damp to have fallen upon our Wings, which has hindered us from rising above certain

Heights. The Arts of Painting and Statuary began to revive with Learning in *Europe*, and made a great but short Flight; so as for these last hundred Years we have not one Master in either of them, who deserved a Rank with those that flourished in that short Period after they began among us.

It were too great a Mortification to think, That the same Fate has happened to us, even in our Modern Learning, as if the Growth of that, as well as of Natural Bodies, had some short Periods, beyond which it could not reach, and after which it must begin to decay. It falls in one Country or one Age, and rises again in others, but never beyond a certain Pitch. One Man, or one Country, at a certain Time, runs a great Length in some certain Kinds of Knowledge, but lose as much Ground in others, that were perhaps as useful and as valuable. There is a certain Degree of Capacity in the greatest Vessel, and when 'tis full, if you pour in still, it must run out some way or other, and the more it runs out on one side, the less runs out at the other. So the greatest Memory, after a certain Degree, as it learns or retains more of some Things or Words, loses and forgets as much of others. The largest and deepest Reach of Thought, the more it pursues some certain Subjects the more it neglects others . . .

. . . But what would we have, unless it be other Natures and Beings than God Almighty has given us? The Height of our Statures may be six or seven Foot, and we would have it sixteen; the Length of our Age may reach to a hundred Years, and we would have it a thousand. We are born to grovel upon the Earth, and we would fain sore up to the Skies. We cannot comprehend the Growth of a Kernel or Seed, the Frame of an *Ant* or *Bee*; we are amazed at the Wisdom of the one, and Industry of the other, and yet we will know the Substance, the Figure, the Courses, the Influences of all those Coelestial Bodies, and the End for which they were made; we pretend to give a clear Account how Thunder and Lightning (that great Artillery of God Almighty) is produced, and we cannot comprehend how the Voice of a Man is framed, that poor

41

little Noise we make every time we speak. The Motion of the Sun is plain and evident to some Astronomers, and of the Earth to others, yet we none of us know which of them moves, and meet with many seeming Impossibilities in both, and beyond the Fathom of human Reason or Comprehension. Nay, we do not so much as know what Motion is, nor how a Stone moves from our Hand, when we throw it cross the Street. Of all these that most Ancient and Divine Writer gives the best Account in that short Satyr, *Vain Man would fain be wise, when he is born like a Wild Ass's Colt.*[4]

But, God be thanked, his Pride is greater than his Ignorance; and what he wants in Knowledge, he supplies by Sufficiency. When he has looked about him as far as he can, he concludes there is no more to be seen; when he is at the End of his Line, he is at the Bottom of the Ocean; when he has shot his best, he is sure, none ever did nor ever can shoot better or beyond it. His own Reason is the certain Measure of Truth, his own Knowledge, of what is possible in Nature, though his Mind and his Thoughts change every seven Years, as well as his Strength and his Features; nay, though his Opinions change every Week or every Day, yet he is sure, or at least confident, that his present Thoughts and Conclusions are just and true, and cannot be deceived; and among all the Miseries, to which Mankind is born and subjected in the whole Course of his Life, he has this one Felicity to comfort and support him, that in all Ages, in all Things, every Man is always in the right. A Boy of Fifteen is wiser than his Father at Forty, the meanest Subject than his Prince or Governours; and the Modern Scholars, because they have for a hundred Years past learned their Lesson pretty well, are much more knowing than the Ancients their Masters.

But let it be so, and proved by good Reasons; is it so by Experience too? Have the Studies, the Writings, the Productions of *Gresham* College, or the late Academy of *Paris*, outshined or eclipsed the *Lycaeum* of Plato, the

Academy of *Aristotle*, the *Stoa* of *Zeno*, the Garden of *Epicurus*?[5] Has *Harvey* out-done *Hippocrates*, or *Wilkins*, *Archimedes*? Are *D'Avila*'s and *Strada*'s[6] Histories beyond those of *Herodotus* and *Livy*? Are *Sleyden*'s Commentaries[7] beyond those of *Caesar*? the flights of *Boileau* above those of *Virgil*? If all this must be allowed, I will then yield *Gondibert* to have excell'd *Homer*, as is pretended;[8] and the Modern *French* Poetry, all that of the Ancients. And yet, I think, it may be as reasonably said, that the Plays in *Moor-Fields* are beyond the *Olympick* Games; a *Welsh* or *Irish* Harp excels those of *Orpheus* and *Arion*; the Pyramid in *London* those of *Memphis*; and the *French* Conquests in *Flanders* are greater than those of *Alexander* and *Caesar*, as their Operas and Panegyricks would make us believe.

... It may, perhaps, be further affirmed, in Favour of the Ancients, that the oldest Books we have, are still in their Kind the best. The two most Ancient, that I know of in Prose, among those we call Profane Authors, are *Aesop*'s Fables, and *Phalaris*'s Epistles,[9] both living near the same Time, which was that of *Cyrus* and *Pythagoras*. As the first has been agreed by all the Ages since, for the greatest Master in his Kind, and all others of that Sort have been but Imitations of his Original; so I think the Epistles of *Phalaris* to have more Race, more Spirit, more Force of Wit and Genius, than any others I have ever seen, either ancient or modern. I know several Learned Men (or that usually pass for such, under the Name of Criticks) have not esteemed them Genuine, and *Politian* with some others have attributed them to *Lucian*: But I think he must have little Skill in Painting, that cannot find out this to be an Original; such Diversity of Passions, upon such Variety of Actions and Passages of Life and Government, such Freedom of Thought, such Boldness of Expression, such Bounty to his Friends, such Scorn of his Enemies, such Honour of Learned Men, such Esteem of Good, such Knowledge of Life, such Contempt of Death, with such Fierceness of Nature and Cruelty of Revenge, could never be represented but by him that possessed them; and I esteem *Lucian* to have been no more capable of writing, than of acting what *Phalaris* did. In all one writ, you find the Scholar or the Sophist; and in all the other, the Tyrant and the Commander ...

The great Wits among the Moderns have been, in my Opinion, and in their several Kinds, of the *Italians*, *Boccace*, *Machiavel*, and *Padre Paolo*; among the *Spaniards*, *Cervantes* (who writ Don Quixote) and Guevara; among the *French*, *Rablais*, and *Montagne*; among the *English*, Sir *Philip Sidney*, *Bacon* and *Selden*.[10] I mention nothing of what is written upon the Subject of Divinity, wherein the *Spanish* and English Pens have been most conversant and most excelled. The Modern *French* are *Voiture*, *Rochfaucalt*'s Memoirs, *Bussy's Amours de Gaul*,[11] with several other little Relations or Memoirs that have run this Age, which are very pleasant and entertaining ...

4   *From*
SIR WILLIAM TEMPLE
A Defence of the Essay
Upon Ancient and Modern Learning
(1701)

The greatest Modern Inventions seem to be those of the *Load-Stone* and *Gun-powder*;[1] by the first whereof, Navigation must be allowed to have been much improved and extended; and by the last, the Art Military, both at Sea and Land, to have been wholly changed; yet 'tis agreed, I think, that the *Chineses* have had the Knowledge and Use of Gunpowder, many Ages before it came into *Europe*: And besides, both these have not served for any common or necessary Use to Mankind; one having been employed for their Destruction, not for their Preservation; and the other, only to feed their Avarice, or increase their Luxury; Nor can we say, that they are Inventions of this Age, wherein Learning and Knowledge are pretended to be so wonderfully encreased and advanced.

What has been produced for the Use, Benefit, or Pleasure of Mankind, by all the airy Speculations of those, who have passed for the great Advancers of Knowledge and Learning these last fifty Years (which is the Date of our Modern Pretenders) I confess I am yet to seek, and should be very glad to find. I have indeed heard of wondrous Pretensions and Visions of Men, possess'd with Notions of the strange Advancement of Learning and Sciences, on foot in this Age, and the Progress they are like to make in the next: As, The Universal Medicine, which will certainly cure all that have it: The Philosopher's Stone, which will be found out by Men that care not for Riches: The Transfusion of young Blood into old Men's Veins, which will make them as gamesom as the Lambs, from which 'tis to be derived: An Universal Language, which may serve all Mens Turn, when they have forgotten their own: The Knowledge of one anothers Thoughts, without the grievous Trouble of Speaking: The Art of Flying, till a Man happens to fall down and break his Neck: Double-bottom'd Ships, whereof none can ever be cast away, besides the first that was made: The admirable Virtues of that noble and necessary Juice called Spittle, which will come to be sold, and very cheap, in the Apothecarys Shops: Discoveries of new Worlds in the Planets, and Voyages between this and that in the Moon, to be made as frequently as between *York* and *London*: Which such poor Mortals as I am think as wild as those of Ariosto, but without half so much Wit, or so much Instruction; for there, these modern Sages may know, where they may hope in Time to find their lost Senses, preserved in Vials, with those of *Orlando*.[2]

One great Difference must be confessed between the Ancient and the Modern Learning; Theirs led them to a Sense and Acknowledgement of their own Ignorance, the Imbecility of Human Understanding, the Incomprehension even of Things about us, as well as those above us ... Ours leads us to Presumption, and vain Ostentation of the little we have learned, and makes us think, we do or shall know, not only all Natural, but even what we call Supernatural Things; all in the Heavens, as well as upon Earth; more than all mortal Men have known before our Age; and shall know in time as much as Angels.

Socrates was by the *Delphick* Oracle pronounced the wisest of all Men, because he professed that he knew nothing: What would the Oracle have said of a Man that pretends to know every thing? *Pliny* the elder, and most learned of all the *Romans* whose Writings are left, concludes the Uncertainty and Weakness of Human Knowledge, with, *Constat igitur inter tanta incerta, nihil esse certi; praeterquam hominem, nec miserius quicquam nec superbius.*[3] But sure, our Modern Learned, and especially the Divines of that Sect, among whom it seems, this Disease is spread, and who will have the World 'to be ever improving, and that nothing is forgotten that ever was known among Mankind', must themselves have forgotten that Humility and Charity are the Virtues which run through the Scope of the Gospel; and one would think they never had read, or at least never minded, the first Chapter of *Ecclesiastes*, which is allowed to have been written, not only by the Wisest of Men, but even by Divine Inspiration; where Solomon tells us, *The Thing that has been, is that which shall be, and there is no new Thing under the Sun; Is there any Thing whereof it may be said, See, this is new? It has been already of old Time which was before us: There is no Remembrance of former Things, neither shall there be any Remembrance of Things that are to come, with those that shall come after.*[4]

These, with many other Passages in that admirable Book, were enough, one would think, to humble and mortify the Presumption of our Modern *Sciolists*,[5] if their Pride were not as great as their Ignorance; Or if they knew the rest of the World any better than they know themselves.

WILLIAM WOTTON
Reflections upon Ancient and Modern Learning
(1694)

From Chapter XIII
On the Logick and Metaphysicks
of the Ancient Greeks

Since all that has been said in the Second and Third Chapters, concerning the *Ethics*, *Politicks*, *Eloquence* and *Poesie* of the Ancient *Græcians*, belongs to them in their most flourishing Ages, a great Part of the Subject Matter of this Enquiry has already been dispatched. The remaining Parts of their Knowledge may be reduced by these Four Heads: *Logick*, *Metaphysicks*, *Mathematicks* and *Physiology*. *Logick* is the *Art of Reasoning*; but by it Men commonly understand the Art of Disputing, and making Syllogisms; of Answering an Adversary's Objections dexterously, and making such others as cannot easily be evaded: In short, of making a plausible Defence, or starting probable Objections, for or against any Thing. As this is taught in the Schools, it is certainly owing to the Ancients: *Aristotle's Organum* is the great Text by which Modern *Logicians* have framed their Systems; and nothing, perhaps, can be devised more subtile in that captious Art, than the *Sophisms* of the Ancient *Stoicks*. But as *Logic* is truly the Art of Reasoning justly, so as not only to be able to explain our own Notions, and prove our own Assertions, clearly and distinctly, but to carry our Speculations further than other Men have carried theirs, upon the same Arguments; it has not only been much cultivated by Modern Philosophers, but as far pursued as ever it was by the Ancients: For hereby have the late Enquiries been made into *Physical*, *Metaphysical* and *Mathematical* Matters, the Extent whereof is hereafter to be examined. Hereby the

Ancient *Mathematicians* made their Discoveries, and when they had done, they concealed their Art; for, though we have many noble Propositions of theirs, yet we have few Hints how they found them out; since the Knowledge of the fore-going Books in *Euclid's Elements* is necessary to explain the Subsequent, but is of little or no use to help us to find out any Propositions in the subsequent Books, (which are not immediate Corollaries from what went before) in case those Books had been lost. Whether the Moderns have been deficient in this noble Part of *Logick*, may be seen by those who will compare *Des Cartes's Discourse of Method*, Mr Lock's *Essay of Humane Understanding*, and *Tschirnhaus's Medicina Mentis*, with what we have of the Ancients concerning the *Art of Thinking*. Such a Comparison would not be to the Disadvantage of those Modern Authors; for, though it may be pretended, that their Thoughts and Discoveries are not entirely new in themselves, yet to us, at least, they are so, since they are not immediately owing to ancient Assistance, but to their own Strength in Thinking, and Force of Genius.

From Chapter XV
Of several instruments invented
by the Moderns, which have helped
to advance Learning

Having now enquired into the State of *Mathematicks*, as they relate to *Lines* and *Numbers* in *general*, I am next to go to those Sciences which consider them as they are applied to *Material Things*. But these being of several Sorts, and of a vast Extent, taking in no less than the whole Material World, it ought to be observed, that they cannot be brought to any great Perfection, without Numbers of Tools, or Arts, which may be of the same Use as Tools, to make the Way plain to several Things, which otherwise, without their Help, would be inaccessible.

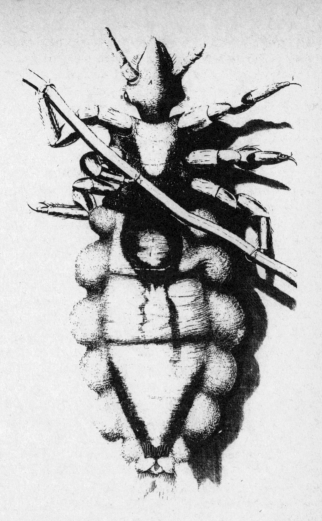

'A Louse holding a human hair': from Robert Hooke's *Micrographia* (1665). Cf. Pope's *Dunciad*, IV, 53–4:

> O! would the Sons of Men once think their Eyes
> And Reason giv'n them but to study *Flies*?

and *Gulliver's Travels*, II, iv: 'I could see distinctly the Limbs of these Vermin with my naked Eye, much better than those of an *European* Louse through a Microscope.'

Of these Tools, or Instruments, some were anciently invented, and those Inventions were diligently pursued: Others are wholly new. According to their Uses, they may be ranged under these Two General Heads: (1) Those which are useful to all Parts of Learning, though perhaps not to all alike. (2) Those which are particularly subservient to a Natural Philosopher, and a Mathematician. Under the first Head one may place *Printing, Paper of Rags*, and *Engraving*. Under the latter come *Telescopes*, *Microscopes*, the *Thermometer*, the *Baroscope*, the *Air-Pump*, *Pendulum-Clocks*, *Chymistry*, and *Anatomy*. All these, but the two last, were absolutely unknown to the Ancient *Greeks* and *Romans*. *Chymistry* was known to the *Greeks*, and from them carried to the *Arabs*. *Anatomy* is, at least, as old as *Democritus*[1] and *Hippocrates*; and doubtless, among the *exact Ægyptians*, something older.

From Chapter XVII
Of Ancient and Modern Anatomy

Anatomy is one of the most necessary Arts to open to us Natural Knowledge of any that was ever thought of. Its Usefulness to Physicians was very early seen; and the *Greeks* took great Pains to bring it to Perfection. Some of the first Dissectors tried their Skill upon living Bodies of Men, as well as Brutes. This was so inhumane and barbarous a Custom, that it was soon left off: And it created such an Abhorrence in Mens Minds of the Art it self, that in *Galen*'s Time even dead Bodies were seldom opened; and he was often obliged to use Apes instead of Men, which sometimes led him into great Mistakes . . .

Here I shall beg leave to descend to Particulars, because I have not seen any Comparison made between *Ancient and Modern Anatomy*, wherein I could acquiesce, whilst some, as Mr *Glanvile* and some others who seem to have copied from him, have allowed the Ancients less than was their Due . . .

Hippocrates took the Brain to be a Gland. His Opinion was

nearer to the Truth than any of his Successors; but he seems to have thought it to be a similar Substance, which it evidently is not. And therefore, when several Parts of it were discovered not to be glandulous, his Opinion was rejected. *Plato* took it to be Marrow,[2] such as nourishes the Bones; but its Weight and Texture soon destroyed his Notion, since it sinks in Water wherein Marrow swims; and is hardened by Fire, by which the other is melted. *Galen* saw a little farther . . .

But the manner of the forming of the *Animal Spirit* in the Brain was wholly unknown. In Order to the Discovery whereof, *Malpighius*[3] by his Microscopes found that the Cortical Part of the Brain consists of an innumerable Company of very small Glandules, which are all supplied with Blood by Capillary Arteries; and that the Animal Spirit, which is separated from the Mass of the Blood in these Glandules, is carried from them into the *Medulla Oblongata* through little Pipes, whereof one belongs to every Gland, whose other End is inserted into the *Medulla Oblongata*, and that these Numberless Pipes, which in the Brain of some Fishes look like the Teeth of a small Ivory Comb, are properly that which all Anatomists after *Piccolhomineus*[4] have called the *Corpus callosum*, or the Medullar Part of the Brain. This Discovery destroys the Ancient Notions of the Uses of the Ventricles of the Brain, and makes it very probable that those Cavities are only Sinks to carry off excrementitious Humours, and not Store-Houses of the Animal Spirit: It shows likewise how little they knew of the Brain who believed that it was an uniform Substance . . .[5]

From Chapter XXVI
Of Ancient and Modern Natural Philosophy

Having gone through with the most considerable Branches of *Natural and Mathematical Knowledge*, I am now to enquire into the Comparative Excellency of Ancient and Modern

Books of Philosophy, thereby to see in which of them Nature, and its Operations, are explained best. Here I shall first enquire into the several *Methods of Philosophizing*; and afterwards, into the Intrinsic Worth of the Doctrines themselves. *Moderns* here are taken in a very strict Sence. I shall mention none who have made any *Entries upon this noble Stage of Nature* above LXXX Years ago, since the time of those first Flights of the Restorers of Learning, that are so exceedingly applauded by Sir *William Temple*. For *Natural Philosophy* was the last part of Knowledge which was cultivated with any particular Care, upon the Revival of Learning; though *Natural History*, which is a principal Ground-work, had been long before increasing, and a considerable Heap of Materials had been collected, in order to the Work.

As for *Modern Methods of Philosophizing*, when compared with the *Ancient*, I shall only observe these following Particulars. (1) No Arguments are received as cogent, no Principles are allowed as current, amongst the celebrated Philosophers of the present Age, but what are in themselves intelligible; that so a Man may frame an Idea of them, of one sort or other. Matter and Motion, with their several Qualities, are only considered in Modern Solutions of Physical Problems. *Substantial Forms, Occult Qualities, Intentional Species, Idiosyncrasies, Sympathies and Antipathies of Things*, are exploded; not because they are Terms used by Ancient Philosophers, but because they are only empty Sounds, Words whereof no Man can form a certain and determinate Idea. (2) Forming of Sects and Parties in Philosophy, that shall take their Denominations from, and think themselves obliged to stand by the Opinions of any particular Philosophers, is, in a manner, wholly laid aside. *Des Cartes* is not more believed upon his own Word, than *Aristotle*: Matter of Fact is the only thing appealed to; and Systems are little further regarded, than as they are proper to instruct young Beginners, who must have a general

Notion of the whole Work, before they can sufficiently comprehend any particular Part of it; and who must be taught to reason by the Solutions of other Men, before they can be able to give Rational Solutions of their own: In which Case, a false Hypothesis, ingeniously contrived, may now and then do the Service of a true one. (3) *Mathematics* are joined along with *Physiology*, not only as Helps to Men's Understandings, and Quickners of their Parts, but as absolutely necessary to the comprehending of the Oeconomy of Nature, in all her Works. (4) The *New Philosophers*, as they are commonly called, avoid making general Conclusions, till they have collected a great Number of Experiments or Observations upon the Thing in hand; and, as new Light comes in, the old Hypotheses fall without any Noise or Stir. So that the Inferences that are now a-days made from any Enquiries into Natural Things, though perhaps they be set down in general Terms, yet are (as it were by Consent) received with this tacit Reserve, *As far as the Experiments or Observations already made, will warrant.*

How much the pursuing of these Four Things will enlarge *Natural Philosophy*, is easie to guess. I do not say, that none of these things were anciently minded; but only, that they were not then so generally put in practice. The great Men of Antiquity often exprest themselves in unintelligible Cant: They chiefly aim'd at being Heads of particular Sects: Few of their Natural Philosophers were great Mathematicians: And they did in general establish Hypotheses without a sufficient Fund of Experiments and Observations whereupon to build them ... Many a Man that cannot demonstrate any *one* single Proposition in *Euclid*, takes it now for granted, that Geometry is of infinite Use to a Philosopher; and it is believed now upon Trust, because it is become an Axiom amongst the Learned in these Matters. And if it had been so received in *Galen's* Time,[6] or by those more Ancient Authors whom *Galen* and his Contemporaries followed, or pretended at least to follow, as their Patterns; such as *Hippocrates*, whom all

53

Sides reverenced, *Herophilus*, *Erasistratus*, *Asclepiades*,[7] and several more, there would have been no need of any Excuses for what he was doing; since his Readers being accustomed to such sort of Reasonings, would either readily have understood them, or acquiesced in them as legitimate Ways of Proof. If Three or Four Mathematical Terms were so affrighting, how would those learned Discourses of *Steno* and *Croone*, concerning Muscular Motion, have moved them?[8] How much would they have been amazed at such minute Calculations of the Motive-strength of all the Muscles in the several general sorts of Animals, as require great Skill in Geometry, even to understand them, which are made by *Borellus*, in his Discourses *of the Motion of Animals*?[9] It is not enough, in this Case, to quote a Saying or two out of some great Man amongst the Ancients; or to tell us, that *Plato* said, long ago, *That God Geometrizes in all his Works*; as long as no Man can produce anyone Ancient Essay upon anyone Part of Physiology, where Mathematical Ratiocinations were introduced to salve those *Phænomena* of Natural Things, upon which it was possible to talk plausibly without their Help. At least, it is certain, That they contented themselves with general Theories, without entring into minute Disquisitions into the several Varieties of Things, as is evident in the two Cases already alledged, *of Vision* and *Muscular Motion*.

Now as this Method of Philosophizing laid down above, is right, so it is easie to prove, that it has been carefully followed by Modern Philosophers. My Lord *Bacon* was the first great Man who took much pains to convince the World that they had hitherto been in a wrong Path, and that Nature her self, rather than her Secretaries, was to be addressed to by those who were desirous to know much of her Mind. Monsieur *Des Cartes*, who came soon after, did not perfectly tread in his Steps, since he was for doing too great a part of his Work in his Closet, concluding too soon, before he had made Experiments enough; but then to a vast Genius he joined exquisite Skill in Geometry, and working upon Intelligible Principles in an Intelligible Manner, though he very often failed of one Part of his End, namely, a right Explication of the *Phænomena* of Nature; yet by marrying Geometry and Physics together, he put the World in Hopes of a Masculine Off-spring in process of Time, though the first Productions should prove abortive. This was the state of Natural Philosophy, when those great Men who, after King *Charles* IId's Restoration, joined in a Body, called by that Prince himself, the ROYAL SOCIETY, went on with the Design; they made it their Business to set their Members awork to collect a perfect History of Nature, in order to establish thereupon a Body of Physicks. What has been done towards it by the Members of that Illustrious Body, will be evident to those who consider that *Boyle*, *Barrow*, *Newton*, *Huygens*, *Malpighius*, *Leeuwenhoek*, *Willughby*, *Willis*,[10] and Abundance more already named amongst the great Advancers of real Learning, have belonged to it: If it shall be thought too tedious an Undertaking, to examine all their Writings, Mr *Boyle's Works*, Monsieur *Les Clerc's Physics*, any one good *System of the* Cartesian *Philosophy*, Monsieur *Rohault's*[11] for Instance, or to comprehend all under one, a Book intituled, *Philosophia Vetus & Nova ad Usum Scholæ accommodata*, may be consulted, and then there will be no difficulty to determine on which Side the Verdict ought to be given; in the last Book especially it is evident how very little the Ancients did in all Parts of Natural Philosophy, and what a great Compass it at present takes, since it makes the Comparison I all along appeal to.

Thus, it seems to me to be sufficiently plain, That the Ancients Knowledge in all Matters relating to *Mathematics* and *Physics*, was incomparably inferior to that of the Moderns. These are Subjects, many of them at least, which require great Intenseness of Thought, great Strength and Clearness of Imagination, even only to understand them; how much more then to invent them?

THOMAS SPRAT
The History of the Royal Society of London
(1667)

The next Philosophers, whom I shall touch upon, are the *Chymists*,[1] who have been more numerous, in this later Age, then ever before. And without question, they have lighted upon the right Instrument of great productions, and alterations: which must for the most part be perform'd by Fire. They may be divided into three rancks: Such, as look after the knowledge of Nature in general: Such, as seek out, and prepare Medicines: and such, as search after riches, by Transmutations, and the great *Elixir*. The two first, have been very successful, in separating, compounding, and changing the parts of things: and in shewing the admirable powers of Nature, in the raising of new consistencies, figures, colors, and vertues of Bodies. And from their labors, the true *Philosophy* is like to receive the noblest Improvements. But the pretensions of the Third kind, are not onely to indow us, with all the benefits of this life, but with Immortality it self. And their success has been as small, as their design was extravagant. Their Writers involve them in such darkness; that I scarce know, which was the greatest task, to understand their meaning, or to effect it. And in the chase of the *Philosopher's Stone*, they are so earnest, that they are scarce capable of any other thoughts: for that if an Experiment lye never so little out of their rode, it is free from their discovery: as I have heard of some creatures in *Africk*, which still going a violent pace straight on, and not being able to turn themselves, can never get any prey, but what they meet just in their way. This secret they prosecute so impetuously, that they believe they see some footsteps of it, in every line of *Moses*, *Solomon*, or *Virgil*. The truth is, they are downright *Enthusiasts* about it. And seeing we cast *Enthusiasm* out of

Divinity it self, we shall hardly sure be perswaded, to admit it into Philosophy . . .

. . . And now it is much to be wonder'd, that there was never yet such an *Assembly* erected, which might proceed, on some standing constitutions of Experimenting. There have, 'tis true, of late, in many parts of *Europe*, some Gentlemen met together, submitted to Common Laws, and form'd themselves into *Academies*. But it has been, for the most part, to a far different purpose: and most of them only aim'd at the smoothing of their Style, and the Language of their Country. Of these, the first arose in *Italy*; where they have since so much abounded, that there was scarce any one great City without one of these *combinations*. But that, which excell'd all the other, and kept it self longer untainted from the corruptions of speech, was the *French Academy* at *Paris*.[2] This was compos'd of the noblest Authors of that Nation: and had for its *Founder*, the *Great Cardinal de Richelieu*: who, amongst all his cares, whereby he establish'd, and enlarged that *Monarchy* so much, did often refresh himself by directing, and taking an account of their progress. And indeed in his own life, he found so great success of this Institution, that he saw the *French Tongue* abundantly purifi'd, and beginning to take place in the Western World, almost as much, as the *Greek* did of old, when it was the Language of Merchants, Souldiers, Courtiers, and Travellers. But I shall say no more of this *Academy*; that I may not deprive my Reader of the delight of perusing their own *History*, written by *Monsieur de Pelisson*:[3] which is so masculinely, so chastly, and so unaffectedly done, that I can hardly forbear envying the *French Nation* this honor: that while the *English Royal Society* has so much out-gone their *Illustrious* Academy, in the greatness of its undertaking, it should be so far short of them in the abilities of its *Historian*. I have onely this to allege in my excuse; that as they undertook the advancement of the Elegance of Speech, so it became their *History*, to have some resemblance to their enterprize: Whereas the intention of ours, being not the artifice of Words, but a bare knowledge of things; my fault may be esteem'd the less, that I have written of *Philosophers*, without any ornament of *Eloquence* . . .

. . . Nor would I have this new *English Academy*, confin'd only to weighing Words, and Letters: But there may also be greater Works found out for it. By many signs we may guess, that the Wits of our Nation, are not inferior to any other; and that they have an excellent mixture of the Spirit of the *French*, and the *Spaniard*: and I am confident, that we only want a few more standing Examples, and a little more familiarity with the Ancients, to excel all the Moderns. Now the best means, that can be devis'd to bring that about, is to settle a fixt, and *Impartial Court* of *Eloquence*; according to whose Censure, all Books, or Authors should either stand or fall. And above all, there might be recommended to them one Principal Work, in which we are yet defective; and that is, the compiling of a History of our late *Civil Wars*. Of all the labors of mens Wit, and Industry, I scarce know any, that can be more useful to the World, then *Civil History* . . . There lye now ready in Bank, the most memorable Actions of Twenty years: a Subject of as great Dignity, and Variety, as ever pass'd under any Mans hands: the peace which we injoy, gives leisure and incouragement enough: The effects of such a Work would be wonderfully advantageous, to the safety of our Country, and to *His Majesties* Interest: for there can be no better means to preserve his Subjects in obedience for the future, than to give them a full view of the miseries, that attended rebellion . . .

From The Second Part

Thus they [the Royal Society] have directed, judg'd, conjectur'd upon, and improved *Experiments*. But lastly, in these, and all other businesses, that have come under their care; there is one thing more, about which the *Society* has

58

been most solicitous; and that is, the manner of their *Discourse*: which, unless they had been very watchful to keep in due temper, the whole spirit and vigour of their *Design*, had been soon eaten out, by the luxury and redundance of *speech*. The ill effects of this superfluity of talking, have already overwhelm'd most other *Arts* and *Professions*; insomuch, that when I consider the means of *happy living*, and the causes of their corruption, I can hardly forbear recanting what I said before; and concluding, that *eloquence* ought to be banish'd out of all *civil Societies*, as a thing fatal to Peace and good Manners. To this opinion I should wholly incline; if I did not find, that it is a Weapon, which may be as easily procur'd by *bad* men, as *good*: and that, if these should onely cast it away, and those retain it; the *naked Innocence* of vertue, would be upon all occasions expos'd to the *armed Malice* of the wicked. This is the chief reason, that should now keep up the Ornaments of speaking, in any request: since they are so much degenerated from their original usefulness. They were at first, no doubt, an admirable Instrument in the hands of *Wise Men*: when they were onely employ'd to describe *Goodness, Honesty, Obedience*; in larger, fairer, and more moving Images: to represent *Truth*, cloth'd with Bodies; and to bring *Knowledg* back again to our very senses, from whence it was at first deriv'd to our understandings. But now they are generally chang'd to worse uses: They make the *Fancy* disgust the best things, if they come sound, and unadorn'd: they are in open defiance against *Reason*; professing, not to hold much correspondence with that; but with its Slaves, *the Passions*: they give the mind a motion too changeable, and bewitching, to consist with *right practice*. Who can behold, without indignation, how many mists and uncertainties, these specious *Tropes* and *Figures* have brought on our Knowledg? How many rewards, which are due to more profitable, and difficult *Arts*, have been still snatch'd away by the easie vanity of *fine speaking*? For now I am warm'd with this just Anger, I cannot with-hold my self, from betraying the shallowness of all these seeming Mysteries; upon which, *we Writers*, and *Speakers*, look so bigg. And, in few words, I dare say; that of all the Studies of men, nothing may be sooner obtain'd, than this vicious abundance of *Phrase*, this trick of *Metaphors*, this volubility of *Tongue*, which makes so great a noise in the World. But I spend words in vain; for the evil is now so inveterate, that it is hard to know whom to *blame*, or where to begin to *reform*. We all value one another so much, upon this beautiful deceipt; and labour so long after it, in the years of our education: that we cannot but ever after think kinder of it, than it deserves. And indeed, in most other parts of Learning, I look on it to be a thing almost utterly desperate in its cure: and I think, it may be plac'd amongst those *general mischiefs*; such as the *dissention* of Christian Princes, the *want of practice in* Religion, and the like; which have been so long spoken against, that men are become insensible about them; every one shifting off the fault from himself to others; and so they are only made bare common places of complaint. It will suffice my present purpose, to point out, what has been done by the *Royal Society*, towards the correcting of its excesses in *Natural Philosophy*; to which it is, of all others, a most profest enemy.

They have therefore been most rigorous in putting in execution, the only Remedy, that can be found for this *extravagance*: and that has been, a constant Resolution, to reject all the amplifications, digressions, and swellings of style: to return back to the primitive purity, and shortness, when men deliver'd so many *things*, almost in an equal number of *words*. They have exacted from all their members, a close, naked, natural way of speaking; positive expressions; clear senses; a native easiness: bringing all things as near the Mathematical plainness, as they can: and preferring the language of Artizans, Countrymen, and Merchants, before that, of Wits, or Scholars.[4]

III

Church
and State

In his *History of the Royal Society* (1667), Bishop Sprat had remarked that 'the universal Disposition of this Age is bent upon a *rational* religion'. New advances in scientific method commemorated by the *History* supported an increasing demand for clarity and demonstration in matters of religious belief. John Locke's *Reasonableness of Christianity* (1695) and Toland's *Christianity not Mysterious* (1696) each stimulated a heated controversy which continued long after Swift had intervened in the dispute between the orthodox and the freethinkers in such works as the *Remarks on Tindal's Rights of the Christian Church* (1707), the *Argument against Abolishing Christianity* (1708), the sermon on the Trinity and the *Abstract of Collins' Discourse of Free-Thinking* (1713). As Swift shows in such works, one did not have to be a latitudinarian in order to despise contentions over dogma and abstruse theological speculations.

The following extracts, with the exception of the vituperative and intolerant Sacheverell sermon, are all marked by what Sprat mildly termed a 'Disposition' towards a rational religion. What Sprat meant was the search for a universal moral system, stimulated by years of exhausting sectarian disputes, which could remove the contentious elements from religion and replace them by a distillation of clear, demonstrable beliefs acceptable to all reasonable men. In this search discussion centred on the need for liberty of conscience and a scepticism towards the mysteries of revealed religion. The rationalists devalued the outward forms of religion and substituted an optimistic faith in the guidance of individual Reason (whether of the Christian or Brahmin) for the dogma of priests and the authority of scripture writ as officially interpreted.

Swift's position in all this was marked by the caution of a conservative. His defence of the established Church was politically motivated; his attitude towards toleration of dissent was coloured by a frank suspicion of the dissenter's motives. The various conflicting attitudes towards the idea of a State-supported Church—toleration of minority conscience, the political recognition of dissent and the relationship between the individual conscience and the civil power—are all represented here by some of their more extreme exponents. For Sacheverell dissent is a kind of creeping treachery to be eradicated by the State enforcing the monopoly of Anglicanism; for Tindal, at the polar extreme, the idea of a State-supported Church is abhorrent; Hoadly, leader of the Low-Church party, would have the individual conscience separated from the sphere of civil jurisdiction; Wollaston, an intellectual latitudinarian, sees natural religion as an organic manifestation of reason in nature, with no political reference. Taken together, Tindal's *Rights* and Swift's *Remarks* (see notes) illustrate the important clash of deist and High Churchman on the idea of a State religion. Hoadly's tolerant benevolism is in marked contrast to the sceptical pessimism of Hobbes, La Rochefoucauld and Swift himself.

In his attacks on dissenters and freethinkers in the *Tale* Swift was quick to associate their non-conformity with spiritual pride, enthusiasm, madness, or political subversion. All these were viewed as inevitable deviations from the reasonable norm of Anglicanism as represented by Martin. On questions involving political change in general Swift was a gradualist rather than a reactionary: in politics, he stated, 'large Intervals of Time must pass between every

... Innovation, enough to melt down and make it of a Piece with the Constitution' (*Contests and Dissensions*). On religious reform, especially on the question of extending toleration to nonconformists, his position was quite specific and clear-sighted. Though it was nonsense, he stated, to expect every man was 'bound to believe', believers and non-believers alike should at least recognise the distinction between the liberty of private conscience and the necessity for a stable public order. 'Every man, as a member of the commonwealth, ought to be content with the possession of his own opinion in private, without perplexing his neighbour or disturbing the public'. Swift's own religious convictions, accordingly, were to be regulated by his 'impartial reason', which was to be informed and improved as far as his 'capacity and opportunities will permit'. Moderation and the sceptic's awareness of the fallibility of human reason mould his view, and he rejected metaphysical speculation and theological logic-chopping, 'subtleties, niceties, and distinctions', on grounds of practical common sense. To Swift it was not politically expedient to allow the liberty to express in public a minority nonconformist conscience which would perplex the mind of the simple believer and foster the proliferation of sects.

Matthew Tindal's *Rights of the Christian Church* (1706) was dubbed by one of its opponents as the one masterpiece of the deist's 'Antichristian Heresy'. To the High Churchman in Swift it was one of those 'Books that instill pernicious Principles' and tend to 'advance dangerous Opinions, or destroy Foundations', a view shared by Swift's old antagonist Wotton, and by the House of Commons, who ordered the book to be burnt by the public hangman in 1710. The vehement personal lampoon on Tindal in Swift's *Remarks* underscores with personal malice his objections to elements in deist theology which posed a serious threat to the very idea of a State-supported Church of England. Tindal's desire to see Church power in the State minimised and his attack on the system of preferments drove Swift to an Establishment Man's dogmatism in reply:

Employments in a State are a Reward for those who intirely agree with it, &c. For Example, a Man who upon all Occasions declared his Opinion, of a Commonwealth before a Monarchy, would not be a fit Man to have

Employments; let him enjoy his Opinions, but not be in a Capacity of reducing it to Practice.

Tindal's contentions elicit from Swift sentiments similarly motivated to and in complete accordance with those of Archbishop Boulter, champion of the 'English interest' and Protestantism in Ireland. As for Tindal's attack on the High Church claim for an 'Independent Power', or *Imperium in imperio*, in the State, Swift strongly rejects this as never having been seriously advanced by responsible churchmen. It is, Swift states, fatuous to talk of the Church of England as 'a perfect Creature of the Civil Power', since the Church's authority comes from Christ. Only the liberty to exercise that power comes from the state. But Swift left his *Remarks* unfinished: half the work is in the form of annotations, for Swift's chosen weapon was not a formal and argued refutation but the rapier thrust of oblique irony and satire. From this contest ensued the *Argument Against Abolishing Christianity* (1708), a polished and sustained irony on the Church–State relationship which pillories the whole mob of atheists and freethinkers.

The effect of pulpit literature on public opinion and politics in the eighteenth century can scarcely be imagined by the modern reader. Tindal was roughly handled by his enemies; Henry Sacheverell, the most outspoken and extreme opponent of toleration in the High Church party, created a national furore in 1709 by his sermon on *The Perils of False Brethren*. It was delivered at St Paul's at the invitation of the Lord Mayor of London on 5 November, a traditional festival commemorating the Gunpowder Plot against the life of James I in 1605, but also a day on which to celebrate England's deliverance from arbitrary power by the landing of William of Orange at Torbay. In the latter context it was a day dear to the Whigs, a fact which suited Sacheverell's purpose admirably. In his sermon he attacked the notion of liberty of conscience and the Whig government's policy of toleration. His claim that the government had been infiltrated by enemies of Church and State appeared to question the lawfulness of the Revolution of 1688, and hence the Act of Settlement and the Hanoverian succession. Defoe, who had already attacked Sacheverell's Oxford sermon of 1702 in the ill-fated *Shortest Way with the Dissenters* (1702), accused him of resurrecting the 'exploded ridiculous doctrine of non-resistance' and passive obedience, extreme Tory beliefs which had both been rendered unrealistic after the events of 1688. Nevertheless, reaction to Sacheverell's violent attack on the nonconformists was prompt and equally violent. London mobs rioted in support of Sacheverell and burned meeting-houses, rekindling religious feuds in a period of progressive toleration. Sacheverell himself was impeached and brought to trial in Westminster Hall on 27 February 1710. The political outcome of the trial contributed to the downfall of the Whigs in 1710 and helped to unify the Tory party, thereafter even more tightly interlocked with High Churchmen.

Successful prosecution of Sacheverell hinged on proving his contravention of current Whig concepts: the Revolution principles, toleration of dissent, and the right of resistance to an arbitrary monarch. (An extract from the record of Lechmere's speech, which elaborates such points, is item 12 below). As a 'Whig in politics' Swift accepted a constitutional balance of power between king, aristocracy and Commons (a mixed government), and the idea of the king being bound to his people by a mutual contract, which James II had broken. As a 'High Churchman' in religion, and additionally as a member of a minority Anglican clergy in Ireland threatened by the possible repeal of the Test Act, he rigidly opposed the extension of toleration to dissenters because he rejected their claims to political status. Though he disagreed with the extreme Tory position in regarding passive obedience as due not to the king, as Sacheverell had calimed, but to the supreme Magistrate, i.e. the legislative power, in his political defence of the Church of England he was as uncompromising as Sacheverell. *Some Free Thoughts Upon the Present State of Affairs* states:

the Church of England should be preserved entire in all her Rights, Powers and Priviledges; All Doctrines relating to Government discouraged which she condemns; All Schisms, Sects and Heresies discountenanced and kept under due Subjection, as far as consists with the Lenity of her Constitution. Her open Enemies (among whom I include at least Dissenters of all Denominations) not trusted with the smallest Degree of Civil or Military Power; and Her secret Adversaries under the Names of Whigs, Low-Church, Republicans, Moderation-Men, and the like, receive no Marks of Favour from the Crown, but what they should deserve by a sincere Reformation.

It was from fear lest the Whig policy of toleration should damage the Church of England in Ireland that Swift deserted the Whigs for the Tories in 1710.

As leader of the 'low church' divines after 1709 Benjamin Hoadly earned the opprobrium of his High Church colleagues, as the above passage makes clear. The sermon here reproduced in extract sparked off the voluminous and confused 'Bangorian' controversy of 1717–19. As a latitudinarian Hoadly was opposed to priestly privileges and claims by the High Churchmen to a supernatural authority in the State (which Swift strenuously denied). He further objected to their assertions of authority in the matter of scriptural interpretation and to the resulting subjection of individual conscience. But in supporting the dissenter's claims for political equality he seemed to his contemporaries to be advocating a complete separation between Church and State, a move which many, including Swift, believed would pave the way for a chaos of sectarian power struggles. Misinterpretation of Hoadly's rather broadly stated sermon is understandable, for it does not specify the Church of England in its argument, and his definition of the 'Church or Kingdom of Christ' is deliberately wide and pacific; it is 'the Number of Persons who are Sincerely, and Willingly Subjects to Him, as Law-giver and Judge, in all matters relating to Conscience, or Eternal Salvation'. What Hoadly *intended* to discuss was the autonomy of the individual conscience and its independence of the civil magistrate: there are 'no Judges over the Consciences or Religion' of the people except Christ himself. In Hoadley's sermon Christianity is reduced to a moral system whose canons of belief reside in moral qualities—'Sincerity and Common Honesty'—not in exclusive and dogmatic shibboleths.

In stressing the social obligations of charity and forbearance Hoadly demonstrates the common ground between deists and latitudinarians. Samuel Clarke, in his *Discourse concerning the Being and Attributes of God* (1704), insists that genuine deists believe that 'Men . . . are every one obliged to make it their business by an Universal Benevolence, to promote the Happiness of all others . . . to be just and honest, equitable and sincere . . . gentle and easie and affable, charitable and willing to assist as many as stand in need of his help, for the preservation of universal Love and Benevolence amongst Mankind'. The doctrine of benevolence was developed in the work of Shaftesbury (see *An Inquiry concerning*

Virtue, or Merit, 1699; revised in 1711), who, like Henry Fielding, found 'true religion' not in revelation, but in the 'Nature of things' and in the essentially good nature of man. Such developments from the latitudinarian position are in marked contrast to the pessimistic view of the social operation of morality found in Swift's work.

The final extract, from Wollaston's *Religion of Nature Delineated* (1722), discusses the nature of man's reason as the motive element in human morality. Wollaston's definition of man as *animal rationale*, traditional in manuals of logic and used to characterise man as a reasoning animal, was emended by Swift in a letter to Pope[1] about *Gulliver's Travels* to *animal rationis capax*, or man as capable of acting according to reason, but not always doing so. In his unrealistically symmetrical world Wollaston doggedly demonstrates that reason is identical with truth and that to act according to reason is to obey the law of God. In addition, all virtues are rewarded by happiness, if only, he adds, in a future life. As in the work of other extreme rationalists Christianity becomes a moral system in which God is identified with Nature, which in turn is governed mathematically, physically and morally by His laws. But since the observable facts of human misery conflict with such a neat scheme (as they did for Johnson when he read Pope's similarly schematic *Essay on Man*), Wollaston is forced, unconvincingly, to account for the irrational and untidy universe around him. Such a universe is found in the world of the Yahoos. Wollaston's hypothesis that 'there may be some [beings], who are indued with reason, but have nothing higher than that' is paralleled by the cold rationality of Swift's Houyhnhnms. Their perplexing and preposterous combination of an animal body with an almost disembodied rational intellect seems an apt illustration of Wollaston's logical hypothesis of 'the most enormous and worst of all brutes'—i.e. 'brutes with reason'. Swift is not attacking Wollaston specifically, but each is involved in a common debate. For instance, the Houyhnhnm's 'perfection of nature' and rule of reason render a specific religion superfluous for their community. Wollaston's book, published during the period in which *Gulliver's Travels* was being written and a copy of which was in Swift's library, makes no specific reference either to the Bible or to revelation as indispensible elements in natural religion. In his fourth voyage to a land of secular perfection Gulliver's rejection of humanity in preference for the company of horses is used by Swift to ridicule all those in his age, deists included, who seemed, from an entirely orthodox Christian point of view, to be foolishly exalting Reason above faith. Faith recognised the limitations of human reason and cognition. Evidence of man's irrationality cannot be suppressed in real life as Gulliver is allowed to do in the world of the *Travels*. And if to Swift the God-given faculty of Reason was being more honoured in the breach than in the performance, then speculative theologians join the distinguished company of Lovers, Platonicks and 'that Philosopher, who, while his Thoughts and Eyes were fixed upon the *Constellations*, found himself seduced by his *lower Parts* into a *Ditch*' (*The Mechanical Operation of the Spirit*). Some modern critics have seen Swift's final answer to the rational optimism of the deists in his portrait of the bestial and anarchic Yahoos in Gulliver's fourth voyage. In these anthropoids, without even the tincture of reason which the Houyhnhnms can discern in Gulliver, Swift has depicted an image of the rational theologian's nightmare.

Swift's battle over the Church–State question involved attacks on the Deists and freethinkers, on the Whigs for their policy of toleration and apparent disregard for the Anglican supremacy, and on the 'nominal Christians' for their lukewarm allegiance to the established church. Such themes were Swift's concern in letters on the Test Act, in ironical pamphlets and satirical arguments. In short, Swift spoke in the accents of him who 'rattles it out against *Popery*, and *Arbitrary Power*, and *Priest-Craft*, and *High-Church*.' But the pamphlet from which these words are taken shows another (and duller) side of Swift. His *Project for the Advancement of Religion* (1709) proposes to achieve moral reform by encouraging the Prince (i.e. Queen Anne) to practise and advocate Piety and Virtue and to make these the only qualifications for preferment. Here Swift is indeed of the society for the reformation of manners. His scheme proposes censorship of the press and an Office of Censors of public morality. It offers the astonishing preference of hypocrisy over dissent and atheism: 'For, if Religion were once understood to be the necessary Step to Favour and Preferment; can it be imagined, that any Man would openly offend against it, who had the least Regard for his Reputation or his Fortune?' Here was a scheme for using the State (more specifically the Court and the system of public offices) to support the Established Church at every level in society, a scheme of staggering pragmatism on Swift's part, running all the risks of absolutism, corruption and hypocritical conformity, which he attacks elsewhere. His premise is that 'it is often with Religion as it is with Love; which, by much Dissembling, at last grows real': a motive for action equally disabling for a carnal and spiritual union, one would think. In such a scheme the Church–State relationship is as much divorced from ecclesiastical and political theories as in the work of the Deists themselves. Whilst the latter wanted a thorough reformation Swift, at least here, seemed to be content with merely nominal allegiance. Even this was to be preferred to atheism.[2] In a world riddled with scepticism and misguided ingenuity the problem of gaining sufficient orthodoxy for the Anglican compromise evidently warranted (in Swift's mind) the enforcement of at least nominal loyalty, even though this was to be achieved by mechanisms we now associate with totalitarianism.[3]

NOTES

1 See note 2 to Wollaston below, item 10.
2 The best discussion of this astonishing *Project* will be found in Ehrenpreis, *Swift*, II, 276–97. Leland Peterson, in 'Swift's *Project*: a religious and political satire', *PMLA*, lxxxii (March 1967), 54–63, sees the piece as a satirical thrust against the Society for the Reformation of Manners, an exposure of nominal Christianity and a satire designed to embarrass the Whig ministry.
3 See George Orwell's brilliant essay, 'Politics vs. literature: An examination of *Gulliver's Travels*' (1945), in *Collected Essays* (London, 1961), 377–98.

7   From
MATTHEW TINDAL
The Rights of the
Christian Church Asserted ...
(1706)

18.   In a word, Religion is so very necessary for the Support
of human Societys, that 'tis impossible, as is own'd by
Heathens as well as Christians, they can subsist without
acknowledging some invisible Power that concerns himself
with human Affairs; and that the Awe and Reverence of the
Divinity makes Men more effectually observe those Dutys in
which their mutual Happiness consists, than all the Rods and
Axes of the Magistrate. And this is so very obvious, that
Atheists know not how to deny it, and therefore suppose
Religion to be a Politick Device, contriv'd on purpose for the
better regulating of human Societys. And the Storys of
certain Nations being so very barbarous as to entertain no
Religion, are either contradicted by later and better
Observations, or else they are not link'd together in Society,
or are scarce above Brutes in Understanding: So that Men
when they associated on a Civil, were oblig'd to do the same
on a Religious Account, one being necessary for the Support
of the other. Hence it is plain how absurdly some Men argue,
when to gain an Independent Power in Religious Matters,
they wou'd exclude the Magistrate from any Power therein,
on pretence that the Welfare of the Civil Society is his only
Province; since that obliges him to concern himself with all
such, as conduce to the Happiness of Human Societys; which
tho they are the most substantial Parts of Religion, yet I shall
so far comply with Custom, as to call them Civil only, in
distinction from others to which Men appropriate the Name
of Religion. And since Men have generally interwoven into
their Religion some merely speculative Points and particular
Modes of Worship, with certain Rites, Ceremonys, and other
indifferent things; and are so much divided about 'em, that

there's scarce any Country which is not as much distinguish'd by some things peculiar in these, as by its Situation: the Question is, whether the Magistrate has any Power here; which can only be known by examining whether Men had any in the State of Nature over their own or others Actions in these matters.

19.   Nothing at first sight can be more obvious, than that all being under an indispensible Obligation to worship God after the manner they think most agreeable to his Will, and in all Religious Matters whatever to follow the Dictates of their Consciences, none cou'd make over the Right of judging for himself, since that wou'd cause his Religion to be absolutely at the disposal of another.[1] And as none has such a Power over his own Person, as to be able to authorize the Magistrate (were it possible any cou'd be so mad as to desire it) to use him ill for worshipping God as he thought most agreeable to his Will; so he can as little impower him to use another ill upon that account, because none in worshipping God according to his Conscience, or in believing and professing such speculative Matters as he thinks true, does another any Injury; the only thing which in a State of Nature cou'd give one a Right to punish another. Nay, in that State shou'd any have attempted such an absurd thing himself, or intic'd others to do so, he might have been justly treated as a common Disturber and Enemy; and consequently they who by the command of any persecuting Magistrate deprive one of his Life, Liberty or Property on this account, are guilty of as great a Crime as if they had done it of themselves without any Commission from him; because as to these matters Men are still in a State of Nature, without any Sovereign Representative to determine for them what they shall believe or profess: And 'tis impossible that Men should ever submit to Government, but with an Intent of being protected in so necessary a Duty as worshipping God according to Conscience, as well as in any other matter whatever . . .

21.   'Tis contrary to the Honour of God, as well as the

71

Good of Mankind, that any Human Power shou'd exceed these Bounds: since all which God, who commands not Impossibilities, requires of us, is an impartial Examination; and consequently that alone, provided we act agreeably, makes us acceptable to him, and therefore ought to render us so to Men, who can have no Right to fix Rewards and Punishments to things which are not of a moral Nature, because they tend to hinder the grand Duty of Consideration. For Men, when they become capable of chusing their Religion, will be discourag'd, from impartially examining those Opinions to which Preferments are annex'd, for fear of finding 'em False; and frighten'd from considering those to which Punishments are affix'd, lest they find 'em True. And therefore all Awes and Bribes are religiously to be avoided, and the Magistrate to treat all his Subjects alike, how much soever they differ from him or one another in these Matters:[2] since, as the contrary Method can only serve to prejudice those who are to chuse their Religion, so it can have no effect on those who have already made their choice (which for the most part, were it not for these Impediments, wou'd be impartially done) except to make them Hypocrites even in the most solemn Acts of Devotion . . .

24. To go further than this, and to suppose the Magistrate has a Right to use Force for the promoting of Truth in his Dominions, must suppose he has a Right to judge for his Subjects what is Truth, and that they are bound to act according to his Determinations: since a Right to punish People for not acting according to his Determinations, necessarily supposes he has a Right to determine for them . . .

. . . So that all Men in forming themselves into Societys for the Worship of God, are in a natural State, neither Prince nor Priest having any more Power over the Peasant, than he has over either of them; but all are to be govern'd by the same Motives. And tho no Church, more than any other voluntary Society, can hold together, except the Members agree on some Place, on the Persons to officiate, and such-like

Circumstances; yet none has a Right to prescribe to another, but every one has for himself a Negative: So that here's a perfect Equality, for no man has any more power over another, than another has over him; and as no man is capable of being represented by another, every one must judge for himself of the Forms and Modes of Worship, the Doctrines, Rites and Ceremonys of any Church, not only before he joins himself to it, but afterwards. And therefore if the determining of such things, as are necessary to be agreed on in order to form a Congregation for the Worship of God, is to be call'd Church-Government, 'tis impossible any Government can be more popular, because none are oblig'd even by a Majority; but those who cannot go with 'em, are to form themselves into a Church after the best manner they can; and two or three thus *gather'd together in the Name of our Saviour*, have the Promise of *his being with them* . . .

29. What has not a little contributed to make Men suppose there are Umpires, Judges or Governors in Religious as well as Civil Matters, is the Magistrate's annexing Profits and Privileges to the Teachers of his own Religion, exclusively of others: and determining who shall license those that are to have these Advantages, and on what Qualifications; and who shall deprive 'em, and for what causes, and such-like. And the chief of the Clergy being the Magistrate's Deputys in this matter, and all of 'em in most Countrys being, generally speaking, of the Religion to which they find Preferments annex'd, do, in order to bring others right or wrong into the same Sentiments, call this *Establishing their Religion and Church by Law*; and make it Schism, and consequently Damnation, not to be of the Church establish'd by Law: which notwithstanding all the noise and din the Clergy make about it, ought not to bias Men, much less take from 'em their natural Right of judging for themselves in matters of Religion, unless they ought to be in all Countrys of that Religion to which they find these Emoluments annex'd . . .

33. ... Nature makes not a greater difference between Man and Brute, than Government does between Man and Man. That which is free, always causes Light and Knowledg in the World; which must confound Priestcraft, a Bird of Night which flees the open day. On the contrary, that which is arbitrary, so cramps Peoples Understanding, that as it never did, so it never can serve to any other use in Religion than to produce Superstition and Priestcraft in abundance ...

36. ... If the Clergy do not find their Interest in promoting Tyranny, what's the reason that if a Prince is so very weak as to be govern'd by them, they put him on violent and arbitrary Methods, till he either ruins himself, or, which is worse, his Country? And we need not go abroad for Examples; since this happy Nation in the memory of Man has felt two fatal Instances of it, by the Court's being bigotted to such a degree in the Reigns of both Father and Son, as to endeavour to subvert the Civil Constitution for the sake of Church, tho' each Court meant a different Church. So that 'tis all one of what Persuasion they are, whether a *Laud* or a *Peters*,[3] who have the management of the *Bigotted Prince*, since the People as well as the Prince are in like danger of being undone.

37. That this was the Ruin of King *James*, is fresh enough in our Memory; and we need go no further to prove this the chief cause of his Father's unhappy Suffering, than a Book lately publish'd in his Vindication: which (tho' printed so many years after, and in all likelihood with more Partiality than the Author himself was guilty of) plainly enough discovers that those unnatural Wars were occasion'd by the Usurpations of High Church; who to maintain the Pomp and Power of their Hierarchy, put the Court upon such oppressive and arbitrary Measures as were insupportable to the best-natur'd People in the World.

From this Conduct of the High-flown Clergy, some have taken the Liberty to compare a High-Church Priest in

Politicks to a Monkey in a Glass-shop, where as he can do no good, so he never fails of doing Mischief enough.[4]

8 *From*
HENRY SACHEVERELL
The Perils of False Brethren
(1709)

... whosoever presumes to Innovate, Alter, or Misrepresent any Point in the Articles of the Faith of our Church, ought to be Arraign'd as a Traytor to our State; Heterodoxy in the Doctrines of the one, naturally producing, and almost necessarily inferring Rebellion, and High Treason in the other, and consequently a Crime that concerns the Civil Magistrate, as much to Punish and Restrain, as the Ecclesiastical. However this Assertion at first View may look like an Highflown Paradox, the Proof of it will fully appear in a few Instances. The grand Security of our Government, and the very Pillar upon which it stands, is founded upon the steady Belief of the Subject's Obligation to an Absolute, and Unconditional Obedience to the Supreme Power, in all things lawful, and the utter Illegality of Resistance upon any Pretence whatsoever. But this Fundamental Doctrine, notwithstanding its Divine Sanction in the Express Command of God in Scripture, and without which, it is impossible any Government of any Kind, or Denomination in the World should subsist with Safety, and which has been so long the Honourable and Distinguishing Characteristick of Our Church, is now, it seems, quite Exploded, and Ridicul'd out of Countenance, as an Unfashionable, Superannuated, nay (which is more wonderful) as a Dangerous Tenet, utterly Inconsistent with the Right, Liberty, and Property, of the PEOPLE; who, as our New Preachers, and New Politicians teach us, (I suppose by a New and Unheard of Gospel, as well as Laws) have in Contradiction to Both, the Power

75

invested in Them, the Fountain and Original of it, to Cancel their Allegiance at pleasure, and call their Sovereign to account for High Treason against his Supreme Subjects forsooth; nay to Dethrone and Murder Him for a Criminal, as they did the Royal Martyr by a Judiciary Sentence. And, what is almost Incredible, presume to make their Court to their Prince, by maintaining such Anti-monarchical Schemes. But, God be Thanked! neither the Constitution of our Church or State, is so far Alter'd, but that by the Laws of Both (still in Force, and which I hope for ever will be) these Damnable Positions, let 'em come either from Rome, or Geneva, from the Pulpit, or the Press, are condemn'd for Rebellion, and High Treason. Our Adversaries think they effectually stop our Mouths, and have us Sure and Unanswerable on this Point, when they urge the Revolution of this Day in their Defence. But certainly They are the Greatest Enemies of That, and His Late Majesty, and the most Ungrateful for the Deliverance, who endeavour to cast such Black and Odious Colours upon Both. How often must they be told, that the King Himself solemnly Disclaim'd the Least Imputation of Resistance in His Declaration; and that the Parliament declar'd, That they set the Crown on his Head, upon no other Title, but that of the Vacancy of the Throne? And did they not Unanimously condemn to the Flames (as it justly Deserv'd) that Infamous Libel, that would have Pleaded the Title of Conquest, by which Resistance was suppos'd? so Tender were they of the Regal Rights, and so averse to infringe the least Tittle of our Constitution! We see how ready these Incendiaries are to take the least Umbrage, to charge their own Cursed Tenets on the Church of England, to Derive their Guilt upon it, and Quit Scores with it for Their Iniquity! Thus do they endeavour to draw Comparisons, and to Justify the Horrid Actions and Principles of Forty One,[1] which have been of late Years, to the Scandal of Our Church, and Nation, so Publickly Defended, not only by the Agents and Writers of the Republican Faction, but by some that have the

76

Confidence to Style themselves Sons, and Presbyters of the Church of England; who in open Defiance of the most peremptory Declarations of God in Scripture, (never to be evaded by any Shifts or Misinterpretations) and the Universal Doctrine, and Expositions of the Catholick Church upon it in all Ages, with the Express Testimony, and Concurrence of Our Church, from its Reformation down to the present Times, corroborated with the Sense of Our Legislature, so unexceptionably confirm'd in Our Laws, Dare, in Despight and Contempt of all this Evidence, manifestly Defend the Resistance of the Supreme Power, under a New-fangl'd Notion of Self-Defence; the only Instance they show of Shame, that they dare not YET maintain Rebellion by its Proper Name . . .

These FALSE BRETHREN in Our Government, do not singly, and in private spread their Poyson, but (what is lamentable to be spoken) are suffer'd to combine into Bodies, and Seminaries, wherein Atheism, Deism, Tritheism, Socinianism,[2] with all the Hellish Principles of Fanaticism, Regicide, and Anarchy, are openly profess'd and taught, to corrupt and debauch the Youth of the Nation, in all Parts of it, down to Posterity, to the present Reproach, and future Extirpation of Our Laws, and Religion. Certainly the Toleration was never intended to Indulge, and cherish such Monsters, and Vipers in our Bosom, that scatter Their Pestilence at Noon-day, and will rend, distract, and confound, the firmest and Best-settl'd Constitution in the World. In short, as the English Government can never be secure on any other Principles, but strictly those of the Church of England, so I will be bold to say, where any Part of it is Trusted in Persons of any Other Notions, They must be False to Themselves, if They are True to Their Trusts; or if They are True to Their Opinions, and Interests, must Betray That Government They are Enemies to upon Principle. Indeed, We must do 'em that Justice, to confess, That since the Sectarists have found out a Way (which their Forefathers, God knows, as Wicked as they were, would have Abhorr'd) to swallow not only Oaths, but Sacraments, to Qualifie themselves to get into Places, and Preferments; these Sanctify'd Hypocrites can put on a shew of Loyalty, and seem tolerably Easy in the Government, if they can Engross the Honours and Profits of it: But let Her Majesty reach out Her Little Finger to touch their Loyns, and these sworn Adversaries to Passive Obedience, and the Royal Family, shall fret themselves, and Curse their Queen, and their God, and shall look upwards. And so much for Our Political FALSE BRETHREN, 'till I come to speak with 'em again by and by . . .

II. Secondly, To lay before You the great Peril, and Mischiefs of these FALSE BRETHREN in Church and State; which I shall endeavour to do, by Proving that They Weaken, Undermine, and Betray in themselves, and Encourage, and put it in the Power of Our Profess'd Enemies, to Overturn, and Destroy the Constitution and Establishment of Both.

1. And First, as to the Church. But here it is very Necessary to Premise, That by the Church of England, We are to understand the True Genuine Notion of it, as it stands Contradistinguish'd in its Establish'd Doctrine, Discipline, and Worship, from all other Churches, and Schismaticks, who would Obtrude upon us, a Wild, Negative Idea of a NATIONAL CHURCH, so as to Incorporate Themselves into the Body, as True Members of it; Whereas 'tis evident that this Latitudinarian, Heterogeneous Mixture of all Persons of what different Faith soever, Uniting in Protestancy, (which is but one single Note of the Church of England) would render it the most Absurd, Contradictory, and Self-Inconsistent Body in the World. This Spurious, and Villainous Notion, which will take in Jews, Quakers, Mahometans, and any thing as well as Christians, as ridiculously incongruous as 'tis, may be first observ'd, as One of Those Prime, Popular Engines, our FALSE BRETHREN have made use of to Undermine the very Essential

78

Constitution of our Church; which as it stands Guarded with its own Sacred Fences, with her only True Sons in her Bosom, may defy all the Malice of the Devil, and her Enemies, to prevail against her. But such is her hard Fortune, her Worst Adversaries must be let into her Bowels, under the holy Umbrage of Sons, who neither Believe her Faith, Own her Mission, submit to her Discipline, or Comply with her Liturgy. And to admit this Religious Trojan Horse, big with Arms and Ruin, into our Holy City, the Streight Gate must be laid quite open, her Walls, and Inclosures pull'd down, and an High-Road made in upon her Communion, and this pure Spouse of Christ Prostituted to more Adulterers than the Scarlet Whore in the Revelations. Her Articles must be Taught the Confusion of all Senses, Nations, and Languages, to render her a Babel, and Desolation. This was indeed the ready way to fill the House of God, but with what? With Pagan Beasts, instead of Christian Sacrifices, with such Unhallow'd Loathsome, and Detestable Guests, as would have Driv'n out the Holy Spirit of God with Indignation. This Pious Design of making our House of Prayer a Den of Thieves, of Reforming Our Church into a Chaos, is well known to have been Attempted several times in this Kingdom, and lately within our Memory, when all things seem'd to Favour it, but that Good Providence, which so happily Interpos'd, against the Ruin of Our Church, and Blasted the long-projected Scheme of these Ecclesiastical Achitophels.[3] A Scheme so Monstrous, so Romantic, and Absurd, that 'tis hard to say, whether it had more of Villany, or Folly in it, and which even the Sectarists of all sorts (who will not be satisfy'd with any thing less than Sovereignty) Exploded, and Laugh'd at, as Ridiculous, and Impracticable. It was doubtless a Wise way to Exemplify Our Brotherly Love and Charity for the Souls of Men, to put both Them, and Ourselves into a Gulph of Perdition, by throwing up the Essentials of Our Faith, and the Uniformity of Our Worship . . .

2. Thus we see how Dangerous these FALSE BRETHREN are to Our Church, which is so Great, and Considerable a Branch of our Civil Constitution, that the Support of Our Government depends upon its Welfare, and what Affects That must strike at the Foundation of Our State; Innovations in either, tending to the Subversion of their Laws, and the Unsettling the Establishment, and consequently to Anarchy and Confusion . . .

FALSEHOOD always implies Treachery; and whether That is a Qualification for any One to be Trusted, especially with the Guardianship of our Church, or Crown, let our Governors consider . . .

. . . That the Old Leaven of their Fore-Fathers is still Working in their Present Generation, and that this Traditional Poyson still remains in this Brood of Vipers, to Sting Us to Death, is sufficiently Visible, from the Dangerous Encroachments They now make upon our Government, and the Treasonable Reflections They have Publish'd on Her Majesty, God bless Her! Whose Hereditary Right to the Throne, They have had the Impudence to Deny, and Cancel, to make Her a Creature of their own Power; and that by the same Principles They plac'd a Crown upon Her, They tell Us, They (That is, the Mob) may Reassume it at their Pleasure. Nay, now they have Advanc'd themselves from the Religious Liberty Our Gracious Sovereign has Indulg'd them, to Claim a Civil Right, as they Term it, and to Justle the Church out of Her Establishment, by Hoisting their Toleration into its Place; and to convince Us what alone will satisfy 'em, insolently Demand the Repeal of the Corporation, and Test Acts, as an Ecclesiastical Usurpation, which, indeed, under Her Majesty (whom God long Preserve for its Comfort and Support!) is the only Security the Church has to Depend upon.

9   From
BENJAMIN HOADLY
*A Sermon Preach'd
before the King*
(1717)

1. As the *Church* of *Christ* is the *Kingdom of Christ*, *He*
himself is *King*: and in this it is implied, that *He* is himself the
sole *Law-giver* to his *Subjects*, and himself the sole *Judge* of
their *Behaviour*, in the Affairs of Conscience and *Eternal
Salvation*. And in this Sense therefore, *His Kingdom is not of
this World*; that He hath, in those Points, left behind Him, no
visible, humane *Authority*; no *Vicegerents*, who can be said
properly to supply his Place; no Interpreters, upon whom his
Subjects are absolutely to depend; no *Judges* over the
Consciences or Religion of his People. For if this were so,
that any such absolute *Vicegerent Authority*, either for the
making *new Laws*, or interpreting *Old* Ones, or *judging* his
Subjects, in *Religious* Matters, were lodged in any Men upon
Earth; the Consequence would be, that what still retains the
Name of the *Church* of *Christ*, would not be the *Kingdom of
Christ*, but the *Kingdom* of those Men, vested with such
Authority. For, whoever hath such an *Authority* of making
Laws, is so far a *King*: and whoever can add new Laws to
those of *Christ*, equally obligatory, is as truly a *King*, as
Christ himself is. Nay, whoever hath an *absolute Authority* to
interpret any written, or spoken Laws; it is *He*, who is truly
the *Law-giver*, to all Intents and Purposes; and not the Person
who first wrote, or spoke them.

In humane Society, the *Interpretation* of *Laws*, may, of
necessity, be lodged, in some Cases, in the Hands of Those
who were not originally the *Legislators*. But this is not
absolute; nor of bad consequence to *Society*: because the
Legislators can resume the *Interpretation* into their own
Hands, as they are Witnesses to what passes in the World;
and as They can, and will, sensibly interpose in all those

Cases, in which their Interposition becomes necessary. And therefore, They are still properly the *Legislators*. But it is otherwise in *Religion*, or the *Kingdom* of *Christ*. He himself never interposeth, since his first Promulgation of his *Law*, either to convey *Infallibility* to Such as pretend to handle it over again; or to assert the true *Interpretation* of it, amidst the various and contradictory Opinions of Men about it. If *He* did certainly thus interpose, He himself would still be the *Legislator*. But, as *He* doth not; if such an absolute *Authority* be once lodged with Men, under the Notion of *Interpreters*, *They* then become the *Legislators*, and not Christ; and *They* rule in their own *Kingdom*, and not in *His*.

It is the same thing, as to Rewards and Punishments, to carry forward the great End of his *Kingdom*. If any Men upon Earth have a *Right* to add to the *Sanctions* of his *Laws*; that is, to increase the Number, or alter the Nature, of the *Rewards* and *Punishments* of his Subjects, in Matters of Conscience, or Salvation: They are so far *Kings* in his stead; and Reign in *their own* Kingdom, and not in *His*. So it is, whenever They erect *Tribunals*, and exercise a *Judgment* over the Consciences of Men; and assume to Themselves the Determination of such Points, as cannot be determined, but by *One* who knows the Hearts; or, when They make any of their own Declarations, or Decisions, to concern and affect the State of Christ's Subjects, with regard to the Favour of God: this is so far, the taking *Christ's Kingdom* out of *His* Hands, and placing it in their own . . .

If therefore, the *Church* of *Christ* be the *Kingdom* of *Christ*; it is essential to it, that *Christ* himself be the Sole *Law-giver*, and Sole *Judge* of his Subjects, in all points relating to the favour or displeasure of *Almighty God*; and that All His *Subjects*, in what Station soever they may be, are equally *Subjects* to *Him*; and that No One of them, any more than Another, hath *Authority*, either to make *New Laws* for *Christ*'s Subjects; or to impose a sense upon the *Old* Ones, which is the same thing; or to *Judge*, Censure, or Punish, the

Servants of *Another Master*, in matters relating purely to *Conscience*, or *Salvation*. If any Person hath any other Notion, either thro' a long Use of Words with Inconsistent Meanings, or thro' a negligence of Thought; let him but ask himself, whether the *Church* of *Christ* be the Kingdom of *Christ*, or not: And, if it be, whether this Notion of it doth not absolutely exclude all other *Legislators* and *Judges*, in matters relating to Conscience, or the favour of God; or, whether it can be *His* Kingdom, if any Mortal Men have such a Power of *Legislation* and *Judgement* in it . . .

2. From what hath been said it appears that the *Kingdom* of *Christ*, which is the *Church* of *Christ*, is the *Number* of Persons who are Sincerely, and Willingly, *Subjects* to *Him*, as *Law-giver* and *Judge*, in all matters truly relating to Conscience, or Eternal Salvation. And the more close and immediate this Regard to *Him* is, the more certainly and the more evidently true it is, that They are of his *Kingdom*. This may appear fully to their own Satisfaction, if They have recourse to *Him* himself, in the *Gospel*; if They think it is a sufficient Authority that He hath declared the *Conditions* of their *Salvation*, and that No Man upon Earth hath any Authority to declare any other, or to add one tittle to them . . .

3. This will be *Another observation*, that it evidently destroys the *Rule* and *Authority* of *Jesus Christ*, as *King*, to set up any Other *Authority* in *His Kingdom*, to which His Subjects are indispensably and absolutely obliged to Submit their Consciences, or their Conduct, in what is properly called Religion. There are *some* Professed Christians, who contend openly for such an *Authority*, as indispensably obliged All around Them to *Unity* of Profession; that is, to Profess even what They do not, what They cannot, believe to be true. This sounds so grossly, that *Others*, who think They act a glorious part in opposing such an Enormity, are very willing, for their own sakes, to retain such an *Authority* as shall oblige Men, whatever They themselves think, though not to profess what They do not believe, yet, to forbear the *profession* and

publication of what They do believe, let them believe it of never so great Importance...

The *Peace* of *Christ's Kingdom* is a manly and Reasonable *Peace*; built upon Charity, and Love, and mutual forbearance, and receiving one another, as God receives us. As for any other *Peace*; founded upon a Submission of our *Honesty*, as well as our *Understandings*; it is falsely so called. It is not the *Peace* of the *Kingdom* of *Christ*; but the *Lethargy* of it: and a *Sleep unto Death*, when his *Subjects* shall throw off their relation to *Him*; fix their subjection to *Others*; and even in Cases, where They have a right to see, and where They think They see, his Will otherwise, shall shut their Eyes and go blindfold at the Command of *Others*; because those *Others* are not pleas'd with their Enquiries into the Will of their great Lord and Judge.

10   From
WILLIAM WOLLASTON
The Religion of Nature
Delineated
(*1725*)

XI. *To be governed by reason is the general law imposed by the Author of nature upon them, whose uppermost faculty is reason: as the dictates of it in particular cases are the particular laws, to which they are subject.* As there are beings, which have not so much as sense, and others that have no faculty above it; so there may be some, who are indued with reason, but have nothing higher than that. It is sufficient at present to suppose there may be such. And then if reason be the *uppermost* faculty, it has a right to controll the rest by being *such*. As in sensitive animals sense commands gravitation and mechanical motions in those instances, for which their senses are given, and carries them out into spontaneous acts: so in rational animals the gradation requires, that reason should command sense.

It is plain, that reason is of a commanding nature: it joins this, condemns that, only allows some other things, and will be paramount ... if it is at all. Now a being, who has such a determining and governing power so placed in his nature, as to be essential to him, is a being certainly framed to be governed by that power. It seems to be as much designed by nature, or rather the Author of nature, that rational animals should use their reason, and steer by it; as it is by the shipwright, that the pilot should direct the vessel by the use of the rudder he has fitted to it. The rudder would not be there, if it was not to be used: nor would reason be implanted in any nature only to be not cultivated and neglected. And it is certain, it cannot be used, but it must command: such is its nature.

It is not in one's power deliberately to resolve not to be governed by reason. For ... if he could do this, he must either have some reason for making that resolution, or none. If he has none, it is a resolution, that stands upon no foundation, and therefore in course falls: and if he has some reason for it, he is governed by reason. This *demonstrates* that reason must govern.

XII. *If a rational being, as such, is under an obligation to obey reason, and this obedience, or practice of reason, coincides with the observation of truth, these things plainly follow.*

1. ... to him nothing can be right, that interferes with reason, and nothing can interfere with truth, but it must interfere with reason. Such a harmony is there between them. For whatever is known to be true, reason either finds it, or allows it to be such. Nothing can be taken for true by a rational being, if he has a reason to the contrary. 2. That there is to a rational being such a thing as *religion* which may also upon this further account properly be called *natural*. For

85

certainly to obey the law, which the Author of his being has given him, is religion: and to obey the law, which He has given or reveald to him by making it to result from the right use of his own natural faculties, must be to him his *natural religion*. 3. A careful observation of truth, the way to happiness, and the practice of reason are in the issue the same thing. For, of the two last, each falls in with the first, and therefore each with other. And so, at last, natural religion is grounded upon this triple and strict alliance or union of *truth*, *happiness*, and *reason*; all in the same interest, and conspiring by the same methods, to advance and perfect human nature: and its truest definition is, *The pursuit of happiness by the practice of reason and truth*.

II. *He, that well examins himself, I suppose, will find these things to be true.*

1. That there are *some* things *common* to him not only *with sensitive animals* and *vegetables*, but also with *inanimate matter*: as, that his body is subject to the general law of gravitation; that its parts are capable of being separated, or dislocated; and that therefore he is in danger from falls, and all impressions of violence.

2. That there are *other* things *common* to him with *vegetables* and *sensitive animals*: as, that he comes from a seed (such the original *animalculum*[1] may be taken to be); grows, and is preserved by proper matter, taken in and distributed through a set of vessels; ripens, flourishes, withers, decays, dies; is subject to diseases, may be hurt, or killed; and therefore wants, as they do, nourishment, a proper habitation, protection from injuries, and the like.

3. That he has *other* properties *common* only to *him* and the *sensitive tribe*: as, that he receives by his senses the notice of many external objects, and things; perceives many affections of his body; finds pleasure from some, and pain from others; and has certain powers of moving himself, and acting: *that is*, he is not only obnoxious to hurts, diseases, and

the causes of death, but also *feels* them; is not only capable of nourishment, and many other provisions made for him, but also *injoys* them; and, beside, may *contribute* much himself to either his injoyments, or his sufferings.

4.   That *beside these* he has *other faculties*, which he doth not apprehend to be either in the inert mass of matter, or in vegetables, or even in the sensitive kind, at least in any considerable degree; by the help of which he investigates truth, or probability, and judges, whether things are agreeable to them, or not, after the manner set down in sect. III. or, in a word, that he is *animal rationale*[2] . . .

III.   *If he doth find these things to be so, then if he will act as he ought to do* (*that is, agreeably to* truth *and* fact) *he must do such things as these*.

1.   *He must subject his sensual inclinations, his bodily passions, and the motions of all his members to reason*; *and try every thing by it*. For in the *climax* set down he cannot but observe, that as the principle of *vegetation* is something above the *inertia* of mere matter, and *sense* something above that again; so reason must be something above all these: or, that his uppermost faculty is *reason*. And from hence it follows, that he is one of those beings mentioned sect. III. prop. XI. and that the great *law* imposed upon him is to be *governed by reason*.

Any man may prove this to himself by experiment, if he pleases. Because he cannot (at least without great violence to his nature) do any thing, if he has a greater reason against the doing of it than for it. When men do err against reason, it is either because they do not (perhaps *will* not) advert, and use their reason, or *not enough*; or because their faculties are defective.

And further . . . to endeavour to act according to right reason, and to endeavour to act according to truth are in effect the same thing. We cannot do the one, but we must do the other. We cannot act according to truth, or so as *not to deny any truth*, and that is we cannot act *right*, unless we endeavour to act according to *right reason*, and are led by it.

Therefore not to subject one's *sensitive* inclinations and passions to *reason* is to *deny* either that he is rational, or that reason is the supreme and ruling faculty in his nature: and that is to desert mankind, and to *deny* himself to be what he knows himself by experience and in his own conscience upon examination to be, and what he would be very angry if any body should say he was not.

If a *beast* could be supposed to give up his *sense* and activity; neglect the calls of hunger, and those appetites by which he (according to his *nature*) is to be guided; and refusing to use the powers, with which he is indued in order to get his food and preserve his life, lie still in some place, and expect to grow, and be fed like a *plant*; this would be much the same case, only not so bad, as when a *man* cancels his *reason*, and as it were strives to metamorphize himself into a *brute*. And yet this he does, who pursues only sensual objects, and leaves himself to the impulses of appetite and passion. For as in that case the *brute* neglects the law of *his nature*, and affects that of the order *below* him: so doth the *man* disobey the law of *his nature*, and put himself under that of the *lower* animals: to whom he thus makes a defection.

If this be so, how wretchedly do they violate the *order* of nature, and transgress against *truth*, who not only *reject* the conduct of reason to follow sense and passion, but even make it *subservient* to them; who use it only in finding out means to effect their wicked ends, but never apply it to the consideration of those ends, or the nature of those means, whether they are just or unjust, *right* or *wrong*? This is not only to *deviate* from the path of nature, but to *invert* it, and to become something *more* than *brutish*; *brutes with reason*, which must be the most enormous and worst of all brutes. When the *brute* is governed by sense and bodily appetites, he observes *his proper* rule; when a *man* is governed after that manner in defiance of reason, he *violates* his: but when he makes his rational powers to *serve* the brutish part, to assist and promote it, he heightens and increases the *brutality*, inlarges its field, makes it to act with greater force and effect, and becomes a *monster* . . .

I must confess however, that our *passions* are so *very apt* to grow upon us, and become exorbitant, if they are not kept under an *exact discipline*, that by way of prevention or caution it is advisable rather to affect a *degree* of apathy, or to recede *more* from the worse extreme. This very proposition itself, which, when *reason* is absent, places *sense* and inclination in the chair, obliges not to permit the reins to our passions, or give them their full career; because if we do, they may (and will) carry us into such *excesses*, such *dangers* and *mischiefs*, as may sadly affect the sensitive part of us: that part itself, which now governs. They ought to be watched, and well examind; if *reason* is on their side, or stands neuter, they are to be heard (this is all, that I say): in *other cases* we must be deaf to their applications, strongly guard against their emotions, and *in due time* prevent their rebelling against the sovereign faculty.

IV

Politics and Parties

The following extracts are clustered around three related topics: the existence, function and definition of the Whig and Tory parties; the widespread notion of the 'mixed' (and, it was thought, peculiarly English) *style* of government in which there is a mixture of monarchy, aristocracy and democracy; and the *functional* characteristics of the 'balanced constitution', in which the executive is balanced by the legislative through a co-operation of King, Lords and Commons. All these issues were of vital importance to the development of England following the Glorious Revolution. Many believed that parties were a curse on the nation: few disputed the blessings of the two latter characteristics. Swift offered his prepared positions notably in the *Contests and Dissensions* and in the *Examiner* papers, *The Sentiments of a Church of England Man* and ultimately in *Gulliver's Travels*.

Though the precise composition of political parties up to 1702 eludes simple definition, there is no doubt that the very existence of Whig and Tory obsessed Swift and his contemporaries. In her speech from the throne in May 1702 Queen Anne prayed to be delivered from 'the mercyless men of both partys' and protested 'All I desire is, my liberty in encouraging and employing all those that concur faithfully in my service, whether they are called Whigs or Tories, not to be tied to one, nor the other.' Those of the Tory persuasion (especially Swift and Bolingbroke) publicly deplored the existence of parties as divisive and fundamentally unnecessary barriers to the expression of national unity and the national will. Each privately acknowledged the assertion that the seed of party loyalty lay in human personality and vigorously joined the partisan battle. Scandalous caricatures of each others' views were adopted by both parties.

The Tories, assuming that they represented the true national interest, accused the Whigs of being a pressure group for factional interests; the Whigs saw themselves defending the people's rights against arbitrary power, Popery and/or religious monopoly by the Established Church. In 1708, when Swift was moderately Whiggish, he claimed in the *Sentiments* that there was a post-Revolutionary agreement between the parties on basic issues such as 'Loyalty to the Queen, the Abjuration of the *Pretender*, the Settlement of the Crown in the *Protestant* Line; and a *Revolution Principle* . . .; Affection to the Church Established, with Toleration of *Dissenters*.' In the same year the Whig Burnet also claimed (*History of My Own Time*), 'in every corner of the nation the two parties stand, as it were, listed against one another.' Swift indeed was arguing a desirable fiction in the teeth of a hard-pressing reality: he observed that 'the Spirit of Faction' had broken 'all the Laws of Charity, Neighbourhood, Alliance and Hospitality; destroyed all Ties of Friendship, and divided Families against themselves'.

Contemporary moments of crisis sharpened the lines of party division: in 1710 the fourth article of impeachment charged Sacheverell that 'as a public incendiary, he persuades her Majesty's subjects to keep up a distinction of faction and parties'. After 1714, when the Tory party was out of office, tainted by Jacobitism and without effective parliamentary leadership, Tories such as Swift saw the continuation of the 'party' issue as evidence of Walpole's duplicity in maintaining division in order to retain office. Yet even within the Whig camp, Pope noted in 1717, internal strife was manifest and bitter: 'The Political State is under great divisions, the

Parties of Walpole and Stanhope are as violent as Whig and Tory' (*Correspondence*, I, 407). Small wonder is it that the detached and urbane King of Brobdingnag in *Gulliver's Travels* finds the question of a man's Whig or Tory loyalty a subject of condescending amusement, an example of human folly. At the court of Lilliput Swift reduces *all* ambitious politicians to the level of performing monkeys and proclaims the identity of purpose in the two parties by nearly identical names: *Tramecksan* allegorises the High Church Tories, *Slamecksan* the Low Church Whigs. Yet it was only in the fantasy world of Gulliver that Swift could escape the reality of party politics.

Originally the formation of party politics dated from the Exclusion Crisis of 1679–81, which had focussed the inseparable political and religious loyalties into two camps. Before the Revolution of 1688 Tory loyalties were characterised by a belief in divine hereditary right, passive obedience and loyalty to the Anglican Church. The Whigs, broadly speaking, were prepared to reject the first of these in order to ensure a Protestant succession after Charles II's death, and Locke evolved their theoretical platform of government by consent and defined the rights of resistance. The Exclusion Crisis forced these two broad positions into opposition and isolated certain fundamentals, such as the Whig stand on freedom of worship for Protestant Dissenters. After 1688 the Tory notion of divine right and passive obedience became theoretically untenable: James II had been deposed and the crown bestowed on a foreigner, who was a Calvinist and no direct descendent. Restrictions were placed on the King's power by the Bill of Rights (1689) and the Toleration Act realised some of the Whig claims for Dissent. Clear lines of party loyalty were broken up by the national crisis in 1688, but had firmly been reformed by 1702 and the accession of Anne.[1]

At times Swift felt keenly the tensions between personal friendship and party loyalty in a world of constantly shifting political dogmas. In the *Sentiments of a Church of England Man* (1708) the whole question of a man's political allegiance had been subordinated to a concern for *personal* integrity: 'I should think that, in order to preserve the Constitution entire in Church and State, whoever hath a true Value for both, would be sure to avoid the Extremes of Whig for the Sake of the former, and the Extremes of Tory on account of the Latter.'

When he was writing for the *Examiner* paper Swift reinforced his choice of the middle way by an argued case. In propagandising Harley's ministerial policy of moderation Swift found a congenial task, for it appeared to offer a way out of the party monopoly of truth: 'there is a very good Word, which hath of late suffered much by both Parties; I mean MODERATION.' Halifax's *Character of a Trimmer* (1688) had elaborated the thesis of uncommitted moderation for post-Revolutionary society and suggests the kind of political integrity above party politics which is sometimes discernible as a nostalgic ideal in several Augustan writers. Halifax, like Swift, regarded the existence of political parties as an affront to the right-thinking man of independent mind; his Trimmer pragmatically states, however:

If there are two Parties, a man ought to adhere to that which he disliketh least, though in the whole he doth not approve it; for whilst he doth not list himself in one or the other Party he is looked upon as such a straggler that he is fallen upon by both. Therefore a man under such a misfortune of singularity is neither to provoke the world, nor disquiet himself by taking any particular station.

For Halifax God himself was a Trimmer, moderating between his two attributes of mercy and justice: the rest naturally follows—that the English constitution was a trimmer between the extremes of arbitrary power and mob rule, where the monarch, in order to safeguard the flexible operation of a mixed and balanced constitution, stays above party feuds, thus balancing the necessary prerogative of the virtuous prince ('law' and 'authority') and the 'natural' rights of the people.

Whilst it was difficult enough to hold such views *before* 1688, for Tories such as Swift after 1714 such ideas were positively Utopian, or at least Brobdingnagian. Increasingly after 1720, Walpole seemed immovably ensconced in a pervasive Whig oligarchy (later dubbed the 'Robinocracy'); the Whiggish George seemed a far cry from Halifax's notion of the virtuous, detached prince; and government had come to be dominated by the party issue (as Rapin was to point out in his *Dissertation* in 1717). Accordingly, in Gulliver's third voyage we meet the scientists who have thought of solving the divisive party issue by performing lobotomies on politicians, cancelling out partisan loyalties by the mutual transplantation of brains fevered by partisan strife: a physical solution to an exasperating and apparently permanent ideological problem.[2]

Anne's reign was indeed studded with political events which revealed the sometimes stark antagonism between the Whigs and Tories.[3] The crisis in 1701–2 over the Protestant succession (again in 1714); dissensions in Convocation, the organ of church government, which had made it unworkable since the beginning of her reign; the Occasional Conformity Bill; peace negotiations with France in 1711–12. None of these raised so much heat as the Sacheverell affair of 1710, when the Whigs decided to prosecute the inflammatory and anti-ministerial sermons of this extreme Tory preacher. The central fact of this trial was that it elicited a vital debate on the Revolution principles and the nature of authority in the State. In the event the Whigs' plan misfired: it appeared that the Whigs were attempting to try Sacheverell's High Church Tory beliefs in order to discredit them; his trial enlisted vociferous popular support and united the Tory party under the old slogan 'the Church in danger'. The importance of the trial for the Whigs may be seen in the report of the prosecuting speech of Lechmere. With an eye on guaranteeing the future Protestant succession he is concerned to unite feeling against Sacheverell by stating his case with dogmatic clarity and an assumption of universal concurrence in the principles of 1688. Thus he steers a careful course: loyalty to the Church of England, but toleration for dissent; allegiance to the monarch, together with a jealously guarded right to resist in defence of individual liberties. Resistance itself is now 'part of the ancient legal Constitution' of the English government. In impugning this right of resistance in 1688 Sacheverell is seen to have discredited William III (the deliverer from arbitrary power) and the subsequent Protestant succession in Anne. Sacheverell's defence was skilfully conducted with the help of Swift's friend Atterbury and Harcourt: his derisory sentence of three years suspension from preaching was received as a Tory victory, much-needed in their disunified state and doubtless a factor in their coming to power under the moderate Harley in 1710.[4]

In his *Dissertation upon the Whigs and Tories* (1717) Rapin was prompt to admit the difficulties in assigning precise definitions to the terms Whig and Tory. As Swift had put it in the *Sentiments of a Church of England Man*, the problem lay in the 'generally scandalous views mutually flung about, that the Whigs were all for Presbytery, Catholicism, a Commonwealth and arbitrary Power' and the Tories were all for 'Episcopacy, as an Apostolical Institution' and abhorred Republicanism. With the independent view of an outsider Rapin was initially well placed to judge their titles by their apparent functions, and his lucid analysis of the infrastructure of the Whig and Tory groups takes account of the way in which component parts were stirred by particular issues which by no means always moved the parties as a whole. Some extreme Tories might be willing to support the Pretender; most were embarrassed by the small noisy band of parliamentary Jacobites. Some Whigs were extreme Republicans; most were happy with a Protestant monarch. As Tindal pointed out in an introductory note to his translation of Rapin's *Dissertation*, the political rivalries between Whig and Tory had taken on European significance as a result of the Treaty of Utrecht—'the adherents of France are Tories, and her enemies Whigs', as he bluntly puts it. Rapin's consistent point in his *Dissertation* is that the present excellence and future stability of English political society depend on men of moderate persuasion in both parties, and on that curiously English form of 'mixed' government. Around the 'true Englishmen', i.e. the moderates, revolve the extremes of Church–Tories (High Flyers) and Republican Whigs, obstructions to the fulfilment of England's political destiny. Though Rapin does not discredit party loyalty his hard-headed analysis of political motivation recognises self-interest as its driving force, and each party's existence may be viewed as an illustration of the failings of human nature, for

it is not easy to observe a just neutrality, because it is difficult to be without ambition and avarice. Those who stand neuter ... are neither preferred nor trusted, by reason that one of the parties are always in power, and have nothing more at heart than the advancing their friends, or gaining some of their adversaries.

a sentiment in accord with Halifax and Swift's thinking.

Rapin's outline of England's 'mixed' government, a combination and balance of monarchy, aristocracy and democracy, features prominently in Bolingbroke's *Dissertation upon Parties* (1733–4). The aim of Rapin had been objective analysis, his viewpoint moulded by his moderation: Bolingbroke's treatise was in part a covert attack on Walpolean Whigs from the standpoint of an opposition Tory. His praise of the English constitution as a dynamic mixture threatened by Whig domination and the 'moneyed interest' is thus an apology for a view of society which resisted change in certain economic aspects. Swift and Bolingbroke each found disagreeable the increasing concentration of wealth in the hands of the money traders—stock jobbers, speculators, etc.—though Bolingbroke could see the value of merchants who were building England's commercial empire by trade. Each feared that the political power of money would be divorced from its social responsibilities, traditionally vested in and exercised by the aristocracy. Thus the parallels which Bolingbroke draws between the grandeur of Rome and, by implication, England under the previous Tory administration up to 1714 (when he himself was its secretary of state) are calculated to reflect badly upon the contemporary corruption, venality and constitutional imbalance of Walpole's administration.[5]

Apart from the fictional Brobdingnagian monarchy in *Gulliver's Travels*, Swift's most carefully prepared defence of the balance of power in a mixed constitution is found in *A Discourse of the Contests and Dissensions between the Nobles and Commons in Athens and Rome* (1701). Here the balance of power between mob, party and potentate, or commons, nobles and king, is seen as the antidote to the infection of party and factional power. Its title clearly indicates its method—parallel history. The essential characteristic of this genre is that history is used to teach by example (see Bolingbroke's *Letters on the Study and Use of History*, 1735), to warn by authoritative precedent (since what has happened in the past may happen again), and to lend inevitability to the commentator's analysis of a contemporary situation. Swift's *Discourse* and Bolingbroke's *On the Policy of the Athenians* (1732) refine the device of parallel history to a high degree of political polemic: each uses Athenian history, the former being a defence of the impeached Whig lords, the latter a Tory attack on the power of the Whig Walpole. Bolingbroke's essay is a purer example of the genre, in the sense that the *Policy of the Athenians* mentions no contemporary events or personalities and may be read feasibly as an innocent antiquarian exercise. But in both cases the crucial relevance is achieved by their timing. Swift's *Discourse* was substantially composed 'in a few weeks', though was probably overtaken by events;[6] Bolingbroke's essay was part of *The Craftman*'s anti-Whig propaganda at a time when Walpole's power seemed absolute.

As a technique of indirect comment parallel history is related to the political allegory of *Gulliver's Travels*: each permits the transposition of a complex and inimical contemporary situation into simpler terms and allows criticism to be covert. Bolingbroke gains a certain elevation of style and argumentative dignity by using Athenian history (as does Swift in the *Discourse*), but his view of Walpole as the tyrannical Pericles is limited by its given historical context, however forceful a denunciation may result. Swift's image of Walpole as Flimnap in the voyage to Lilliput is not controlled by the demands of an actual and historic situation: his allegorical presentation gives him permanent imaginative life and, to his redoubled shame, he becomes the generic figure of the cringing politician. Thus historical allusion is at the centre of the total meaning. Swift's view of history is the same as Dryden's. In his *Life of Plutarch* (1683) Dryden claimed that History

helps us to judge of what will happen, by shewing us the like revolutions of former times. For mankind being the same in all ages, agitated by the same passions, and moved to action by the same interests, nothing can come to pass but some precedent of the like nature has already been produced, so that having the causes before our eyes, we cannot easily be deceived in the effects, if we have judgement enough to draw the parallel.

NOTES

1 See further Geoffrey Holmes, *British Politics in the Age of Anne* (Macmillan, London, 1967), pp. 20–1, and 47.
2 Cf. Halifax's note in *Of Parties*: 'Party cutteth off one half of the world from the other, so that the mutual improvement of men's understandings by conversing, etc., is lost, and men are half undone when they lose the advantage of knowing what their enemies think of them' (Halifax: *Complete Works*, ed. J. P. Kenyon, Penguin, Harmondsworth, 1969, p. 209).
3 For Swift's discussion of the 'Cant-words of *Whig* and *Tory*', see *Examiner* 43 (1711), *Prose*, III, 162–7.
4 See Geoffrey Holmes, *The Trial of Dr Sacheverell* (Methuen, London, 1973), chapter X.

5   Walpole's characteristic method of retaining political control was
    through patronage and placemen. *The Craftsman* published a list of
    offices held by Walpole and his relatives from 1722: 'First Lord of
    the Treasury, Mr Walpole. Chancellor of the Exchequer, Mr
    Walpole. Clerk of the Pells, Mr Walpole's son. Customs of London,
    second son of Mr Walpole, in Reversion. Secretary of the Treasury,
    Mr Walpole's brother. Postmaster-General, Mr Walpole's brother.
    Secretary to Ireland, Mr Walpole's brother. Secretary to the
    Postmaster-General, Mr Walpole's brother-in-law.' Quoted in J. H.
    Plumb, *The First Four Georges* (Batsford, London, 1956), p. 74.
6   See *Prose*, VIII, 119 and Ehrenpreis, *Swift*, II, 44–8 for the
    circumstances surrounding the composition of the *Discourse*.

11   From
HALIFAX
The Character of a Trimmer
(1688)

When all is said, there is a natural 'reason of state'—an
undefinable thing, grounded upon the common good of
mankind—which is immortal, and in all changes and
revolutions still preserveth its original right of saving a nation
when the letter of the law perhaps would destroy it, and, by
whatsoever means it moveth, carrieth a power with it that
admitteth of no opposition, being supported by Nature, which
inspireth an immediate consent at some critical times into
every individual member to that which visibly tendeth to the
preservation of the whole; and this being so, a wise Prince,
instead of controverting the right of this 'reason of state', will
by all means endeavour it may be of his side, and then he will
be secure.

Our Trimmer cannot conceive that the power of any Prince
can be lasting but where it is built upon the foundation of his
own unborrowed virtue . . .[1]

. . . Our Trimmer admireth our blessed constitution, in
which dominion and liberty are so happily reconciled. It
giveth to the Prince the glorious power of commanding
freemen, and to the subjects the satisfaction of seeing that

power so lodged as that their liberties are secure. It doth not allow the Crown such a ruining power as that no grass can grow wherever it treadeth, but a cherishing and protecting power—such a one as hath a grim aspect only to the offending subjects, but is the joy and the pride of all the good ones; their own interest being so bound up in it as to engage them to defend and support it. And though in some instances the King is restrained, yet nothing in the government can move without him. Our laws make a true distinction between vassalage and obedience, between devouring prerogatives and a licentious ungovernable freedom; and as, of all the orders of building, the composite[2] is the best, so ours, by a happy mixture and a wise choice of what is best in others, is brought into a form that is our felicity who live under it, and the envy of our neighbours that cannot imitate it. The Crown hath power sufficient to protect our liberties. The people have so much liberty as is necessary to make them useful to the Crown. Our government is in a just proportion—no tympany,[3] no unnatural swellings either of power or liberty. And whereas, in all overgrown monarchies, reason, learning, and inquiry are banished and hanged in effigy for mutineers; here they are encouraged and cherished, as the surest friends to a government established upon the foundation of law and justice.

When all is done; those who look for perfection in this world may look as long as the Jews have done for their Messias, and therefore our Trimmer is not so unreasonably partial as to free our government from all objections. No doubt there have been fatal instances of its sickness, and, more than that, of its mortality for some time; though by a miracle it hath been revived again. But, till we have another mankind, in all constitutions that are bounded, there will ever be some matter of strife and contention; and, rather than want pretences, men's passions and interests will raise them from the most inconsiderable causes. Our government is like our climate. There are winds which are sometimes loud and unquiet, and yet, with all the trouble they give us, we owe a great part of our health to them; they clear the air, which else would be like a standing pool, and, instead of a refreshment, would be a disease to us . . .

. . . Our Trimmer is a friend to Parliaments, nothwithstanding all their faults and excesses, which of late have given such matter of objection to them. He thinketh that though they may at some times be troublesome to authority, yet they add the greatest strength to it under a wise administration. He believeth no government is perfect except a kind of omnipotency reside in it, to be exercised upon great occasions.[4] Now this cannot be attained by force alone upon the people, let it be never so great. There must be their consent, too, or else a nation moveth only by being driven—a sluggish and constrained motion, void of that life and vigour which is necessary to produce great things . . .

. . . What is there in this that is so criminal as to deserve the penalty of that most singular apothegm, *A Trimmer is worse than a rebel*? What do angry men ail to rail so against moderation? Doth it not look as if they were going to some very scurvy extreme that is too strong to be digested by the more considering part of mankind? These arbitrary methods, besides the injustice of them, are (God be thanked!) very unskilful too, for they fright the birds, by talking so loud, from coming unto the net that is laid for them. When men agree to rifle a house, they seldom give warning or blow a trumpet.

But there are some small statesmen who are so full charged with their own expectations that they cannot contain. And kind Heaven, by sending such a seasonable curse upon their understandings, hath made their ignorance an antidote against their malice. Some of these cannot treat peaceably; yielding will not satisfy them, they will have men by storm. There are others who must have plots to make their service necessary, and have an interest to keep them alive, (since they are to live upon them), and persuade the King to retrench his own greatness so as to shrink into the head of a Party; which is the betraying him into such an unprincely mistake, and to such a wilful diminution of himself, that they are the last enemies he ought to allow himself to forgive. Such men, if they could, would prevail with the sun to shine only upon them and their friends, and to leave all the rest of the world in the dark ...

They should consider there is a soul in that great body of the people, which may for a time be drowsy and unactive; but when the Leviathan[5] is roused, it moveth like an angry creature, and will neither be convinced nor resisted. The people can never agree to show their united powers till they are extremely tempted and provoked to it; so that to apply cupping-glasses[6] to a great beast naturally disposed to sleep, and to force the tame thing, whether it will or not, to be valiant, must be learnt out of some other book than Machiavelli, who would never have prescribed such a preposterous method. It is to be remembered, that if princes have law and authority on their side, the people on theirs may have nature, which is a formidable adversary. Duty, justice, religion, nay, even human prudence too, biddeth the people suffer everything rather than resist; but our corrupted nature, wherever it feeleth a smart, will run to the nearest remedy. Men's passions are in this case to be considered as much as their duty, let it be never so strongly enforced; for if their passions are provoked, they being as much a part of us as any of our limbs, they lead men into a short way of arguing, that admitteth no distinctions, and from the foundation of self-defence they will draw inferences, that will have miserable effects upon the quiet of a Government.

... Our Trimmer, therefore, inspired by this Divine virtue, thinketh fit to conclude with these assertions:—That our climate is a Trimmer between that part of the world where men are roasted, and the other where they are frozen; that our church is a Trimmer between the frenzy of fanatic visions and the lethargic ignorance of Popish dreams; that our laws are Trimmers between the excesses of unbounded power and the extravagance of liberty not enough restrained; that true virtue hath ever been thought a Trimmer, and to have its dwelling in the middle between the two extremes; that even God Almighty Himself is divided between His two great attributes, His mercy and His justice.[7] In such company, our Trimmer is not ashamed of his name, and willingly leaveth to the bold champions of either extreme, the honour of contending with no less adversaries than nature, religion, liberty, prudence, humanity and common sense.

12   From
NICHOLAS LECHMERE
Speech at the Sacheverell Trial
(1710)

That when a Preacher of the Gospel, and a Minister of the Church of *England*, even under the then happy Establishment, should thus publickly condemn the Foundations on which it stood, in Defiance of Her Majesty and the great Council of the Nation then sitting in Parliament, it becomes an indispensible Duty upon them, who appear'd in the Name and on the Behalf of all the Commons of Great Britain, not only to demand their Lordships Justice on such a Criminal, but clearly and openly to assert their Foundations.

He crav'd Leave to remind their Lordships of the Condition of Things in both Kingdoms, immediately preceding the late Revolution; The Case he said was stated and recorded, between the late King *James* and the Subjects of both Kingdoms, in the several Declarations of the Rights of both Nations made by them at that Time;

That he would forbear to aggravate the Miscarriages of that unhappy Prince, further than by saying, That it was declar'd in the Preamble to the Bill pass'd in *England, That by the Assistance of Evil Counsellors, Judges and Ministers, employ'd by him, he did endeavour to subvert and extirpate the Protestant Religion, the Laws and Liberties of the Kingdom, in the several Instances there enumerated*: And in that passed in the Kingdom of *Scotland* it stood declared, *That, by the Advice of Evil Counsellors, he did invade the Fundamental Constitution of that Kingdom, and alter'd it from a Legal limited Monarchy, to an Arbitrary Despotick Power.*

Their Lordships, on that Occasion, might again consider the ancient Legal Constitution of the Government of this Kingdom, from which it would evidently appear to them, that the Subjects of this Realm had not only a Power and Right in themselves to make that Resistance, but lay under an indispensable Obligation to do it.

The Nature of their Constitution being that of a limited Monarchy, wherein the supreme Power was communicated and divided between Queen, Lords and Commons, tho' the Executive Power and Administration were wholly in the Crown. The Terms of such a Constitution did not only suppose, but express an Original Contract, between the Crown and the People, by which that Supreme Power had been (by mutual Consent, and not by Accident,) limited and lodg'd in more Hands than one; and the uniform Preservation of such a Constitution for so many Ages, without any fundamental Change, demonstrate the Continuance of the same Contract:

That the Consequences of such a Frame of Government were obvious; that the Laws were the Rule to both, the common Measure of the Power of the Crown, and of the Obedience of the Subject; and if the Executive Part endeavour'd the Subversion, and total Destruction of the Government, the Original Contract was thereby broke, and the Right of Allegiance ceased; that Part of the Government, thus fundamentally injur'd, having a Right to Save or

Recover that Constitution, in which it had an Original Interest.

And, the Nature of such an Original Contract of Government prov'd, that there was not only a Power in the People, who have inherited that Freedom, to Assert their own Title to it, but they were bound in Duty to transmit the same Constitution to their Posterity.

That it was misspending their Lordships Time to Illustrate that particular, which was an Eternal Truth, essential to the Government it self, and not to be defaced, or destroy'd, by any Force or Device . . .

. . . That the many Laws pass'd since, more particularly those for the Settlement of the Crown and Succession, were so many repeated Declarations of their late Majesty's, and Her Majesty then on the Throne, together with the Representative Body of the Nation, in Confirmation of their Ancient Constitution; Nay, they had higher Testimonies to appeal to, the many glorious Successes with which God Almighty had blessed the Arms of Her most Sacred Majesty, employed in Defence of the Arms of Resistance, were so many Testimonies from Heaven in their Vindication.

Their Lordships might take Notice on what Grounds the Doctor [Sacheverell] continu'd to assert the same Position in his Answer . . . the Commons thought he had, by his Answer, highly aggravated his Crime, by charging so pernicious a Tenet, as that of absolute unlimited Non-Resistance, to be a Fundamental Part of the Government, and by asserting that as the Doctrine of the Church of *England*.

That it was a great Reproach to the Excellency of the Constitution, to impute such Principles to it as inevitably infer'd its Destruction; and an equal Dishonour to the Crown of the Realm, the great Glory of which was to be set over and govern a Nation of Free-born Subjects, the meanest of which had an Inheritance in the Government and the Laws equal with the greatest.

They likewise esteem'd it an high Reflection on Religion it

self, and the Church of *England*, to charge its purest Doctrines, with such Constructions, by which all Irreligion and Oppression would be Authoriz'd.

That, the Commons must for ever consider themselves under the strongest Obligations of Gratitude to their great Deliverer, to assert the Honour and Justice of that Resistance, by which he had rescu'd an Oppress'd People from inevitable Destruction; and thought they should not deserve the Name of Subjects of *Great Britain*, or the least Blessing of so good a Government, if at that time before their Lordships, and for ever after, they did not assert, in the most strenuous manner, the Honour and Justice of that Resistance which had brought about the late happy Revolution. And upon that Foundation it was, that they doubted not but their Lordships would in a Parliamentary way fasten a Brand of indelible Infamy on that enslaving Tenet by which it hath been condemn'd . . .

. . . That, The Commons, esteem'd the Toleration of Protestant Dissenters to be one of the earliest and happiest Effects of the late Revolution, wisely calculated for the Support and strengthening the Protestant Interest, the great End of the Revolution it self.

They remember'd, with the highest Gratitude to Her Majesty, Her Royal Resolution declar'd from the Throne, to preserve it inviolably;[1] and they observ'd their Lordships, that it appear'd to them, from a Report on their own Journals of a Conference between both Houses, on the Bill against *Occasional Conformity* (not meant to enlarge the Liberties of Protestant Dissenters) That the Persecution of Protestants was, in the Preamble to that Bill, declar'd *to be the contrary to the Christian Religion, and the Doctrine of the Church of* England, *and that the Act of Toleration ought to be kept inviolably*; and the Commons found no Exception then taken by their Lordships to that Declaration, but on the contrary, many Expressions from both Houses, highly extolling the

Policy and good Effects of that Law.

Their Lordships would perceive, from the Evidence of the Commons, many plain Declarations of the Prisoner in Maintenance of that Article; but offer'd it to their Lordships, as a further Evidence, that the Doctor most shamefully arraign'd the Memory of a Prelate, Eminent for his Zeal to the Protestant Religion, for his compassionate Intercessions with Queen *Elizabeth*, in favour of Dissenting Protestants;[2] a Reflection plainly meant by him to cast an Odium on the Act of Toleration, and on the then Fathers of the Church, so Eminent for their Charity and Moderation; and from the Applauses he gave to the Severities shown by that Queen, he Illustrated the Calumny thrown by him on Her present Majesty, and Her Approbation of the Toleration: Their Lordships might please duly to consider the Malignity of Expressions meant to condemn so good a Law, then standing in its full Force, and to encourage the Unchristian Principles of Persecution . . .

But the Commons crav'd Leave to observe, that the Independent Power, or Jurisdiction of the Church, or of Ecclesiastical Judges, being the Doctrine advanc'd by the Prisoner, was not less dangerous; as it stood in utter Defiance and Contradiction of *Magna Charta*, and the Laws of the Land; was destructive of the Legal Supremacy of the Crown and Legislature, a Violation of the Oath of Supremacy, contrary to the Principles of the Reformation, and the Doctrine and Interest of the Church of *England*,[3] of which he was a member.

13   From
PAUL DE RAPIN-THOYRAS
A Dissertation on the Rise,
Progress, Views, Strength, Interests,
and Characters of the two Parties
of the Whigs and Tories
(1717)

The Government of *England* is of a particular kind, of which
there is not the like at present in all the world. It is, however,
the same which was formerly established in all the Kingdoms
of *Europe*, formed out of the ruins of the *Roman* Empire. The
present difference between *England*, and other States, in this
respect, is owing to this, that the *English* have preserved the
form of their Government ever since their settling in Great
Britain; whereas in other nations, it has been lost by degrees,
or extremely altered. This Government, which has so long
subsisted in this island, appears, in some respects,
Monarchical, in others, Republican; and yet, properly
speaking, it is neither. It cannot be called purely Monarchical,
since the Nobility and the People have a share in the
Legislative Power jointly with the King, nor can the King
impose any tax, without the people's consent. Neither is it
Republican, since there is a King, who exercises the sovereign
authority, who disposes, as he pleases, of all places and
dignities ecclesiastical, civil, or military; and can make peace
or war, without consulting his Subjects. It would be therefore
in vain to pretend to describe this Government, by the usual
names of Monarchy, Aristocracy, Democracy, which agree
not with it. It is a mixed Government, differing from, and yet
composed of, all three. The prerogatives of the Sovereign, and
the privileges of the Nobles and People, are so tempered
together, that they mutually support one another. At the same
time, each of the three powers, concerned in the Legislature,
may insuperably obstruct the attempts of one or both the
others, to render themselves independent. In short, it is very

near the same form of Government, established by the *Saxons* in *Germany*, by the *Francs* in *Gaul*, by the *Visigoths* in *Spain*, by the *Ostrogoths*, and after them, by the *Lombards* in *Italy*. These northern nations introduced this Government into the most southern parts of *Europe*, when they settled there, and founded new States upon the ruins of the *Roman* Empire . . .

The *English* in general are extremely jealous of their Laws and Liberties, nor are they less so of their Religion. This is what I think I may venture to affirm, though some of them seem indifferent as to the latter. But, thanks be to God, these are far from being the majority. Now it would have been very difficult for the Pretender, advanced to the Throne by foreign aid, professing a religion contrary to the national, and guided by rank Torys, to keep himself within the bounds of Moderation, necessary to gain the hearts of his subjects, without which a King of *England* can never sit firmly on his Throne. However, without staying to guess what might have happened, let us only observe that the rank and rigid Torys have been disappointed. Not only, the Pretender is not King, but his hopes of becoming so were never less.[1] King George is in peaceable possession of his Crown; the Torys are humbled, and the Whigs, lately oppressed, are now at the top of the Wheel.

After this brief account of the rise and progress of the Torys and Whigs, it will not perhaps be unacceptable to the Reader to know more particularly the views, interests, strength, and characters of the two Parties. For this purpose the different branches before-mentioned must be carefully distinguished. It is therefore necessary to repeat here that the two parties may be considered under two different relations; namely, with respect to the State, and with regard to the Church. I shall first speak of the State-Torys and Whigs, after which, I shall consider them with respect to religion.

The State-Torys are, as I said, divided into two branches, one of which may in *French* be called, *Rank*. In *England* they are known by the name of High-Flyers. This Idea, taken from Birds that by soaring above the common flight, lose themselves in the clouds, is very suitable to men, who cannot contain themselves within the limits of the established Government. These are for having the sovereign absolute in *England*, as he is in *France* and some other Countries, and for erecting his will into law. They regard not what I have said in the beginning of this Dissertation, that all the governments at this day in *Europe* were originally like that established in *England*; and consequently there is no reason why the *English* should imitate nations who have suffered it to be lost, or at least very much altered. It may be imagined that in such a Country as *England*, this party cannot be very numerous, and yet they are very considerable for three reasons. First, because the heads of this party are persons of the highest rank, and commonly favorites and ministers of State, or such as hold the greatest offices at Court, and the most eminent dignities in the Church. These men, who would not willingly put themselves under the conduct of others, being thus advantageously situated, become, generally, the leaders of all the Tory-Party. They manage them as they please, not only for the advantage of the whole party, but chiefly for their own particular ends. Thus very often, under pretence of acting for the interest of the party, their proceedings tend only to their own advantage, and the Torys are led by them much farther than most of them desire. It is this which gives occasion to many persons to accuse all the Torys of being for arbitrary power, though it is certain that only the High-Flyers are chargeable with this principle. But 'tis no great fault, it seems, to ascribe to a whole party what is done by their leaders.

Secondly, This particular branch of Torys is considerable, in that, when they are in the ministry, they ingage the Church-Torys strenuously to maintain the Doctrine of Passive-Obedience, which goes a great way towards gaining the people to their party. They insinuate to the Episcopal Ministers, that they have only in view the ruin of the

Presbyterians, and under that pretense cause them to preach a Doctrine, the consequence of which extends to all the subjects. This was experienced in the reigns of *Charles* II, of *James* II, and of Queen *Anne*, towards the conclusion.

Lastly, the Party of the High-Flyers becomes very powerful, when, as it frequently happens, they are supported by the King, and then it is that the liberty of the nation is in danger. Proofs of this, have been seen in the reigns of *James* II, and *Charles* I, *Richard* II, *Edward* II, and *Henry* III; for the High-Flyers are more antient than is imagined.

The second branch of the State-Torys is composed of those I called moderate. These are for having the King enjoy all his Prerogatives, but they pretend not, with the High-Flyers, to sacrifice him to the privileges of the subject. They are true *Englishmen*, who have the welfare of their country at heart, and are for preserving the constitution transmitted to them by their ancestors. They have often sav'd the State, and will again save it, when in danger from the rank Torys or Republican-Whigs, by opposing with all their power those who shall attempt to alter the Government. It would be injustice, to confound them with the High-Flyers under the general denomination of Torys.

As there are two branches of State-Torys, so there are two of State-Whigs, namely, Republican, and moderate Whigs. The republican Whigs are the remains of the party of the long Parliament which endeavoured to turn the Government into a Commonwealth. These at present are so inconsiderable, that they serve only to strengthen the other Whigs with whom they usually join. The Torys would persuade the publick, that all Whigs are of this kind. And in like manner the Whigs would have it believed that all Torys are High-Flyers. But this is only an artifice to render one another mutually odious.

The second branch of the State-Whigs contains the moderate Whigs, who are nearly allied to the moderate Torys in principle; and consequently are to be considered as true *Englishmen*, who desire, the Government may be maintained upon its antient foundations. Herein they would be exactly like the moderate Torys, were it not that these incline more to the King, and the moderate Whigs to the Parliament. The moderate Whig is perpetually hindering the People's rights from being invaded, and sometimes even takes precautions at the expence of the Crown. By him the Triennial Act[2] was procured, with some others, which 'tis needless to mention, to prevent the abuse of the royal power. Hence it is evident that the High-Flyers have no greater enemy than the moderate Whig, and that these two branches of Whigs and Torys properly form the opposition between the State-Torys and State-Whigs. These last laugh at Passive-Obedience when its consequences are carried too far. Their Principle is, that the royal power has its bounds, which cannot be transgressed, without injustice. Consequently they believe, that whenever the Sovereign exceeds his prerogatives, he may be resisted by his subjects. Hence it is easy to infer, they do not think the King can dispense with the laws.

What has been said is sufficient to show that the moderate state-Whigs and Torys are almost of the same sentiments. Their being of different parties proceeds from their mutual fear that either may make the ballance incline too much to the King's or the Parliament's side. It is not therefore strange, that these two branches of the opposite parties, unite in the pressing exigencies of the State. For, their views equally point to the preservation of the Government; though often they pursue their end by different paths. Accordingly, since the union of these two branches upon the death of King *William*, they have remained inseparable, and the moderate Whig and Tory form almost the same party, under the common appellation of Whig. I dare not however affirm that there are not yet moderate Torys who keep by themselves, and are unwilling to be confounded with the Whigs.

It must be remembered that hitherto I have only spoke of the Torys and Whigs in relation to the Government, without any regard to religion. I take care not to confound things which ought to be carefully distinguished. It is not true that all church-men are Torys, or all Presbyterians, Whigs in point of Government, as is commonly imagined. Many Presbyterians are in this respect of the same principles with the moderate Torys, and would not be less concerned to see the King stripped of his Prerogatives, than the subject of his privileges. In like manner, many Church-men, even Bishops themselves, are Whigs, very good Whigs as to the Government, and as considered in opposition to the High-Flyers, which shows the necessity of distinguishing State-Torys and Whigs, from Church-Whigs and Torys . . .

From what has been said concerning the several branches of Whig and Tory, it is easy to gather that these two names are very obscure and equivocal terms, because they convey, or ought to convey to the mind different ideas, according to the subject discoursed of. For instance, if I hear it said, that the Torys and Whigs are at great enmity, this raises in my mind an idea comprehending all the several branches of Whigs and Torys in general. But if I am told, the Torys are for having the King absolute and independent, or that the Whigs would be glad the regal power were abolished, my idea can only extend to the High-Flyers and the Republican Whigs. The rest of the Whigs and Torys would doubtless be offended at any such imputations. In like manner, if I hear that the Torys had rather see a Papist on the Throne than a Protestant, favourable to the Whigs, I should injure the Torys in general, by imputing such a thought to them, which can only be entertained by the Popish and some rigid Church-Torys, and perhaps some High-Flyers . . .

Thus the names of Torys and Whigs convey to the mind certain confused ideas, which few are capable of rightly distinguishing. But this difficulty still increases, when it is considered that the same person may be either Whig or Tory, according to the subject in hand. A Presbyterian, for instance, who wishes the ruin of the Church of *England*, is certainly for that reason in the Whig party. But if this Presbyterian opposes with all his power the attempts, of some of his party, against the regal authority, it cannot be denied that he is in that respect a true Tory. In like manner, when the Church only is concerned, the Episcopal-party are to be considered as Torys. But how many even of these are Whigs with respect to the Government? Nor have Foreigners only such confused ideas in this matter; the *English* themselves are liable to them. Nothing is more frequent than to hear a Whig charging all the Torys in general with an intention to destroy the rights and liberties of the subject; and a Tory arraigning the Whigs without distinction, as utter enemies to the Church and State. Every man uses this confusion of ideas, occasioned by the names of Whig and Tory, to accuse his adversaries of what is most odious in both parties . . .

Interest . . . is the principal motive which actuates the two parties, and this is but too apparent . . .

There are thousands of good *Englishmen*, without doubt, who grieve to see their country thus rent with divisions, and would gladly embrace all expedients to put a stop to them.[3] But it is not easy to observe a just neutrality, because it is difficult to be without ambition and avarice. Those who stand neuter, as I said, are neither preferred nor trusted, by reason that one of the parties are always in power, and have nothing more at heart than the advancing their friends, or gaining some of their adversaries. Consequently there can be no posts or offices for men, from whom the prevailing party can expect no manner of service. Moreover, how can a man be neuter between two parties, each of whom represent their adversaries as designing those evils which are most apt to fill men with fears, I mean, the destruction of the religion they profess, and the dissolution of a Government, which alone, in their opinion, can render subjects happy? A man must be very insensible not to be moved with such dangers, when convinced of their reality.

All *Englishmen* therefore are not to bear the blame of these unnatural divisions, but only those who cherish them for their own private interest.

HENRY ST JOHN,
VISCOUNT BOLINGBROKE
A Dissertation upon Parties:
Letter XVII
(1733–4)

SIR:—The great alteration we have spoken of, in property and power, brought our constitution, by slow degrees, and through many struggles and dangers, so near the most perfect idea of a free system of government, that nothing would be now wanting to complete it, if effectual means were found of securing the independency of parliament against corruption, as well as it is secured against prerogative. Our kings have lost little of the gaudy plumage of the crown. Some of their superfluous power, indeed, hath been bought, and more hath been wrested from them. Notwithstanding which, it is a very demonstrable truth, that the crown must sit lighter and more secure on the head of a wise prince, (and no constitution provides for, though every constitution should provide against, a weak prince,) since the great change of property and power in favor of the commons, than ever it did before. Our kings are no longer exposed, as some of the greatest of them have been, to the insults of turbulent, ambitious lords, or haughty prelates. It is no longer in the power of a few factious noblemen to draw armies into the field, and oblige their prince to fight for his crown, to fight to gain it, and to fight to keep it; as Edward the Fourth did, I think, in nine pitched battles. To make the prince uneasy, or insecure, as we are now constituted, the whole body of the people must be uneasy under his government. A popular king of Great Britain will be always not only easy and secure, but in effect absolute. He will be, what the British constitution alone can make any prince, the absolute monarch of a free people; and this popularity is so easily acquired, a king gains the public confidence and affection at so cheap a rate, that he must be poor indeed in all the kingly virtues, who does not purchase them, and establish true popularity upon them . . .

. . . But the great advantage we are to insist upon here, which hath arisen to the whole nation from the alteration in the state of property and power, is this: that we have been brought by it to the true poise of a mixed government, constituted like ours on the three simple forms. The democratical power is no longer kept under the same dependencies; and if a house of commons should now fail to assert that independent share in the supreme legislative power, which the constitution assigns to this assembly, it could not proceed alone, as it might and sometimes did formerly, from the nature of tenures, and many other unavoidable restraints; it would proceed from the corruption of particular men, who threw themselves into a voluntary dependency. The democratical power of our constitution is not sufficient to overtop the monarchical and aristocratical; but it is sufficient to counterwork and balance any other power by its own strength, and without the fatal necessity of favoring the ambition of the crown against the lords, or that of the lords against the crown. Nay more, as our government is now constituted, the three estates have not only one common interest, which they always had; but they have, considered as estates, no separate, contradictory interest. Our constitution gives so much grandeur, so much authority and power to the crown, and our parliaments give so immense a revenue, that no prince hath any real interest to desire more, who looks on himself as the supreme magistrate of a free people; for if we suppose inordinate ambition, or avarice, to make part of his character, these passions are insatiable: but then for this very reason, because they are so, there ought to be no account held of them; and though a prince may measure his demands, a people, who are in their senses, will never measure their concessions by them.

The property of the commons is not only become far superior to that of the lords upon the whole, but in the detail there are few, very few, instances to be produced of greater shares of private property amongst the latter, than amongst the former; and as the property of the commons is greater, so it is equally free. There are no badges of servitude on one side; no pretence of any superiority, except those of title and rank, on the other. The peers are, in some points, I speak it with all the respect due to them, commoners with coronets on their coats of arms; and affecting to act as such, it is plain they desire very wisely to be taken for such, on many occasions. The interests of these two estates then, with regard to property, are the same; and their particular rights and privileges are now so well ascertained, and so distinguished, that as the proximity of their interests of one sort should always unite them, so the distance of those of another sort cannot easily make them clash. In short, these two orders, according to the present constitution, (and how different is it from that of Rome, or, in the last respect, even from that of Spain, not to mention that of France?) have no temptation, and scarce the means, of invading each other: so that they may the better, and the more effectually, employ their vigilance, and unite their efforts, whenever it shall be necessary, against the encroachments of the crown, from whose shackles they have both emancipated themselves, whether the attempts to impose these shackles again are carried on by prerogative, or by the more formidable enemy of liberty, corruption.

15   *From*
VISCOUNT BOLINGBROKE
On the Policy of the Athenians
(1732)

... they had the misfortune for several years, to groan under the government of a set of ministers, who were too intent upon their own interest to have any serious regard for the welfare of the public; though that was the constant subject of their own praises; and the better to carry on their selfish and mischievous designs, and divert the people of Athens from looking into their conduct, they not only promoted continual dissensions amongst them, under the different distinctions of favourers or opposers of the former tyranny of Pisistratus;[1] but they likewise engaged them, on one side or the other, in every quarrel that arose, not only in Greece, but in Asia and places at the greatest distance, upon the smallest pretences of ancient alliances, or kindred with their ancestors; by which means they wasted their strength and riches in many fruitless and unnecessary foreign expeditions, for no other purpose than to make a parade of their power at sea; and which had no other effect than to increase the envy and jealousy of their neighbours.

To support such extraordinary and extravagant expenses, they were obliged to raise almost as great and heavy impositions as they did in the time of the Persian war, to the great decay of trade and impoverishment of the people; and though this was coloured with the specious pretences of extinguishing all remains of the former war, and settling a solid and lasting peace; yet it did not prevent the frequent murmurs and complaints of the public; nor were there wanting persons who vigorously and honestly opposed measures which were so visibly destructive of the true interest and safety of Athens; measures which it would have been impossible to have continued, if the heads of the faction who got possession of the government, had not found means to delude the people, from time to time, with the great advantages they were every day to receive from an universal, established peace, by which they were to be delivered from all apprehensions of the return of Hippias,[2] or any of his descendants; and the balance of power was for ever to be secured to the Athenians; a notion which had been so successfully propagated in Athens, and so much intoxicated the minds of the people, that there was no imposition so gross which their leaders could not pass upon them under this pretence; and it was the never-failing argument for silencing all oppositions, and removing all objections to the most chimerical projects, or unreasonable propositions in their public assemblies.

Athens was daily languishing under this unhappy management, which would have brought certain ruin upon her in the end, without the calamity of the Peloponesian war; for nothing prevented it but the continual struggles of her great men to supplant one another. This kept them in some awe, and restrained them from doing all the mischief which they had both in their inclination and power; so that the preservation of Athens for some time, may be said to be owing, in a great measure, to the short continuance of those in the administration.

But Cimon, Aristides and Tolmidas,[3] with several other considerable men of real merit and abilities, who, notwithstanding some failings, had done their country very great and eminent services; these men, I say, happening to go off the stage very near one another, left the field open to Pericles,[4] who first subverted their constitution, and then erected to himself an arbitrary power, which ended in the destruction of Athens.

He was a gentleman of a private fortune, but unmeasurable ambition, which made him stick at nothing to advance himself in the state. For this purpose he set out on the foot of liberty, and courted the affections of the people, by pretending a zeal for their interests upon all occasions; but when he had once made himself considerable by these methods, he threw off the mask, and treated them with the utmost insolence; by turns betraying all those who trusted him, and knowing no friendships or enmities, but such as favoured or opposed his corrupt purposes. He gave a very remarkable instance of this, with regard to Cimon, a noble Athenian of great parts and integrity, but one whom Pericles hated and constantly opposed, for keeping him under that subordination which became his station and character. Yet Cimon afterwards falling under a prosecution from the people, he screened[5] him in the public assembly, and then made a bargain with him to share the government between them; but took an opportunity to revenge himself in the ruin of his son Lacedaemonius, after his father's death.

As he was master of great volubility of tongue, with a knack of speaking plausibly in public, and had joined to this a very daring and consummate assurance; so he knew perfectly well how to improve them to his own advantage in supporting any proposition, right or wrong, as it best suited his present purpose; for nothing was more common than to see him in one assembly with great zeal confuting his own arguments in a former one; and he never scrupled to contradict the most certain truths, or to assert the most notorious falsehoods in order to carry his point, though sure to be discovered a few hours afterwards, having always an evasion ready at hand.

But notwithstanding the great opinion which he seemed to entertain of his own eloquence and cunning, he was convinced they would prove but a very feeble and short-lived support to him, without some better assistance. He therefore made use of all his art and contrivance to work himself into the administration of the public revenues, in which he had the good luck to succeed, after the death of Aristides; who, having been long treasurer of Greece, did not leave enough money behind him to defray the expenses of his own funeral. —Happy had it been for Athens, if Pericles had succeeded him in his noble qualities, as well as employment. But his character was the reverse of the good Aristides, and his administration one continued scene of rapine and profusion. Thus did he establish his power on a much more lasting foundation than his predecessors, by applying himself to the foibles and vices of mankind, which are too often the surest hold upon them; for though it is not to be imagined but that many corruptions had sprung up during the former disorders and weakness of the government; yet some remains of the modesty and virtue of their ancestors had hitherto restrained the Athenians from an open and avowed prostitution of their integrity; but Pericles, by the licentious distribution of bribes and bounties amongst the people, soon extinguished all sentiments of their former honesty and love of their country, which he treated as the most ridiculous fanaticism; and all the endeavours of a few to oppose this torrent of iniquity were the public and standing jest of his conversation.

This extravagant and unnatural flow of the public money by degrees introduced that spirit of expense and luxury amongst all ranks of men, under the mistaken notion of politeness, which consumed the estates of the best families in Athens, and soon made them so necessitous, that forgetting their ancient honours and the dignity of their birth, they were not ashamed to become the known pensioners of Pericles, living in as abject a dependence upon him as the meanest of the people.[6]

Thus was universal corruption spread over the whole state; and, to complete their misfortune, the very money which was reserved for the necessities of war only, was spent in debauching the minds of the people, and what was designed for their preservation, turned to their destruction.

As Pericles was not qualified by his rank to be of the assembly of the Areopagus;[7] (the great and supreme judicature of Athens;) so to remove every obstacle to his ambition, he employed all his art to undermine their authority, and by degrees drew all public business of consequence to the popular assemblies; where, by the assistance of bribes, pensions, and employments, which were all at his disposal, he was secure of carrying everything almost without opposition[8] . . .

. . . But it would have been impossible for him to have withstood the general clamour and demand of the people for bringing him to justice, if he had not had recourse to a new artifice, which no minister before him had the assurance to attempt. This was a proposal for allowing him ten talents for secret-service money;[9] which, though no very great sum, yet as it was understood, and even acknowledged by himself, to be the wages of iniquity, it was giving a public sanction to corruption, and was a precedent, that at once quite overturned all the ancient checks and controls, by which their ancestors had, in the strictest manner, guarded against the embezzlement of public money; the disposal of which was, by this stroke, put into the absolute power of him, who was at the head of the treasury; for, under this cover, he had the most unlimited scope to supply any expenses, under pretence of the public service.

One would think that nothing more could have been desired to gratify the most insatiable thirst of power and dominion; but such were the extravagant expenses of Pericles, in unprofitable negotiations abroad, and satisfying the craving importunities of his dependents at home, who always rose in their demands in proportion to the difficulties, in which they saw him engaged, and the want he had of their service, that though he feared no repulse to the most unreasonable demand of new supplies, yet being conscious himself of his exorbitant expenses, he began to be ashamed that the people should see what money he consumed. He therefore resolved to make one bold step more, to secure himself of a fund, which would at once fully answer his purposes and conceal his profusions. This he put in execution, by seizing upon the sacred treasure at Delos,[10] which was deposited there by the common consent of the states of Greece, to be kept inviolable, never to be touched but in case of the utmost extremity, and that not without their unanimous advice and consent.

Such an open violation of the public faith raised the clamours of all Greece upon Pericles . . .

It ought, however, to be remembered, for the honour of that learned state, that the most celebrated wits and poets of Athens endeavoured to open the eyes of their countrymen, and animate them against Pericles, by exposing his conduct in satirical poems and invectives, but they were too far gone in luxury and corruption to recover their ancient spirit, being continually soothed in their vices by a set of profligate writers, whom Pericles had picked up and employed in his service.[11] These fellows were so abandoned, that they not only made a jest of liberty, and justified all the methods of arbitrary government, but put their patron in competition with Jupiter himself, and flattered him with the appelation of Olympius, at the same time that he was precipitating the destruction of their country.

Thus we see that the overgrown power, ambition and corruption of one man brought ruin upon the most flourishing state in the universe; and there are not wanting instances of the like kind in history to convince us that the same conduct will have the same consequences in all ages and all nations.

V

The State
of Ireland

Few exponents of the linguistic views of the Royal Society came as close to achieving the required 'Mathematical plainness' in their published work as Sir William Petty. His work as a statistician, or political economist, demanded and received precision, clarity, and an emphasis on definition which had been stressed by Bacon and by Petty's friend, Thomas Hobbes. Conscious that his work was still at the pioneer stage, Petty took pains to describe his methodology and to place it squarely in the mainstream of the new science. In the Preface to *Political Arithmetic* (1690), he wrote:

The Method I take ... is not yet very usual; for instead of using only comparative and superlative Words, and intellectual Arguments, I have taken the course (as a Specimen of the Political Arithmetic I have long aimed at) to express myself in Terms of *Number*, *Weight*, or *Measure*; to use only Arguments of Sense, and to consider only such Causes, as have visible Foundations in Nature.

The purpose of Petty's survey was to quantify the problem of Ireland's precarious economy within the context of England's mercantile demands. His tools were observation and description: hypotheses and deduction were to be based strictly on mathematical calculations. Such elements moulded a recognisable style—the projector's style which Swift was to adopt for his model in his most brilliantly sustained satire, *A Modest Proposal* and, to a less spectacular extent, in *A Short View of the State of Ireland*.

Petty's solution to Ireland's misery—the transportation of a million people to England—was wholesale, arbitrary, and Hobbesian in its untroubled disregard of individual liberties. Notions of consent on the part of the victims of such a scheme simply do not arise and, as Molyneux' *Case* indicates, the mercantilist theories of the day could easily accommodate a scheme as outrageous as Petty's. Ireland, like other English colonies in the seventeenth century, was assumed to be totally dependent on the rule of the mother country, and its prime duty was in serving the latter's exclusive interests. Much penal legislation enforced the point. In Petty's *Treatise*, inevitably, people and cattle are concurrently discussed as items of exploitable national wealth, and it is not difficult to see the possibilities for satiric inversion in the trope: 'people are the riches of a nation', an economic commonplace of the day. William Horsley, in *The Universal Merchant* (1753), crudely summarised the position thus: 'Numbers of People are the Wealth of a Nation because where they are plenty, they must work cheap.'[1] When reading Petty's essay it is easy to confuse the lands with the hands, the herds with the herdsmen. When reading Swift's bitter satire the inhumanity of the projector's scheme is neatly disguised by a perfect parody of his disinterested logic and careful computations.

It is unnecessary to point out that Petty was not an ironist. Yet he once suggested that the ultimate solution to the perennial problem of Ireland lay in its depopulation and total submersion beneath the sea. Such a comment indicates the enormity of Ireland's situation, for it is the despairing economist's analogue to the indignant satirist's fantasy of cannibalism in *A Modest Proposal*. Petty's *Treatise*, however, seriously aimed at the 'National Union of both Kingdoms and Peoples', and 'a Perpetual Peace and Settlement of Ireland'. Equally, Swift's *Proposal* is focussed on Ireland's miseries: implicit in Swift's choice of indirect rhetoric (parody and satire) is the assumption that only extreme

124

remedies stand any chance of affecting a situation which had driven even the experts such as Petty to outrageous solutions. Thus the indignation in the *Proposal* goes far beyond the local effect of satirising the style of the projector: many such schemes had failed, and Swift's parody is therefore an artistic and moral response to the paradoxes and distortions which existed in a real situation. The choice of parody as a vehicle for Swift's feelings is itself a token of his despair. When such a rhetorical choice was inappropriate, that is, when Swift was obliged to treat the same situation in a sermon (in the *Causes of the Wretched Condition of Ireland*, *Prose*, IX, 199–209), his style is less tensed, more direct and straightforward.

Swift was certainly acquainted with Petty's *Political Anatomy of Ireland* (completed in 1672 and published in 1691) and the *Political Arithmetic* (1676;1690), but the extract chosen here is from the unpublished *Treatise of Ireland*. Petty submitted this work to James II (and Pepys) in 1687: it was designed to represent the Protestant interest in Ireland at a time when James was pursuing violent Catholic policies. Its politically controversial nature, and its unfinished state thus prevented its publication until 1899.[2] Nevertheless it is chosen here precisely because of its controversial nature and because it supplies a more pointed example of the projector's style to which Swift's concerns were addressed in the *Proposal*. By comparison, the style of Petty's *Anatomy* and *Arithmetic*, though known to Swift, is more diffuse and statistical in approach.

The terminology and method of Swift's *Modest Proposal* and *Short View* relate precisely to the type of economic treatise developed by Petty. But Swift's *Answer to the Craftsman*, which proposes an ironic version of Petty's scheme, is an almost perfect parody even in the detail of tone. Having calculated the ratio of acres to graziers the *Answer* goes on to state:

These Eight Thousand Four Hundred Families may be divided among the four Provinces, according to the Number of Houses in each Province; and making the equal Allowance of Eight to a Family, the Number of Inhabitants will amount to Sixty Seven Thousand Two Hundred Souls; to these we are to add a Standing Army of Twenty Thousand *English*, which, together with their Trulls, their Bastards, and their Horse-boys, will, by a gross Computation, very near double the Count, and be very near sufficient for the Defence and Grazing of the Kingdom, as well as to

125

enrich our Neighbours, expel Popery, and keep out the Pretender. And lest the Army should be at a Loss for Business, I think it would be very prudent to employ them in collecting the publick Taxes for paying themselves and the Civil List.

I advise, that all the Owners of these Lands should live constantly in *England*, in order to learn Politeness, and qualify themselves for Employments: But, for fear of increasing the Natives of this Island, that an annual Draught, according to the Number born every Year, be exported to whatever Prince will bear the Carriage; or transplanted to the *English* Dominions on the American Continent, as a Screen between his Majesty's *English* Subjects and the savage *Indians*.[3]

This is stinging. The Answerer in fact proposes to schematise what is indeed already happening to Ireland: absentee landlords and emigration forced by poverty and exploitation were already hard facts of Irish life. To make it even harder the proposal suggests a garrison of troops and their associates equal in number to almost half the troublesome population. And all this from one whose sense of Ireland's *actual* degradation is scandalised by those who claimed to see improvement. The bitterness is ironically conveyed by its opposite, a jaunty confidence in its 'present happy Condition' and a patriotic 'Love and Esteem' for 'this noble Island'. The idiom of the economist is shot through, here and in *A Modest Proposal*, with a sense of moral outrage.

NOTES

1 See J. T. Boulton, 'Arbitrary power: an eighteenth century obsession', *Studies in Burke and his Time*, IX, 3 (1968), 905–26.

2 For a note on the publication history see C. H. Hull, *Economic Writings of Sir William Petty*, 2 vols. (Cambridge University Press, 1899), II, 546–8.

3 *Prose*, XII, 175–6. Even Swift's sense of outrage proved an underestimation of Ireland's anguished future. Cf. Cecil Woodham-Smith, *The Great Hunger: Ireland 1845–9* (Hamish Hamilton, London, 1962) and, of course, the current sectarian violence.

16   *From*
SIR WILLIAM PETTY
Treatise of Ireland:
An Essay in Political Arithmetic
(1687)

How to enable the People of England
and Ireland to spend 5 Millions
worth of Commodities more than now:
And how to raise
the present Value of the Lands
and Goods of Ireland
from 2 to 3

This is to be done. 1. By bringing one Million of the present
1300 Thousand of the People out of Ireland into England,
tho' at the Expence of a Million of Money. 2. That the
remaining 300 Thousand left behind be all Herdsmen and
Dairy-Women, Servants to the Owners of the Lands and
Stock Transplanted into England; all aged between 16 and 60
years, and to quit all other Trades, but that of Cattle, and to
import nothing but Salt and Tobacco.[1] Neglecting all
Housing, but what is fittest for these 300 Thousand People,
and this Trade, tho' to the Loss of 2 Millions-worth of
Houses. Now if a Million of People be worth 70l. per Head
one with another, the whole are worth 70 Millions; then the
said People, reckon'd as Money at 5 per Cent. Interest, will
yield 3 Millions and a half per Ann. (3.) And if Ireland send
into England 1 Million and a half worth of Effects (receiving
nothing back) Then England will be enriched from Ireland,
and otherwise, 5 Millions per Ann. more than now: Which, at
20 Year's Purchase, is worth one Hundred Millions of
Pounds Sterling, as was propounded . . .

How to take away all the Evils
arising from Differences of Births,

Extractions, Languages, Manners,
Customs, Religion, and Laws,
and Pretence whatsoever

1. There is no Person or Party in Ireland, of what religion soever, who denies the King of England to be King of Ireland also.

2. Whereas there are Disputes concerning the Superiority of Parliament; now there will need no Parliament in Ireland to make Laws among the Cow-Herds and Dairy-Women: Nor indeed will there be any Peers, or Free-holders, at all in Ireland, whereof to make a Parliament.

3. There will be little Pomp or Expence in the Chief Governor &c. the onely Business being to regulate the simple Cattle Trade to the best common Advantage.

4. The Courts of Judicature may be much abated, for that there will be little or no Variety of Cases or Actions.

5. The Officers of Ports will need onely to keep an Account of Exportation, where there are no Importations, or very little or simple.

6. The Work of the Clergy will require little intricate Learning or School-Divinity.

7. The 267 Thousand Catholicks may be such as can all speak English, and who will take English Names.

8. The Lands upon the down-Survey[2], may also have English Names put upon them.

9. The Transplanters into England may do the same.

10. The 300 Thousand left in Ireland are all Servants to those who live in England, having no Property of their own, in Land or Stock.

11. Money need be but little and that Local.

12. Cloths may be uniform, and withal equal, and also most commodious for the People's Employments.

13. The Catholic Priests may be English-men.

14 The 15000 militia Men being 1/10 of the whole Number

of Men, may serve by Turns as Soldiers every tenth Year.

15. The 4000 Men at Sea in 40 small Ships are enough to begirt Ireland, or to keep a Guard between the North of Ireland and Scotland: as also between Scilly and Kingsale, as the beginning of a real Mare Clausum.

16. The Lands may be valu'd according to the annual Increase of Flesh produceable from the same, restraining and reducing all other Respects to that one.

17. Controversies concerning Estates in Ireland, may be determined in England, where the Pretenders are now to live.

18. Whereas it may be offensive to make Estimates of the Number of Men slain in Ireland for the last 516 Years; and of the Value of the Money and Provisions, sent out of England thither; Of the Charge of the last Warr begun Anno 1641; The Value of the Wasting and Dispeopling the Countrey, Charges at Law for the last 30 Years &c. We say that the same may be all spared, Since all may be probably remedied and forgotten by the Means and Methods above-mentioned . . .

An appendix of objections to this essay, with answers to the same

First that the Transplantation of a Million of People is Impractible and Utopian.

Answer.

1st. It has been already said that the Charges thereof needs not to exceed 20 shillings per head at a Medium between Poor and Rich, Great and Small; and from the Middle of Ireland to the Middle of England supposed to be 120 Miles of Land in Distance.

2. Forty small Vessels of about Sixty Tuns each (which are easily had) will perform this whole Work in Five Year's Time.

3. The Freight per head need not exceed Two Shillings, and the Travelling Charges by Land at one Penny per Mile needs not be above Ten Shillings, Leaving Eight Shillings for Extraordinaries.

4. There will be found Undertakers enough, to regulate this Matter, and bring the Charges thereof to a Certainty, which may amount to 200 Thousand Pounds per Ann. to be advanced for Five Years out of the Public Revenue, and reimbursed, as shall elsewhere be shown.

The second Objection, That the Cattle-Trade above-propounded is also impracticable.

Answer

1. The Lands and Cattle are the same as now, wanting onely a new Application to each other.

2. A Council of Fitting Persons must make this Application, by Pitching the Number of each Species of Cattle, for every Sort of Land within the whole Territory of Ireland.

3. The same may pitch the Number of Cow-Herds, Shepherds, Dairy-Women, Slaughter Men and others, which are fit and sufficient to manage the Trade of exported Cattle dead or alive, of Hydes, Tallow, Butter and Cheese, Wool and Sea-fish &c.

4. To appoint the Foreign Markets and Ports where each Commodity is to be shipped and sold, to provide Shipping and to keep Account of the Exportation above-mentioned, and of the imported Salt, Tobacco, with a few other Necessarys.

5. When the whole Number, to be left in Ireland, is adjusted, then to pitch how many of them shall be English, or such as can speak English, and how many Irish, how many Catholiques and how many others, without any other respect, than the Management of this Trade, for the common Good of all the Owners of these Lands, and it's Stock indifferently.

6. Forasmuch as it is intended to allow each Servant to this Trade 20 Nobles per Ann. out of the Grand Commodities aforenamed, it is also intended to allow them Land for Corn and Gardenage with River-Fishing, Wild-Fowl and Hunting.

7. To keep up Part of the neglected Houses, till England be fully Peopled with 12 Millions . . . at 3 Acres per head.

8. To appoint the Foot-Militia and Horse-Guards.

9. To carry away the Young Children and superannuated Persons.

The 3rd. Objection, That Men will not conform to this Change, tho' tending to the General, and their own Particular, Good, out of a mere Caprice and Perverseness.

Answer.

1. If the Owners of Ireland may hereby raise their Concernments from 2 to 3 in Value, If the Landlords of England may hereby increase the Worth of their Lands from 3 to 4, And if the King may advance his Revenue from 4 to 5; and that the Church may receive a Supplyment out of Ireland of 100 Thousand Pounds per Ann. I suppose that particular Men will not long persist in their Perverseness and Humor; Or (if they do) that a Parliament of England, may cure this Evil, in both Kingdoms, as kind Parents may correct the Children whom they Love. . . .

The fourth Objection, that this Transplantation and Change of Trade amounts to an Abolishment of the Irish Nation: Which will be Odious to them, and not compensable by all the Benefits abovementioned.

Answer.

1. That this Proposal was intended for a Union of the two Nations, which is a real Blessing to both, according to that of *Faciam eos in Gentem Unam*:[3] Whereas the Curse of a Civil Warr is, to divide one intire Nation into two Nations: As the Irish Commotions Anno 1641 actually did. Now if the two Nations be brought into one, the Name of the lesser Nation must needs be abolished, whilst the Thing and Substance is exalted. For

1. In this Case the Irish Names of Lands and Men are lay'd down, and English taken up in their Rooms.

2. The Cabineers of Ireland, which are Ten to One of all the others, will be removed out of their wretched Beastlike habitations; unfit for making Merchantable Butter and

Cheese, and the Manufacture of Wool and Linnen out of the best Materials.

3. They will be set upon more pleasant and profitable Imployments in England.

4. They will be entertained there with greater Variety of agreeable Objects and Exercises.

5. They will be nearer the King, who hath a Kindness for them, with full Liberty of Conscience.

6. They will be safe from any Re-Conquest, which may be fatal to them.

7. They will be ingrafted and incorporated into a Nation more Rich, Populous, Splendid, and Renowned than themselves, for Letters, Arms, and other Atchievements.

8. This Transplantation will make the People of Ireland to be a real Addition (whereas they had been hitherto a Diminution and Counterpoize) to the Power of England, and for above 500 Years a vast Expence of it's Blood and Treasure.

The 5th Objection, That Changing the present Proportions between Catholicks and others in England (now 230 for one) to that of Nine for One, will be very formidable to the Protestants of England, and apt to create dangerous Fears and Jealousies in them.

Answer.

1. Altho' I never intended to complicate Religion with the Matters of this Essay, yet I may intimate that, by the late Changes in Ireland, of the Government, Army, Judicatures, Sherriffs, Jurys, and by bringing together and concentrating all the Catholick Powers; and by Publishing a Design of making the Catholicks there as considerable in their Wealths, as in their Numbers; which has caused the Price of Lands and houses and Cattle so to fall, and the English Artizans and Money so to diminish, As that the whole of Ireland, in this Year 1687, is fallen from 3 to 2 of what the same was worth Anno 1683, and will probably cause a Fall in his Majesty's Revenue from about 7 to 6. I say, I might intimate from the

Premisses that some Remedy is necessary.[4]

2. Moreover the imagined Benefit of making Ireland an Asylum, by the present Method, for all the King's Catholic Subjects, in case of an angry-Heterodox Successor to the Crown, is not comparable to the Danger of Ireland's Revolt and Reconquest.

Lastly, Whether the present united State of Catholicks in Ireland will make more Catholicks in his Majesty's whole Dominions, than the Transplantation here propounded, I know not, seeing no manifest cogent Reasons for either Opinion. Onely it is certain it will make Six and Thirty Times more Catholicks in England, than now there are, but not one more in the whole.

Wherefore if what concerns Religion be doubtful, let the same be left to God, whose peculiar Work it is; and let what is Obvious and Certain concerning the Wealth, Strength, Splendor, and Honor, of both Nations be consider'd according to Sense and Reason, to which God has left these Matters . . .

Postscript

If in this Jealous Age this Essay should be taxed of an Evil Design to Wast and Dispeople Ireland, We say that the Author of it intends not to be *Felo de se* [i.e. a suicide] and propound something quite contrary, by Saying it is naturally possible in about 25 Years to double the Inhabitants of Great Britain and Ireland and Make the People full as many as the Territory of those Kingdoms can with tolerable Labor afford a competent Livelihood unto: Which I prove thus, (vizt)

1. The sixth Part of the People are teeming Women of between 18 and 44 Years old.

2. It is found by Observation That but 1/3 Part of between 30 and 40[%] of the teeming Women are Marryed.

3. That a Teeming Woman, at a Medium, bear a child every two Years and a half.

4. That in Mankind at London, there are 14 Males for 13 Females, and because Males are prolific 40 Years, and Females but 25, there are in Effect 560 Males for 325 Females.

5. That out of the Mass of Mankind there dyes one out of 30 per Annum.

6. That at Paris, where the Christnings and the Births are the same in Number, the Christnings are above 18,000 per Annum, and consequently the Births at London, which far exceed the Christnings there, cannot be less than 19,000 where the Burials are above 23,000.

As for Example.

Of 600 People, the Sixth Part (vizt 100) are teeming Women, which (if they were all marry'd) might bear 40 Children per Ann. (vizt) 20 more than do dye out of 600, at the rate of one out of 30; and consequently in 16 Years the Increase will be 320, making the whole 920. And by the same Reason, in the next 9 Years, the said 920 will be 280 more, in all 1200, vizt double of the Original Number of 600.

Upon these Principles, if there be about 19,000 Births per Ann. at London, the Number of the marry'd teeming Women must be above 38,000; and of the whole Stock of the Teeming Women must be above 114,000, and of the whole People Six Times as many vizt 684,000; which agrees well enough with 696,000, which they have been elsewhere computed to be.

To conclude it is naturally possible, that all teeming Women may be marry'd, since there are in Effect 560 Males to 325 Females; and since Great Britain and Ireland can with moderate Labor food and other Necessaries to near double the present People or to about 20 Millions of heads, as shall when Occasion requires it, be demonstrated . . .

William Molyneux: The Case of Ireland (1697/8)

In 1692 William King, Bishop of Derry (later Archbishop of Dublin and Swift's ecclesiastical superior) was involved in litigation to prevent the London Society from leasing waste-land in his diocese to Presbyterians. The Irish Lords supported King's suit, but their decision was overruled by the House of Lords in England. With the immediate purpose of supporting King, but with the far more important object of asserting Ireland's constitutional equality with regard to England, William Molyneux undertook what was to become a classic antimercantilist work. By means of exhaustive historical precedents the *Case* demonstrated that Ireland, though united with England through the Crown, was independent of the English parliament and could only be bound by legislation to which it had freely consented. Writing to his friend John Locke in 1698, Molyneux explained that the *Case* was 'done in haste' and 'intended to overtake the proceedings at *Westminster*; but it comes too late for that'. Westminister's decision was unaffected by the *Case*, and the act for restricting the Irish wool trade was passed. Yet though the *Case* failed in its short term aims, it became the manual of all those who rejected English claims to ascendancy and was reprinted eleven times in the following century.

As Molyneux himself acknowledges with some pride (and, due to anonymous publication, with some uncertainty also), the *Case* draws heavily for its political philosophy, its argument, even for some of its imagery, on Locke's *Two Treatises of Government*, particularly in the crucial passages on consent. In its turn the *Case* supplied Swift with arguments and precedents for the *Drapier's Letters* and constituted the theoretical authority behind a comment such as this, from the *Short View of Ireland*: 'Thus, we are in the Condition of Patients who have Physick sent them by Doctors at a Distance, Strangers to their Constitution, and the Nature of their Disease.'[1]

Though much of its method of arguing by historical precedent is lifeless now, Molyneux' *Case* is not without its moments. A common technique in its argument is to shame the English government by running down a seemingly reasonable proposition to its logical (and usually arbitrary or cruel) consequences. Even such an apparently moderate appeal as the following must have been read with a twinge of apprehension in 1698, barely ten years after the Revolution:

... we have as Antient and Express an Authority for our present Constitution of Parliaments in *Ireland*, as can be shown in *England*. And

I believe it will not be thought Adviseable in these latter Days to break in upon *Old Settled Constitutions*: No one knows how fatal the Consequents may be.

In addition, as Robbins points out, the *Case* put forward a theory of the natural inherent rights of man which, in terms of its consequences for other dependent English colonies, quite overshadowed its immediate service to Ireland at the turn of the century.[2]

Though agreeing with Molyneux on the question of Ireland's constitutional equality, Swift did not repudiate the mercantilist theory which demanded her colonial subjection. In *Intelligencer* 19 he outlined his limited brief: 'what is lawful for a subject of Ireland, I profess I cannot determine.' Since the theoretical spade-work had been done already by Molyneux, Swift could simply refer to him in support of his cause and then concentrate on the human and libertarian fronts: 'What I did for this Country was from perfect Hatred of Tyranny and Oppression' (*Prose*, XIII, 111–13). Among the opponents of the antimercantilist views expressed in Molyneux were Charles Davenant, Arthur Dobbs,[3] and Swift's patron, Sir William Temple.

It should not be forgotten that Swift in Ireland was a member of a privileged minority of Anglo-Irish Protestants based on Dublin officialdom. Ireland's colonial status meant that all the important government and church posts were made and held by the 'English interest.' Indeed, during the first half of the eighteenth century only one Irish-born vice-gerent, the Duke of Ormonde, held office (1703-7; 1711-12). Lords Lieutenant, like most landlords, usually resided in England. Legislation dating from Poynings Law had made Ireland virtually defenceless against the imposition of legal and economic restrictions by the Westminster parliament, and more recent acts penalising Irish woollen, cattle and navigational activities further enforced her dependence. The only effective resistance to England's legislative domination came from the Anglo-Irish group which included Molyneux and which was led by William King. Swift was the unofficial spokesman of this group after 1720. But his campaign dates from the early *Story of an Injured Lady* (1707), *A Letter Concerning the Sacramental Test Act* (1709) and *A Proposal for the Universal Use of Irish Manufacture ... Utterly Rejecting Every Thing wearable that comes from England* (1720). The *Drapier's Letters* (1724), *A Short View of Ireland* (1728) and *A Model Proposal* (1729) contain his best work in the Irish campaign.

After the early 1730s Swift wrote no more Irish tracts: as he put it in a letter, 'I would not prescribe a dose for the dead' (*Correspondence,* IV, 266). Far back in 1673 Sir William Temple had reiterated the commonplace that 'the true and natural Ground of Trade and Riches, is Number of People, in Proportion to the Compass of Ground they inhabit' *(An Essay upon the Advancement of Trade in Ireland).* Swift's version of this maxim in 1737 spelled out his ultimate feeling of desperation: Ireland, he said, 'is the only Christian Country where People contrary to the old Maxim, are the Poverty and not the Riches of the Nation'.[4]

NOTES

1 See also Swift's letter to Peterborough, *Correspondence,* III, 134.
2 For further discussion, see Caroline Robbins, *The Eighteenth-Century Commonwealthman* (Harvard University Press, Cambridge, Mass, 1961).
3 Charles Davenant (1656-1714), political economist, son of the dramatist Sir William D'Avenant. He published works on taxation, trade, and on political questions, e.g. *Essays on the Ballance of Power* (1701). Arthur Dobbs (1689-1765), Irish author of *Essay on the Trade and Imports of Ireland* (1729, 1731), appointed surveyor-general in Ireland by Walpole in 1730.
4 *A Proposal for Giving Badges to the Beggars of Dublin, Prose,* XIII, 135. There is a full discussion of Swift's Irish Tracts and their relationship with other figures in the Anglo-Irish group in O.W. Ferguson, *Jonathan Swift and Ireland* (Illinois University Press, Urbana, Ill., 1962).

17 From
WILLIAM MOLYNEUX
The Case of Ireland
(1697/8)

It may seem a strange Doctrine, that any one should have a Power over the *Life* of another Man, and not over his *Estate*;

but this we find every Day, for tho' I may *kill* a Thief that sets on me in the High Way, yet I may not take away his *Money*; for 'tis the *Brutal Force* the Aggressor has used, that gives his Adversary a Right to take away his *Life*, as a noxious Creature: But 'tis only Damage sustain'd that gives Title to another Man's *Goods*.

It must be confess'd that the Practice of the World is otherwise, and we commonly see the Conqueror (whether *Just* or *Unjust*) by the Force he has over the Conquer'd, compels them with a Sword at their Breast to stoop to his Conditions, and submit to such a Government as he pleases to afford them. But we enquire not now, what is the *Practice,* but what *Right there is to do so*. If it be said the Conquered submit by their own *Consent*; then this allows *Consent* necessary to give the Conqueror a Title to Rule over them. But then we may enquire, whether Promises extorted by *Force* without *Right,* can be thought *Consent*, and how far they are *obligatory*; and I humbly conceive that they *bind not at all*. He that *forces* my Horse from me, ought presently to *restore* him, and I have still a *Right* to retake him: So he that has *forced* a Promise from me, ought presently to *restore* it, that is, quit me of the *Obligation* of it, or I may chuse whether I will perform it or not: For the *Law of Nature* obliges us only by the *Rules* she prescribes, and therefore cannot oblige me by the *Violation* of her Rules; such is the Extorting any thing from me by Force.

From what has been said, I presume it pretty clearly appears, that an *Unjust* Conquest gives *no Title* at all; That a *Just* Conquest gives Power only over the *Lives* and *Liberties* of the *Actual Opposers*, but not over their *Posterity* and *Estates*, otherwise than as before is mentioned; and not at all over those that did *not Concur* in the Opposition.

They that desire a more full Disquisition of this Matter, may find it at large in an Incomparable *Treatise*, concerning the *True Original Extent and End of Civil Government*, Chap. 16. This Discourse is said to be written by my

Excellent Friend, JOHN LOCKE, Esq; Whether it be so or not, I know not; This I am sure, whoever is the Author, the greatest Genius in *Christendom* need not disown it.[1] . . .

...We have heard of late much Talk in *England* of an *Original Compact* between the *King* and *People* of *England*; I am sure 'tis not possible to shew a more fair *Original Compact* between a *King* and *People*, than this between *Henry* the Second, and the *People* of *Ireland*, *That they should enjoy the like Liberties and Immunities, and be govern'd by the same mild Laws, both Civil and Ecclesiastical, as the People of* England.

From all which it is manifest, that there were no Laws imposed on the people of *Ireland*, by an Authority of the Parliament of *England*; nor any Laws introduced into that Kingdom by *Henry* the Second, but by the *Consent* and *Allowance* of the People of *Ireland*. For both the Civil and Ecclesiastical State were settled there, *Regiae sublimitatis Authoritate*, solely by the King's Authority, *and their own good Wills*, as the *Irish* Statute, 11 Eliz. c.I. expresses it. And not only the *Laws* of *England*, but the Manner of *holding Parliaments* in *Ireland* to make Laws of their own (which is the *Foundation* and *Bulwark* of the Peoples *Liberties* and *Properties*) was directed and established there by *Henry* the Second, as if he were resolved that no other Person or Persons should be the Founders of the Government of *Ireland* but himself and the *Consent* of the People, who submitted themselves to him against all Persons whatsoever. . .

By what foregoes, I presume it plainly appears, that by three several Establishments under the three first Kings of *Ireland* of the *Norman Race*, the *Laws and Liberties of the People of England, were granted to the People of Ireland*. And that neither of these three Kings Establish'd those Laws in Ireland by any *Power* of the *Parliament* of *England*, but by the free *Consent, Allowance* and *Acceptance* of the *People of Ireland*. . .

It has ever been acknowledged that the Kingdom of *Ireland* is inseparably annex'd to the Imperial Crown of *England*. The Obligation that our Legislature lies under by *Poyning's Act* 10.*H*.7.c.4.[2] makes this Tye between the two Kingdoms indissoluble. And we must ever own it our Happiness to be thus annexed to *England*: And the Kings and Queens of *England* are by undoubted Right, *ipso facto* Kings and Queens of *Ireland*. And from hence we may reasonably conclude, that if any Acts of Parliament made in *England*, should be of Force in *Ireland*, before they are Received there in Parliament, they should be more especially such Acts as relate to the *Succession* and *Settlement of the Crown*, and *Recognition* of the King's Title thereto, and the *Power* and *Jurisdiction* of the King. And yet we find in the *Irish* Statutes, 28 *Hen*. VIII.c.2. *An Act for the Succession of the King and Queen Ann*; and another, Chap. 5. declaring the King to be *Supream Head of the Church of* Ireland; both which Acts had formerly pass'd in the Parliaments of *England*. So likewise we find among the *Irish* Statutes, *Acts of Recognition of the King's Title to Ireland*, in the Reigns of *Henry* the Eighth, Queen *Elizabeth*, King *James*, King *Charles* the Second, King *William* and Queen *Mary*. By which it appears that *Ireland*, tho' Annexed to the Crown of *England*, has always been look'd upon to be *a Kingdom Compleat within it self*, and to have all Jurisdiction to an *Absolute* Kingdom, belonging and Subordinate to no Legislative Authority on Earth. Tho' 'tis to be noted, these English Acts relating to the Succession, and Recognition of the King's Title, do particularly Name *Ireland*.

As the *Civil* State of *Ireland* is thus *Absolute* within it self, so likewise is our State *Ecclesiastical*, This is manifest by the *Canons*, and *Constitutions*, and even by the *Articles* of the *Church of Ireland*, which differ in some things from those of the *Church of England*. And in all the Charters and Grants of Liberties and Immunities to *Ireland*, we still find this, That *Holy Church shall be Free*, &c. I would fain know what is meant here by the Word *Free*: Certainly if our *Church* be *Free*, and Absolute within itself, our *State* must be so likewise; for how our *Civil* and *Ecclesiastical* Government is now interwoven, every Body knows. But I will not enlarge on this Head, it suffices only to hint it; I shall detain my self to our *Civil Government* ...

... we are all the *same* King's Subjects, the Children of one *Common Parent*;[3] and tho' we may have our *Distinct* Rights and Inheritances absolutely within ourselves; yet we ought not, when these do chance a little to interfere to the Prejudice of one or t'other Side, immediately to treat one another as Enemies; fair amicable Propositions should be proposed, and when these are not hearken'd to, then 'tis time enough to be at Enmity, and use Force.

The last Thing I shall take Notice of, that some raise against us, is, That *Ireland* is to be look'd upon only as a *Colony* from *England*: And therefore as the *Roman Colonies* were subject to, and bound by, the Laws made by the *Senate* at *Rome*; so ought *Ireland* by those made by the *Greater Council* at *Westminster*. Of all the Objections rais'd against us, I take this to be the most extravagant; it seems not to have the least *Foundation* or *Colour* from *Reason* or *Record*: Does it not manifestly appear by the *Constitution* of *Ireland*, that 'tis a *Compleat Kingdom* within it self? Do not the Kings of England bear the *Stile of Ireland* amongst the rest of their Kingdoms? Is this agreeable to the Nature of a *Colony*? Do they use the Title of Kings of *Virginia, New-England*, or *Mary-Land*? Was not *Ireland* given by *Henry* the Second in a Parliament at *Oxford* to his son *John*, and made thereby an *Absolute Kingdom, separate* and wholly *Independent* on *England*, 'till they both came United again in him, after the Death of his Brother *Richard* without Issue? Have not multitudes of Acts of Parliament both in *England* and *Ireland*, declared *Ireland a compleat Kingdom*? Is not *Ireland* stiled in them All, the *Kingdom*, or *Realm* of *Ireland*? Do these *Names* agree to a *Colony*? This on all hands involves so many Absurdities, that I think it deserves nothing more of our Consideration . . .

All Men are by Nature in a State of Equality, in respect of Jurisdiction or Dominion: This I take to be a Principle in it self so evident, that it stands in need of little Proof. 'Tis not to be conceiv'd, that Creatures of the same Species and Rank, promiscuously born to all the same Advantages of Nature, and the Use of the same Faculties, should be subordinate and subject one to another; These to this or that of the same Kind. On this Equality in Nature is founded that Right which all Men claim, of being free from all Subjection to positive Laws, 'till by their own *Consent* they give up their Freedom, by entring into Civil Societies for the common Benefit of all the Members thereof. And on this *Consent* depends the *Obligation* of all *Humane Laws*; insomuch that without it, by the unanimous Opinon of all *Jurists*, no Sanctions are of any *Force*. For this let us Appeal, amongst many, only to the *Judicious* Mr. *Hooker's Ecclesiastical Polity,* Book I. Sect. 10 . . .[4]

To the same purpose may we find the Universal Agreement of all Civilians, *Grotius, Puffendorf,*[5] *Locke's Treat. Government,* &c.

No one or more Men, can by *Nature* challenge any *Right, Liberty* or *Freedom*, or any Ease in *his Property, Estate* or *Conscience,* which all other Men have not an *Equally Just Claim to*. Is *England* a *Free* People? So ought *France* to be. Is *Poland* so? *Turkey* likewise, and all the *Eastern Dominions*, ought to be so: And the same runs throughout the whole *Race of Mankind* . . .

. . . Wherein can it appear, that any Statute made in *England*, was at any time since the Reign of *Henry* the Third, allowed and put in practice in the Realm of *Ireland*, without the *Authority* of the *Parliament* of *Ireland*? . . . If the Religion, Lives, Liberties, Fortunes, and Estates of the Clergy, Nobility, and Gentry of *Ireland*, may be dispos'd of, without their *Privity* and *Consent*, what Benefit have they of

142

any Laws, Liberties, or Priviledges granted unto them by the Crown of *England*? I am loth to give their Condition an *hard Name*; but I have no other Notion of *Slavery, but being Bound by a Law to which I do not consent* . . .

Lastly, The People of *Ireland* are left by this Doctrine in the greatest *Confusion* and *Uncertainty* Imaginable. We are certainly bound to obey the *Supream Authority* over us; and yet hereby we are not permitted to know *Who* or *What* the same is; whether the *Parliament of England*, or *that of Ireland*, or *Both*; and in what Cases the *One*, and in what the *Other*; Which *Uncertainty* is or may be made a Pretence at any time for *Disobedience*. It is not impossible but the different Legislatures we are subject to, may Enact Different, or Contrary Sanctions: Which of these must we obey?

To conclude all, I think it is highly *Inconvenient* for *England* to *assume* this *Authority* over the Kingdom of *Ireland*: I believe there will need no great Arguments to convince the wise Assembly of *English* Senators, how *inconvenient* it may be to *England*, to do that which may make the *Lords* and *People* of *Ireland* think that they are not *Well Used*, and may drive them into *Discontent*. The *Laws* and *Liberties* of *England* were granted above Five hundred Years ago to the People of *Ireland*, upon their Submissions to the Crown of *England*, with a Design to make them *Easie* to *England*, and to keep them in the Allegiance of the King of *England*. How consistent it may be, with true Policy, to do that which the People of *Ireland* may think is an *Invasion* of their Rights and Liberties, I do most humbly submit to the Parliament of *England* to consider. They are Men of *Great Wisdom, Honour*, and *Justice*; and know how to prevent all future *Inconveniences*. We have heard great Out-cries, and deservedly, on Breaking the *Edict of Nantes*,[6] and other Stipulations; How far the Breaking our Constitution, which has been of Five Hundred Years standing, exceeds that, I leave the World to judge . . .

The *Rights of Parliament* should be preserv'd *Sacred* and

Inviolable, wherever they are found. This kind of Government, once so *Universal* all over *Europe*, is now almost *Vanished* from amongst the Nations thereof. Our King's Dominions are the only Supporters of this noble *Gothick Constitution*,[7] save only what little Remains may be found thereof in *Poland*. We should not therefore make so light of that sort of Legislature, and as it were Abolish it in One Kingdom of the Three, wherein it appears; but rather cherish and Encourage it wherever we meet it.

VI

Scientists
and satire

It is widely agreed that Swift failed to see the practical aims and values of the natural sciences of his day. He was not alone among his contemporaries in this blindness, but in Swift's case it was more a case of self-induced myopia. Apart from the information which he undoubtedly gleaned from independent reading in the sciences, throughout his life he was in touch with men of science. His tutor at Trinity College Dublin, St George Ashe, was a founder of the Dublin Philosophical Society and wrote papers on mathematical and astronomical subjects for the Royal Society. Men such as Howard, Molyneux and Sir Andrew Fountaine in their various ways supplied Swift with ready access to the work of physician, mathematician and antiquarian. Dr Arbuthnot, physician to Queen Anne, was a man whose friendship Swift valued above all others: he was both virtuoso and wit, a member of the Royal Society, author of *An Essay on the Usefulness of Mathematical Learning* (1701), and the scourge of quack scientists and pedantic minds in the Scriblerus Club. It is inconceivable that Swift could have respected these men in spite of their scientific pursuits. To satirise science and scientists effectively he was forced to acquire detailed knowledge of his target.

In the event Swift's satire on the modern natural scientists is uneasily balanced between gross absurdities which he knew to exist at the periphery and practical values which he seemed hesitant to acknowledge. His attack on Wotton's scientific apologia (the *Reflections*) in *A Tale* and *The Battle* was prompted not by antagonism at specific experiments but by loyalty to the gentleman-scholar ideals of the humanist Temple. Without this combination of moral and personal loyalties (represented by Temple) his scientific satire is the weaker. Swift readily admitted that the satire on Projectors in *Gulliver's Travels* was not entirely successful, and as far back as 1714 he was writing to Arbuthnot requesting his aid in the Scriblerus satires: 'I could putt together, and lard, and strike out well enough, but all that relates to the Sciences must be from you.'[1] Swift's eclectic mind is nowhere better shown than in his scientific satires. It is wrong to expect discrete and precise sources for each of the foolish projects that Gulliver encounters in his voyage to Laputa. Swift's mind did not work in this way: as Nicolson and Mohler put it, 'Swift's brilliance ... lay less in originality than in ingenious and paradoxical combinations of material he gleaned from others.' Thus the extracts in the following section, however close they appear to their Swiftian fates also show that unique and eclectic magic of Swift's converting imagination.

One incident in Swift's biography seems a natural focus for his attitudes to science. His only known visit to the Royal Society at Gresham College was curiously and accurately prophetic. In December 1710 he wrote to Esther Johnson to describe some of the London sights he had seen. In a large party (including some young children) he had been to the King's menagerie, the asylum of Bedlam, the Royal Society ('but the keeper was not at home'), and had ended the day at 'the Puppet-Show' (*Journal to Stella*, I, 121–2). Caged animals, lunatics, a learned society and a puppet-show all jostled together in his memory: thereafter, and in spite of what Swift knew to the contrary, the pursuants of natural sciences were never clearly discriminated from associated madness and performing spectacle.

In his third voyage Gulliver is transported to Laputa, a bizarre distortion of contemporary reality populated by the fatuous and grotesque theoretical scientists. The Laputians enjoy all the power conferred by science, typically taking it to an extreme in their tyranny of the Balnibarbians by the Flying Island: but they escape none of its terrors, for their astronomers have instilled fears of planetary collisions into the citizenry. Their speculative mania infects Gulliver, who had been 'a Sort of Projector' in his younger days. But the figure of Lord Munodi dominates his respect. Munodi's judgement and taste have created an oasis of Augustan sanity in a desert of sterile intellects.

In his *Essay on Projects* (1697) Defoe defined a project 'according to modern acceptation' as 'a vast undertaking too big to be managed, and therefore likely enough to come to nothing.' Swift's response to projectors is similar and he applies the response to inventors of political, economic, financial and scientific schemes alike. His satire on scientists, however, is firmly located in the contemporary and past activities of the Royal Society. With subtle malice Swift has Gulliver point out that the Academy of Lagado was established 'about Forty Years ago', which would make it roughly contemporary with its Royal Society model, assuming that Gulliver is talking in 1707/8.

Swift's antagonism to the new science has been located in a tradition of such satire which would include Rabelais (*Gargantua and Pantagruel*) and Shadwell (*The Virtuoso*). Pope's *Essay on Man* and Johnson's *Rasselas* similarly exhibit a skepticism of scientific achievement. Yet Swift's acknowledged sensitivity to certain areas of human experience (bodily evacuation, sex and death—most notably in some of his poems) would have been particularly abrased by the scientist's unconcern with moral categories. For example, a typical experimental scientist such as Stephen Hales, though a priest, could collate and link experimental data on the temperature of armpits, milk, urine, the noon-day sun, the 'scorching heat of a hot-bed of horse-dung' in which cucumbers are grown, and go on to experiment with the respiration of dogs and compare the perspiration rate of man and cabbage, and calculate the cubic inches of air in 158 grains of Newcastle coal. To a layman's mind repelled by such minute specialisation and revolted at the absence of human perspective such activity was already ridiculous and needed only slight distortion to be made entirely grotesque. Thus Swift needed only to add a satirical warp to the woof of actual experiments.

The most well-known experimenter in Lagado is the man who had spent eight years on a project for extracting sunbeams from cucumbers, 'which were to be put into Vials hermetically sealed, and let out to warm the Air in inclement Summers'. The first extract below is from Stephen Hales' *Vegetable Staticks*, an investigation into the effect of sunlight in promoting the respiration of plants. These valuable and pioneering experiments were completed, according to Hales, about 1720, read to the Royal Society, but not published until 1727. At most we have an analogy to Swift's experimenter, not a definite source, since it cannot be proved that Swift either knew or did not know of these experiments. Even so the style and method of Hales are typical and illustrate the basis for Swift's satiric parody on their personalities, observations, conclusions, and on their practical irrelevancies. For example, Hales calculates the temperature of cucumber roots and this eventually leads him on at a later stage to an aside about 'the modern invention to convey heated air into rooms thro' hot flues'. Swift's scheme for using cucumbers as a source of heat is seen as a ludicrous expense of human energy without any practical use for humanity. In general he makes the Laputians hopelessly disabled by the demands of practical living: because of their theoretical preoccupations with mathematics they cannot make a suit of clothes to fit Gulliver nor build a house which will stand up. Gulliver explains that their aesthetic sense is similarly dominated by mathematics:

> Their ideas are perpetually conversant in Lines and Figures. If they would, for Example, praise the Beauty of a Woman, or any other Animal, they describe it by Rhombs, Circles, Parallelograms, Ellipses, and other Geometrical Terms; or else by Words of Art drawn from Musick, needless here to repeat . . .

In music and mathematical theory the Laputians are outstanding. They are also obsessive: 'the whole Compass of their Thoughts and Mind, being shut up within the two forementioned Sciences.' For his dinner Gulliver is served 'a Shoulder of Mutton, cut into an Aequilateral Triangle; A Piece of Beef into a Rhomboides; and a Pudding into a Cycloid. The second Course was two Ducks, trussed up into the Form of Fiddles; Sausages and Puddings resembling Flutes and Hautboys, and a Breast of Veal in the Shape of a Harp.' Mathematics and music combine to reduce beauty to a matter of correct geometrical proportions. Mathematics, as Wotton's *Reflections* had shown, was the branch of modern science upon which the Moderns prided themselves most. And in tacking music to mathematics in the mad Academy of Lagado Swift had undoubtedly specific targets. The Royal Academy of Music had been established in 1719 and several members of the Royal Society had written papers on the analogies between music and mathematics. Francis North subjected music to diagrammatic analysis in *Philosophick Essays on Music* in 1677; Dr John Wallis was another. A glimpse of such intellectual endeavours is afforded by a paper by Thomas Salmon entitled *The Theory of Musick reduced to Arithmetical and Geometrical Proportions*, published in the *Transactions* of the Royal Society in 1705 (the second extract below). Together with its attendant illustrations this is an experiment of which the Lagado scientists would have been proud. It is a perfect manifestation of their credo and suggests how close Swift's satire was to reality. In demonstrating that the beauty of music is exclusively the result of combining mathematical proportions Swift's point about the road of theoretical excess leading to the asylum of obsession is well made.

The final extract, St André's *Account of an Extraordinary Effect of the Cholick*, may serve two purposes. In a general way it relates to Swift's use of dissection terminology, particularly in passages where Swift is talking about the method of satire. The 'anatomy of satire' is much more than a suggestive analogy in Swift's hands. In this famous passage from 'A Digression on Madness' the satirist becomes anatomical surgeon:

... in most Corporeal beings, which have fallen under my Cognizance, the *Outside* hath been infinitely preferable to the *In*: Whereof I have been farther convinced from some late Experiments. Last week I saw a woman *flay'd*, and you will hardly believe, how much it alter'd her Person for the worse. Yesterday I ordered the Carcass of a *Beau* to be stript in my Presence; when we were all amazed to find so many unsuspected Faults under one Suit of Cloaths. Then I laid open his *Brain*, his *Heart*, and his *Spleen*; But, I plainly perceived at every Operation, that the farther we proceeded, we found the Defects encrease upon us in Number and Bulk: from all which, I justly formed this Conclusion to myself; that whatever Philosopher or Projector can find out an Art to sodder or patch up the Flaws and Imperfections of Nature, will deserve much better of Mankind, and teach us a more useful Science, than that so much in present Esteem, of widening and exposing them (like him who held *Anatomy* to be the ultimate End of *Physick*.).

Here the satirist and the anatomist are played off against each other. The anatomist is forced to a conclusion which has always been obvious to the satirist: Who needs to be a scientist to learn that a whore and a fop are examples of human vice and folly? The surgery involved in the experiment is superfluous and merely confirms a commonplace: what appears to be the product of experiment and observation turns out to be orthodox moral criticism, and it may be suggested that what Swift is doing here is to satirise those whose concern for merely physical symptoms has blunted their moral sense. As Pope put it in *The Dunciad*, book IV, ll. 453–6), 'The proper Study of Mankind is Man':

O! would the sons of Men once think their Eyes
And Reason giv'n them but to study *Flies*?
See Nature in some partial narrow shape,
And let the Author of the Whole escape.

Swift's general point about experimental scientists is that they neglect the urgent problems of moral philosophy in favour of discrete and partial physical analysis. What Swift does with his basic materials in the Academy of Lagado is indicated by reference to St André's experiment. Gulliver's guided tour round the Academy is interrupted by 'a small Fit of the Cholick'. He relates how

my Conductor led me into a Room, where a great Physician resided, who was famous for curing that Disease by contrary Operations from the same Instrument. He had a large Pair of Bellows, with a long slender Muzzle of Ivory. This he conveyed eight Inches up the Anus, and drawing in the Wind, he affirmed he could make the Guts as lank as a dried Bladder. But when the Disease was more stubborn and violent, he let in the Muzzle while the Bellows was full of Wind, which he discharged into the Body of the Patient; then withdrew the Instrument to replenish it, clapping his Thumb strongly against the Orifice of the Fundament; and this being repeated three or four Times, the adventitious Wind would rush out, bringing the noxious along with it (like Water put into a Pump) and the Patient recovers. I saw him try both Experiments upon a Dog, but could not discern any Effect from the former. After the latter, the Animal was ready to burst, and made so violent a Discharge, as was very offensive to me and my Companions. The Dog died on the Spot, and we left the Doctor endeavouring to recover him by the same Operation.

Understandably, Gulliver does not allow this ghastly mechanistic remedy to be applied to his own ailment and decides to let nature take its course. The detail of using a pair of bellows for this particular piece of quackery Swift could have borrowed from several sources—from Rabelais, from Sprat's account of Hooke's experiment in the *History of the*

Royal Society, from Shadwell's *The Virtuoso*, or from his own earlier use in the satire of nonconformist orators in *A Tale of a Tub*.[2] The effect of adding it is to make monstruous physical mock of the experts, for M St André's observations represent the type of actual endeavours on which Swift embroiders his fantasy. St André attempts to prove that a fallacious theory of contraries exists regarding digestion: in the course of his treatment the patient dies. The cure offered by Swift's projector is theoretically conceivable but absurdly mechanistic: he kills a dog.[3]

By combining material from several sources Swift compounds the projectors' follies to make something new and utterly grotesque. If his satire is undiscriminating, in that it attacks truth and folly together, it is also true that Swift had no intention to be fair-minded. Swift's indictment of the projectors lies not merely in their ridiculousness, but also in their divergence from the norm of practical and theoretical balance offered earlier in the *Travels* by the King of Brobdingnag. Gulliver had here criticised the King for the very unscientific nature of his politics: Gulliver is neatly bypassed by the King's disarming comment, 'that whoever could make two Ears of Corn, or two Blades of Grass to grow upon a spot of Ground where only one grew before; would deserve better of Mankind, and do more essential Service to his Country, than the whole Race of Politicians put together.' In order to criticise politicians Swift used an analogy from the natural sciences. It is the more ironical for Swift thereby denies to the virtuosi of the Royal Society their proper and intended practical aims, which they were soon to fulfil. Swift's particular charge against the scientists of impracticality had already been answered in Wotton's *Reflections*. Modern discoveries such as the compass, microscope, telescope, barometer, the discovery of the blood's circulation, the mechanics of hearing and seeing, etc. are listed. Temple's charge of being motivated by gain is denied:

This is what our Age has seen; and it is not the less admirable, because it cannot be made immediately useful to humane Life: It is an excellent Argument to prove, That it is not Gain alone which biasses the Pursuits of the Men of this Age after Knowledge; for here are numerous Instances of Learned Men, who finding other Parts of Natural Learning taken up by Men, who in all Probability would leave little for Aftercomers, have, rather than not contribute their Proportion towards the Advancement of Knowledge, spent a World of Time, Pains and Cost, in examining the Excrescencies of all the Parts of Trees, Shrubs, and Herbs, in observing the critical Times of the Changes of all sorts of Caterpillars and Maggots, in finding out by the Knife and Microscopes the minutest parts of the smallest Animals, in examining every Crevice, and poring in every Ditch, in tracing every Insect up to its original Egg, and all this with as great Diligence, as if they had an *Alexander* to have given them as many Talents, as he is said to have given to his master *Aristotle*.[4]

An unlooked-for vindication of Swift's savage ridicule of medical credulity among the scientists came barely two months after *Gulliver's Travels* appeared. The King's surgeon-anatomist, the same Nathaniel St André whose article on canine dissection is reproduced here, printed an account of how he had delivered one Mary Tofts of several stillborn rabbits in Godalming. After the ruse was discovered satiric fantasy and strange reality changed places for a while: 'Lemuel Gulliver', the pseudonymous author of 'The Anatomist Dissected' (1727), suggested that St André's astonishing gullibility could only properly be rewarded by promition to 'Anatomist extraordinary to the Court of Laputa'.[5]

NOTES

1 *Correspondence*, II, 46. Swift appears to have turned down Arbuthnot's offer of assistance in connection with the voyage to Laputa: see *Correspondence*, III, 284. Laputa was the last voyage in order of composition. This section is particularly indebted to Marjorie Nicolson and Nora M. Mohler's 'The scientific background of Swift's *Voyage to Laputa*', and 'Swift's flying island in the *Voyage to Laputa*'; both in *Annals of Science*, II (1937), Nos. 3 and 4. For a note on the Laputian word-machine (not discussed here), see Irvin

Ehrenpreis, 'Four of Swift's sources', *MLN*, LXX (1955), 95–100. I have discussed the linguistic context of Swift's Lagadian satire, and related matters, in 'Swift and linguistics: the context behind Lagado and around the Fourth Voyage', *Neophilologus* (1974), LVIII, 4, pp. 425–39.

2 See W. A. Eddy, *Gulliver's Travels: a Critical Study* (1923; reprinted 1963), and Paul Turner's edition of *Gulliver's Travels* (Oxford, 1971), p. 349, note 16.

3 For further discussion of Swift's use of surgical imagery, see Clive T. Probyn, 'Swift and the physicians: aspects of satire and status', *Medical History* (1974), XVIII, 3, 249–61.

4 *Reflections Upon Ancient and Modern Learning* (1694), ch. XXII, 269–70.

5 For further discussion of the episode, see the notes on this passage and S. A. Seligman, 'Mary Toft—the rabbit breeder', *Medical History*, V (1961), 349–60.

18   *From*
STEPHEN HALES
Vegetable Staticks: Or, An Account
of some Statical Experiments
on the Sap in Vegetables.
Being an Essay towards
a Natural History of Vegetation.
Also, a Specimen of An Attempt
to Analyse the Air,
By a Great Variety of
Chymico-Statical Experiments:
Which were read at several Meetings before
the Royal Society
(1726)

Chapter I
Experiment XX

. . . The hottest Sun-shine in the year 1724, gave to the *Thermometer*, exposed to it, a heat equal to that of the blood of animals, *viz*. 64 degrees: And tho' plants endure this and a considerably greater heat, within the tropicks, for some hours each day, yet the then hanging of the leaves of many of them shews that they could not long subsist under it, were they not frequently refreshed by the succeeding evening and night . . .

The common noon-tide heat in the Sun in *July* is about 50 degrees: The heat of the air in the shade in *July* is at a medium 38 degrees. The *May* and *June* heat is, from 17 to 30 degrees; the most genial heat, for the generality of plants, in which they flourish most, and make the greatest progress in their growth. The autumnal and vernal heat may be reckoned from 10 to 20 degrees. The winter heat from the freezing point to 10 degrees.

The scorching heat of a hot bed of horse-dung, when too hot for plants, is 75 degrees and more, and hereabout is probably the heat of blood in high fevers.

The due healthy heat of a hot bed of horse-dung, in the fine mold, where the roots of thriving Cucumber-plants were, in *Feb*. was 56 degrees, which is nearly the bosom-heat, and that for the hatching of eggs. The heat of the air under the glass-frame of this hot-bed was 34 degrees; so the roots had 26 degrees more heat, than the plants above ground. The heat of the open air was then 17 degrees.

. . . The impulse of the Sun-beams giving the moisture of the earth a brisk undulating motion, which watery particles, when separated and rarified by heat, do ascend in the form of vapour: And the vigour of warm and confined vapour, (such as is that which is 1, 2, or 3 feet deep in the earth) must be very considerable, so as to penetrate the roots with some vigour; and as we may reasonably suppose, from the vast force of confined vapor in *Aeolipiles*,[1] in the digester of bones, and the engine to raise water by fire.

If plants were not in this manner supported with moisture, it were impossible for them to subsist, under the scorching heats, within the tropicks, where they have no rain for many months together: For tho' the dews are much greater there, than in these more Northern climates; yet doubtless where the heat so much exceeds ours, the whole quantity evaporated here in a summer's day, is found to exceed the quantity of dew which falls in the night. But the dew, which falls in a hot summer season, cannot possibly be of any benefit to the roots of trees because it is remanded back from the earth, by the following day's heat, before so small a quantity of moisture can have soaked to any considerable depth. The great benefit therefore of dew, in hot weather, must be, by being plentifully imbibed into vegetables; thereby not only refreshing them for the present, but also furnishing them with a fresh supply of moisture towards the great expences of the succeeding day.

'Tis therefore probable, that the roots of trees and plants are thus, by means of the Sun's warmth, constantly irrigated with fresh supplies of moisture; which, by the same means, insinuates it self with some vigour into the roots. For if the moisture of the earth were not thus actuated, the roots must then receive all their nourishment meerly by imbibing the next adjoining moisture from the earth; and consequently the shell of the earth, next the surface of the roots, would always be considerably drier the nearer it is to the root; which I have not observed to be so. And by *Experiment* 18 and 19, the roots would be very hard put to it, to imbibe sufficient moisture in dry summer weather, if it were not thus conveyed to them, by the penetrating warmth of the Sun: Whence by the same genial heat, in conjunction with the attraction of the capillary sap vessels, it is carried up thro' the bodies and branches of vegetables, and thence passing into the leaves, it is there most vigorously acted upon, in those thin plates, and put into an undulating motion, by the Sun's warmth, whereby it is most plentifully thrown off, and perspired thro' their surface; whence, as soon as it is disintangled, it mounts with great rapidity in the free air . . .

Chapter VI

A specimen of an attempt
to analyse the Air
by a great variety
of chymic-statical Experiments,
which show in how great
a proportion Air
is wrought into the composition
of animal, vegetable, and mineral
Substances, and withal how readily
it resumes its former elastick state,
when in the dissolution
of those Substances it is
disingaged from them.

Experiment CXIV

I tyed down a middle sized Dog down alive on a table, and having layed bare his windpipe, I cut it asunder just below the *Larynx*, and fixed fast to it the small end of a common fosset; the other end of the fosset had a large bladder tyed to it, which contained 162 cubick inches; and to the other end of the bladder was tyed the great end of another fosset, whose orifice was covered with a valve, which opened inward, so as to admit any air that was blown into the bladder, but none could return that way; yet for further security, that passage was also stopped with a spiggot.

As soon as the first fosset was tyed fast to the windpipe, the bladder was blown full of air thro' the other fosset; when the Dog had breathed the air in the bladder to and fro for a minute or two, he then breathed very fast, and shewed great uneasiness, as being almost suffocated.

Then with my hand I pressed the bladder hard, so as to drive the air into his lungs with some force; and thereby make his *Abdomen* rise by the pressure of the *Diaphragm*, as in natural breathings: Then taking alternatively my hand off the bladder, the lungs with the *Abdomen* subsided; I continued in

157

this manner, to make the Dog breathe for an hour; during which time I was obliged to blow fresh air into the bladder every five minutes, three parts in four of that air being either absorbed by the vapours of the lungs, or escaping thro' the ligatures, upon my pressing hard on the bladder.

During this hour, the Dog was frequently near expiring whenever I pressed the air but weakly into his lungs; as I found by his pulse, which was very plain to be felt in the great crural artery near the groin, which place an assistant held his finger on most part of the time; but the languid pulse was quickly accelerated, so as to beat fast; soon after I dilated the lungs much, by pressing hard upon the bladder, especially when the motion of the lungs was promoted by pressing alternatively the *Abdomen* and the bladder, whereby both the contraction and dilation of the lungs was increased.

And I could by this means rouse the languid pulse whenever I pleased, not only at the end of every 5 minutes, when more air was blown into the bladder from a man's lungs, but also towards the end of the 5 minutes, when the air was fullest of fumes.

At the end of the hour, I intended to try whether I could by the same means have kept the Dog alive some time longer, when the bladder was filled with the fumes of burning *Brimstone*: But being obliged to cease for a little time from pressing the air into his lungs, while matters were preparing for this additional Experiment, in the mean time the Dog dyed, which might otherwise have lived longer, if I had continued to force the air into his lungs.

Now, tho' this Experiment was so frequently disturbed, by being obliged to blow more air into the bladder twelve times during the hour; yet since he was almost suffocated in less than two minutes, by breathing of himself to and fro the first air in the bladder, he would by Experiment 106 on Candles, have dyed in less than two minutes, when one fourth of the old air remained in the bladder, immediately to taint the new admitted air from a man's lungs; so that his continuing to live thro' the whole hour, must be owing to the forcible dilation of the lungs, by compressing the bladder, and not to the *vivifying spirit of air*. For without that forcible dilation, he had, after the first 5 or 10 minutes, been certainly dead in less than a minute, when his pulse was so very low and weak, which I did not find to be revived barely by blowing 3 parts in 4 of new air from the lungs of a man into the bladder: But it was constantly roused and quickened, whenever I increased the dilations of the lungs, by compressing the bladder more vigorously; and that whether it was at the beginning or end of each 5 minutes, yet it was more easily quickened, when the bladder was at any time newly filled, than when it was near empty.

From these violent and fatal effects of very noxious vapours on the respiration and life of animals, we may see how the respiration is proportionably incommoded, when the air is loaded with lesser degrees of vapours, which vapours do in some measure clog and lower the air's elasticity; which it best regains by having these vapours dispelled by the ventilating motion of the free open air, which is rendered wholesome by the agitation of winds: Thus what we call a close warm air, such as has been long confined in a room, without having the vapours in it carried off by communicating with the open air, is apt to give us more or less uneasiness, in proportion to the quantity of vapours which are floating in it. For which reason the *German* stoves, which heat the air in a room without a free admittance of fresh air to carry off the vapours that are raised, as also the modern invention to convey heated air into rooms thro' hot flues, seem not so well contrived, to favour a free respiration, as our common method of fires in open chimneys, which fires are continually carrying a large stream of heated air out of the rooms up the chimney, which stream must necessarily be supplied with equal quantity of fresh air, thro' the doors and windows, or the cranies of them.

And thus many of those who have weak lungs, but can

breath well enough in the fresh country air, are greatly incommoded in their breathing, when they come into large cities where the air is full of fuliginous vapours, arising from innumerable coal fires, and stenches from filthy lay-stalls and sewers: And even the most robust and healthy in changing from a city to a country air, find an exhilarating pleasure, arising from a more free and kindly inspiration, whereby the lungs being less loaded with condensing air and vapours, and thereby the vesicles more dilated, with a clearer and more elastick air, a freer course is thereby given to the blood, and probably a purer air mixed with it; and this is one reason why in the country a serene dry constitution of the air is more exhilarating than a moist thick air.

19

THOMAS SALMON
*The Theory of Musick
reduced to Arithmetical
and Geometrical Proportions*
(1704)

Sir,

Having had the honour last week of making the trial of a Musical experiment before the Society at *Gresham College*, it may be necessary to give a farther account of it; that the Theory of Musick, which is but little known in this Age, and the practise if it, which is arriv'd at a very great excellency, may be fixed upon the sure foundations of Mathematical certainty. The Propositions, upon which the Experiment was admitted, were: That Musick consisted in Proportions, and the more exact the Proportions, the better the Musick: That the Proportions offer'd were the same that the ancient *Grecians* us'd:[1] That the Series of Notes and Half Notes was the same our Modern Musick aim'd at: which was there exhibited upon fingerboards calculated in Mathematical proportion. This was demonstrated upon a Viol, because the Strings were of the greatest length, and the proportions more easily discern'd; but may be accommodated to any Instrument, by such mechanick contrivances as shall render those sounds, which the Musick requires.

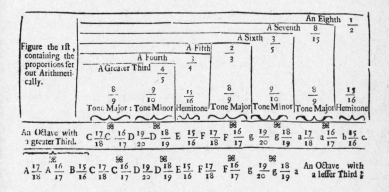

From Thomas Salmon's *The Theory of Musick reduced to Arithmetical and Geometrical Proportions*. This diagram contains 'the proportions set out Arithmetically'.

Cf. *Gulliver's Travels*, III, ch. 2: 'in the common Actions and Behaviour of Life, I have not seen a more clumsy, awkward, and unhandy People, nor so slow and perplexed in their Conceptions upon all other Subjects, except those of Mathematicks and Musick.' For the classical derivation of these ideas, see Plato's *Timaeus*.

The full knowledge and proof of this Experiment may be found in the two following Schemes, wherein Musick is set forth, first Arithmetically and then Geometrically: The Mathematician may, by casting up the proportions, be satisfied, that the five sorts of Half-Notes here set down, do exactly constitute all those intervals, of which our Musick does consist. And afterwards he may see them set forth upon a Monochord, where the measure of all the Notes and Half-Notes comes exactly to the middle of the String. The Learned will find that these are the very proportions which the old *Greek* Authors have left us in their Writings, and the Practical Musicians will testifie, that these are the best Notes he ever heard.

20
NATHANIEL ST ANDRE
An Account of an extraordinary
Effect of the Cholick
(read to the Royal Society 21 March 1717)

The *Peristaltick* Motion[1] of the Intestines is by all Anatomists suppos'd the proper Motion of those Cylindrical Tubes.

The use of this Motion is to propel the Chyle into the *vasa lactea*,[2] and to accelarate the grosser Parts of the Aliment downwards, in order to expel them, when all their nutritive Contents are extracted.

This Motion thus establish'd, it naturally seems to follow that an Inversion of it (call'd for that Reason an *Antiperistaltick Motion*) shou'd force the *Aliments, Bile, pancreatic Juices*, and lastly the *Faeces* to ascend towards the Mouth.

The Cause of this imaginary *Antivermicular* Motion, is assigned to a Stoppage of the Intestin, or to a great length of it being ingaged in the same manner as the Fingers of a Glove are choak'd by inverting the Glove in drawing it off: Or like as a Silk-Stocking, which when 'tis not gartered, falls upon the Foot, and is in a manner strangled, so that some Force is required to bring it up again.

This suppos'd, the *Antiperistaltick Hypothesis* seems at first Sight very natural, and answers most Difficulties. For if the Vermicular Motion accelerates the Contents of the Intestins downwards; the Antivermicular, by the Law of Contraries, should force them upwards towards the Mouth.

Was this Supposition as certain as 'tis generally receiv'd, I shou'd not presume to advance that there is no such thing as an *Antiperistaltick* Motion of the Intestins; nor that the *Miserere mei*[3] is oftner a violent Contraction of the Abdominal Muscles, than a Stoppage or Inversion of the Intestins, as 'tis supposed.

So laying aside all Prevention, let it be granted that this Disease is a violent Contraction of the Abdominal Muscles, as I have already suppos'd it, caus'd by the Redundancy of the Intestins or their Contents. Then comparing the Symptoms of this Disease, with those of the different Kinds of *Hernias*, we shall find by the Analogy of the Parts, Reason and repeated Experience, that the *Chordapsus*,[4] so call'd by *Celsus*,[5] is a Disease in which the Intestins and *Omentum*,[6] at other Times the *Pancreas* or *Spleen*, nay, even the *Mesentery*[7] it self are forc'd through the *Diaphragma* into the *Thorax*.

All these tender Parts being strongly compress'd, by the continual Motion of this Muscle, must by consequence cause the same Accidents as in the *Bubonocele*[8] or compleat *Hernia*, there being no difference in these two Cases; but that the first is a strangling of the *Intestin* by the *Diaphragm*, and the latter a choaking of the Intestins by the *Abdominal Muscles*.

One Example of the many of the like Nature, that I can produce, will much confirm this Assertion, and may serve to convince any Person that is impartial.

The Case is this. A Gentleman that came to Town yesterday was Sevennight in good Health, meeting with some Friends, drank a great deal of new bottled Oat-Ale, after some Pints of Wine. These Liquors fermented so violently in his Stomach and Intestins; that he was taken with a violent *Cholick* the same Night.

In the morning an Apothecary was sent for, who administered a Clyster,[9] and took some Ounces of Blood to relieve the Patient, who complain'd of a great Pain in his left Side.

The Clysters being repeated the Night following, as also

the next Morning, and the Patient growing worse; the Apothecary, without Order of any Physician, gave him a violent Vomit; which operated Eight or Nine Times: This added Fewel to the Fire; and the Patient having from that Time been in a desperate Condition, two eminent Physicians were call'd, who order'd that the Clysters shou'd be repeated: But they not prevailing, I was sent for about six Hours before the Patient died. I found him complaining of a violent Pain in all the Regions of the *Abdomen*; a frequent Inclination to vomit; having a great Difficulty of breathing, together with a very slow Pulse; his Belly being as hard as a Stone, tho' not swell'd.

This last Indication made me conclude, that the Disease was a violent Contraction of the Abdominal Muscles, which had overcome the *Diaphragm*, and that probably the *Intestins* might be forc'd into the *Thorax*.

I was the more confirm'd in this Opinion from the Examples of the like Case, which I shall shortly lay before the Society; upon which I ordered a Fomentation of hot Milk, adding to every Quart a Drachm of *Liquid Laudanum*, which in these Maladies gives great Relief: But before it cou'd be got ready, the Patient expir'd in a violent Convulsion.

My Opinion having being highly censur'd by the two Physicians, I open'd this Gentleman, to justifie my self, or to own my Fault openly, if I had been mistaken: But as the thing happen'd as I conjectured, those Gentlemen will forgive me for taking the Liberty of justifying my self.

In opening this Body, I found the Abdominal Muscles so much contracted, that it was almost impossible to penetrate them with a very sharp Scalpel.

Upon Examination, I found the Stomach empty, and some Parts of the *Duodenum*, but the *Jejunum*[10] and *Ilium*[11] so much distended with the fermented Oat-Ale, that the *Ilium* had four Inches of Diameter, and the *Colon* above eight.

The *Ilium* was also pretty much inflam'd in its inferior part; and all the Valves of the Colon were obliterated, by the great

Distention of that *Intestia*.

But the greatest Disaster was, the Dilation made in the *Diaphragm*, as I suppos'd; made just upon the Chink which remits the intercostal Nerve to the *Viscera* of the *Abdomen*, through which a Portion of the *Colon* was forc'd, and the greatest Part of the *Omentum* and *Pancreas*.

These tender Parts being choak'd, soon inflam'd, a Mortification of them following; and a Rupture of the *Pancreatick Vein* caus'd an internal *Haemorrhage*, which fill'd all the left Cavity of the *Thorax*, insomuch that the whole left lobe of the Lungs was compress'd almost under the *Musculus Scalenus*.[12]

The Quantity of extravas'd Blood was very great, and it was not in the least coagulated.

I have brought the diseas'd Parts with me, to shew the Society the Certainty of this Account ...

VII

The nature of man

Swift believed in the depravity of human nature for a long time before *Gulliver's Travels* was written. Its bleak portrayal of Gulliver's disintegrating personality invited inaccurate charges of its author's misanthropy from those who had rejected the orthodox Christian and Augustinian convictions that man was in essence corrupt. The theology of *Gulliver's Travels*, like the Puritan satire in *A Tale of a Tub*, was old-fashioned in 1726: the optimists were beginning to prevail over the pessimists and Locke's belief in man's natural ability to create an ordered, rational universe (as opposed to Hobbes's assumption of his anarchic nature) had won the minds of many thinking men. The philosophy of the *Travels* is not original and the complexity of the fourth voyage to the land of the Houyhnhnms lies in its use of conventional ideas and symbols which have survived the passing of their sustaining context. Part of what follows in this section is an attempt to revive the intellectual context in which Swift's permutations on the theme of man as risen ape or fallen angel were originally made. This ancient dichotomy had recently surfaced in a debate between Locke and one of his most dogged opponents, Edward Stillingfleet.

In the second edition of his *Essay Concerning Human Understanding* (1694) Locke added a new discussion of a difficult problem – the nature of personal identity. In a later work, *The Reasonableness of Christianity* (1695) Locke traced some of the evils of human society to the authority of an independent power vested in the priesthood free of State control. During this book he omitted the doctrine of the three-person Trinity from his list of 'reasonable' doctrines. Though not a deist on fundamental points (he believed, for instance, in the supernatural elements in religion and also questioned the adequacy of Reason alone in matters of religious belief), Locke was charged with the deistic heresies and was adopted as the inspiration for John Toland's *Christianity Not Mysterious* (1696) in order to support a specifically deist argument. Locke's discussion of *identity* and *person* and Toland's use of Locke's ideas for deist purposes were seized upon and vigorously denounced by Edward Stillingfleet (Lord Bishop of Worcester) in his *Vindication of the Doctrine of the Trinity*, a defence of orthodoxy. In this debate are to be found strands of the intellectual fabric and some of the terminology of Gulliver's perplexing fourth voyage. Here Swift anatomises general human nature through the disintegration in Gulliver of rational poise and the ability to recognise the boundaries between creatures and their normal properties, where God-given Reason is exhibited by horses and human physicality is uncontrollably enacted by creatures conventionally beneath Man on the ladder of creation, apes. The conventional humanist framework which Swift is inverting is illustrated by Pope's lines (Epistle II, ll 1–18) in the *Essay on Man*:

Know then thyself, presume not God to scan;
The proper study of Mankind is Man.
Plac'd on this isthmus of a middle state,
A being darkly wise, and rudely great:
With too much knowledge for the Sceptic side,
With too much weakness for the Stoic's pride,
He hangs between; in doubt to act, or rest,
In doubt to deem himself a God, or Beast;
In doubt his Mind or Body to prefer,
Born but to die, and reas'ning but to err;
Alike in ignorance, his reason such,
Whether he thinks too little or too much:

Chaos of Thought and Passion, all confus'd;
Still by himself abus'd, or disabus'd;
Created half to rise, and half to fall;
Great lord of all things, yet a prey to all;
Sole judge of Truth, in endless Error hurl'd:
The glory, jest, and riddle of the world!

Gulliver is strung between these dichotomies in a world wherein he is denied (or progressively rejects) normal frames of reference.

The section of the Locke–Stillingfleet controversy which is of interest here is the argument about the definition of the term *Man* by means of a discussion of generic and specific terms. How can we be sure, asked Locke, that 'Peter, James and John' are all 'true and real men', when it can be shown that these are merely linguistic signals which are associated by convention with complex ideas of *Man*. What were man's essential as opposed to his accidental properties? In suggesting that man was possibly substantially material Locke had invited Stillingfleet's charge of heresy, since such a proposition seemed to deny the Christian doctrine of the immateriality of the soul, a Hobbesian materialism. Locke had stated that we cannot define the true nature of substance merely by naming it. Moreover, his theory of universals stated that the term *Man* could only describe what is left after every quality possessed by James, John, or Peter (i.e. individual men) but not by all men had been eliminated. Thus the general term denotes the fixed generic essence, whether the term be man, horse, or tree. Man is an animal, but he also possesses the property of Reason: yet, Locke went on to say, it does not follow that any individual man is a reasoning animal by definition. To Stillingfleet's chagrin Locke stated that the property of Rationality does not exist in Peter, James and John, but exists only in

That specifick abstract Nature, which Peter and James for their supposed Conformity to it, are ranked under. For example, Rationality as much as Property as it is of a *Man*, is no *Property* of *Peter*; he was Rational a good part of his Life, could Write and Read, and was a sharp Fellow at a Bargain: But about Thirty, a knock so altered him, that for these Twenty years past, he has been able to do none of these Things, there is to this Day, not so much appearance of Reason in him, as in his Horse or Monkey: and yet he is *Peter* still. (Locke's *Reply to the Bishop of Worcester's Answer to his Second Letter,* 1699, p. 358)

Thus in the case of "poor Peter" there was a problem: where the term *rational man* could not be appropriately applied, could one then maintain that Peter was not a man? There was a lesson here for Gulliver. In the fourth voyage to the land of the Houyhnhnms Gulliver is presented with a perversion of normality, where the conventional logic-book definition of man as *animal rationale* is not enough to distinguish *Man* (since it is here applied to horses) from the animals. Equally, when Gulliver eventually finds the essentially 'Houyhnhnm' virtues of benevolence and friendship exhibited in *human* form (in the Portuguese sea-captain, Pedro de Mendez), he rejects them because he fails to observe the distinction Locke had tried to make to Stillingfleet: he fails to distinguish individual excellence from the generic revulsion which he comes to feel is the definition of the whole human race.

Swift's preoccupation with the distinctions which Locke had been making to Stillingfleet between individual and generic properties is illustrated by his letter to Pope (29 September 1725), written during the final stage of composing *Gulliver's Travels*:

I have ever hated all Nations professions and Communityes and all my love is towards individuals for instance I hate the tribe of Lawyers, but I love Councellor such a one, Judge such a one for so with Physicians (I will not speak of my own Trade) Soldiers, English, Scotch, French; and the rest but principally I hate and detest that animal called man, although I hartily love John, Peter, Thomas and so forth. This is the system upon which I have governed my self many years (but do not tell) and so I shall go on till I have done with them. I have got Materials Towards a Treatis proving the falsity of that Definition *animal rationale*; and to show it should be only *rationis capax*. Upon this great foundation of Misanthropy (though not Timons manner) The whole building of my Travells is erected: And I never will have peace of mind till all honest Men are of my Opinion.[1]

The manner of this passage is totally unlike Gulliver's closing denunciation of humanity in the fourth voyage; he makes no individual exceptions to his general misanthropy. At the end he is left alone instructing his indocible Yahoo family in the ways of the Houyhnhnms. Here is the climax, then, of the process towards complete rational imbalance which has characterised Gulliver's perception of himself and his surroundings.

In the first two voyages the obvious disparity in sizes between himself and his Lilliputian and Brobdingnagian friends makes it easy for Gulliver to perceive and preserve his human identity. The third voyage shakes his faith in speculative reason. The fourth voyage increasingly takes its vantage point from a source outside Gulliver himself. To the Houyhnhnms Gulliver is seen and shown to be merely a superior sort of Yahoo. Chapter three shows that Gulliver's pride in his reason is being assailed and that he is willing to sacrifice anything for the title of rational animal. He remarks to the Grey Horse,

upon my arrival hither, I was as much astonished to see the Houyhnhnms act like rational Beings, as he or his Friends could be in finding some Marks of Reason in a Creature he was pleased to call a *Yahoo*; to which I owned a Resemblance in every Part, but could not account for their degenerate and brutal Nature.

In chapter seven Gulliver is willing for the first time to see himself from another's point of view, and he is ashamed of what he sees: 'there is now an entire Congruity betwixt me and their Yahoos.' After the disgusting embrace which he suffers at the hands of the female Yahoo (chapter 8), he is forced to admit: 'I could no longer deny, that I was a real *Yahoo*, in every Limb and Feature, since the Females had a natural Propensity to me as one of their own Species.' By chapter 10, with his pride in human reason shattered and his physical nature made a source of disgust, Gulliver would willingly shake off his humanity: he is lovingly grateful to the Houyhnhnms that 'they would condescend to distinguish me from the rest of my Species', since he is ashamed of his membership of the 'human Race in general'.

Thus Swift maintains the outline of the generic-specific debate on man's identity to the end of the *Travels*, with Gulliver adopting the reverse of his creator's attitude (as stated in the letter to Pope) and opting for an unattainable and mechanical rationality at the cost of his frail humanity. The preposterous conclusion of Gulliver preferring the company of actual horses to that of his own family is engineered by a Lockean Swift intent on showing the precarious rule of Reason and the inescapably physical elements of human personality. Gulliver leaves his creator, and the perceptive reader, firmly convinced that rationality is still a property of some men (though Gulliver be mad) and that individuals such as the King of Brobdingnag and Pedro de Mendez bear witness to the potential virtue of some men. Locke had argued that external shape is no infallible sign of 'inner' properties (in this case, reason). Swift was to show in *Gulliver's Travels* that in its worst manifestations the Yahoo inhabits us all, and that a human being without sin is neither physically nor even intellectually within human grasp. Locke insists that the world of *words* is distinct from, and is at best only a provisional and approximate description of the world of *things*: for Swift there was a tragic dichotomy between man's moral aspirations and his actual behaviour. The moral tragedy is built upon the ancient foundations of logical error. Aristotle had warned:

Look also to see whether the resemblance be that of a caricature, like the resemblance of a monkey to a man, whereas a horse bears none: for the monkey is not the more handsome creature despite its nearer resemblance to man. Again, in the case of two things, if one is more like the better thing while another is more like the worse, then that is likely to be better which is more like the better ...
... if Man be better than Horse, then also the best Man is better than the best horse. Also, if the best in A be better than the best in B, then also A is better than B without qualification; e.g. if the best man be better than the best horse, then also Man is better than Horse without qualification.[2]

Note: Locke and Stillingfleet cite passages from each other's books in italics. This practice has been retained.

NOTES

1 *Correspondence*, III, 103. The logic-book background is discussed in a brilliant article by R. S. Crane, 'The Houyhnhnms, the Yahoos, and the history of ideas', in *Reason and Imagination*, ed. J. A. Mazzeo (Routledge & Kegan Paul, London, 1962), pp. 231–53.
2 *The Works of Aristotle*, ed. W. D. Ross (Clarendon Press, Oxford, 1928), I. *Categoriae et Interpretatione*, book III.2, 117b. For further discussions see 'Swift and the human predicament', in Clive T. Probyn, ed., *The Art of Jonathan Swift* (Vision Press, London, 1978), pp. 57–80.

JOHN LOCKE
A Letter to
the Bishop of Worcester
(1697)

. . . That the Essences of Things, as they are knowable by us, have a Reality in them, distinct from that of *abstract Ideas* in the Mind, which are *meerly Creatures of the Mind*, I do not see; and we shall farther enquire, in considering your Lordships following Words.

Therefore there must be a real Essence in every Individual of the same kind. Yes, and I beg leave of your Lordship to say, of a different *kind*, too. *For that alone is it which makes it to be what it is.*

That every individual Substance, has a real, internal, individual Constitution, *i.e.* a *real Essence*, that makes it to be what it is, I readily grant. Upon this your Lordship says,

Peter, James *and* John, *are all true and real Men*: Without doubt, supposing them to be Men, they *are true and real Men*, i.e. supposing the Name of that Species belongs to them. And so three *Bobaques*[1] are all true and real *Bobaques*, supposing the Name of that Species of Animals belongs to them.

For I beseech your Lordship to consider, whether in your way of Arguing, by naming them *Peter, James* and *John*, Names familiar to us, as appropriated to Individuals of the Species *Man*, your Lordship does not first suppose them *Men*; and then very safely ask, Whether they be not *all true and real Men*? But if I should ask your Lordship, whether *Weweena, Chuckerey* and *Cousheda*,[2] were true and real Men or no? Your Lordship would not be able to tell me, till I having pointed out to your Lordship the Individuals called by those Names, your Lordship by examining whether they had in them those sensible Qualities, which your Lordship has combined into that complex Idea, to which you give the specifick name *Man*, determin'd them all, or some of them, to be of the Species which you call *Man*, and so to be *true and real Men*; which when your Lordship has determin'd, 'tis plain you did it by that which is only the Nominal Essence, as not knowing the *real* one. But your Lordship farther asks, *What is it makes* Peter, James *and* John, *real Men? Is it the attributing the general Name to them? No certainly; but that the true and real Essence of a Man is in every one of them.*

If when your Lordship asks, What *makes them Men*? Your Lordship used the Word *making* in the proper sense for the efficient Cause, and in that Sense it were true, That the Essence of a Man, *i.e.* the specifick Essence of that Species made a Man; it would undoubtedly follow, That this specifick Essence had a reality beyond that of being only a general, abstract Idea in the Mind. But when it is said, That it is the *true and real Essence of a Man in every one of them, that makes* Peter, James *and* John, *true and real Men*; the true and real meaning of these Words is no more, but that the Essence of that Species, *i.e.* the Properties answering the complex, abstract Idea, to which the specifick Name is given, being found in them that makes them be properly and truly called Men, or is the Reason why they are called Men. Your Lordship adds, *And we must be as certain of this, as we are that they are Men.*

How, I beseech your Lordship, are we certain, That they are *Men*, but only by our Senses, finding those Properties in them which answer the abstract, complex Idea, which is in our Minds of the specifick Idea, to which we have annexed the specifick name *Man*? This I take to be the true meaning of what your Lordship says in the next Words, *viz. They take their denomination of being Men, from that common Nature or Essence which is in them*; and I am apt to think, these Words will not hold true in any other Sense.

Your Lordships Fourth Inference begins thus: *That the general Idea is not made from the simple Ideas, by the meer*

Act of the Mind abstracting from Circumstances, but from Reason and Consideration of the Nature of Things.

I thought, my Lord, That *Reason* and *Consideration* had been *Acts of the Mind, meer Acts of the Mind,* when any thing was done by them. Your Lordship gives a Reason for it, *viz. For when we see several Individuals that have the same Powers and Properties, we thence infer, That there must be something common to all, which makes them of one kind.*

I grant the Inference to be true; but must beg leave to deny that this proves, That the general Idea the Name is annexed to, is not made by the Mind. I have said, and it agrees with what your Lordship here says, That 'The Mind, in making its complex Ideas of Substances, only follows Nature, and puts no Ideas together, which are not supposed to have an Union in Nature; no Body joins the Voice of a Sheep, with the Shape of an Horse; nor the Colour of Lead, with the Weight and Fixedness of Gold, to be the complex Ideas of any real Substances; unless he has a Mind to fill his Head with Chimeras, and his Discourse with unintelligible Words. Men observing certain Qualities always joined and existing together, therein copied Nature, and of Ideas so united, made their complex Ones of Substances, &c.'

Which is very little different from what your Lordship here says, That 'tis from our Observation of *Individuals*, that we come to *infer, That there is something common to them all.* But I do not see how it will thence follow, that the *general* or specifick Idea is not made by the meer Act of the Mind. No, says your Lordship. *There is something common to them all, which makes them of one Kind; and if the difference of Kinds be real, that which makes them all of one Kind must not be a* nominal, *but* real Essence.

This may be some Objection to the Name of *Nominal Essence*; but is, as I humbly conceive, none to the Thing designed by it. There is an internal Constitution of Things, on which their Properties depend. This your Lordship and I are agreed of, and this we call the *real Essence*. There are also certain Complex Ideas, or Combinations of these Properties in Mens Minds, to which they commonly annex specifick Names, or Names of sorts, or *kinds* of Things. This, I believe, your Lordship does not deny. These complex Ideas, for want of a better Name, I have called *Nominal Essences*; how properly, I will not dispute. But if any one will help me to a better Name for them, I am ready to receive it; till then I must, to express my self, use this. Now, my Lord, *Body*, *Life* and the Power of *Reasoning*, being not the *real* Essence of a *Man*, as I believe your Lordship will agree; will your Lordship say, That they are not enough to make the Thing wherein they are found of the kind called *Man*, and not of the kind called Baboon, because the *difference of these Kinds is real*? If this be not real enough to make the *Thing of one kind* and *not of another*, I do not see how *Animal rationale* can be enough *really* to distinguish a *Man* from an *Horse*: For that is but the *nominal*, not *real Essence* of that kind, designed by the name *Man*. And yet, I suppose, every one thinks it *real* enough, to make a *real difference* between that and other *Kinds*. And if nothing will serve the turn, to MAKE Things *of one Kind and not of another*, (which as I have shew'd, signifies no more but ranking of them under different specifick Names) but their real, unknown Constitutions, which are the *real Essences* we are speaking of, I fear it would be a long while before we should have really different kinds of Substances, or distinct Names for them, unless we could distinguish them by these Differences, of which we have no distinct Conceptions. For I think it would not be readily answer'd me, if I should demand, Wherein lies the *real difference* in the internal Constitution of a *Stag* from that of a *Buck*, which are each of them very well known to *be of one Kind*, and not *of the other*; and no Body questions but that the Kinds whereof each of them is, are *really different*. Your Lordship farther says, *And this difference doth not depend upon the complex Ideas of Substances, whereby Men arbitrarily join Modes together in their Minds.*

I confess, my Lord, I know not what to say to this, because I do not know what these *Complex Ideas* of Substances are, *whereby* Men arbitrarily joyn Modes together in their Minds. But I am apt to think there is a Mistake in the Matter, by the Words that follow, which are these: *For let them mistake in their Complication of Ideas, either in leaving out or putting in what does not belong to them; and let their Ideas be what they please, the real Essence of a Man, and an Horse, and a Tree, are just what they were.*

The Mistake I spoke of, I humbly suppose is this, That Things are here taken to be distinguished by their *real Essences*; when by the very way of speaking of them, it is clear, That they are already distinguished by their nominal Essences, and are so taken to be. For what, I beseech your Lordship, does your Lordship mean, when you say, The *real Essence of a Man, and an Horse, and a Tree*, but that there are such Kinds already set out by the signification of these names *Man, Horse, Tree*? And what, I beseech your Lordship, is the Signification of each of these specifick Names, but the complex Idea that it stands for? And that complex Idea is the nominal Essence, and nothing else. So that taking *Man*, as your Lordship does here, to stand for a kind or sort of Individuals, all which agree in that common, complex Idea, which that specifick Name stands for, it is certain that the real Essence of all the Individuals, comprehended under the specifick name *Man*, in your use of it, would be just the same, let others leave out or put into their complex Idea of *Man* what they please; because the real Essence on which that unalter'd complex Idea, *i.e.* those Properties depend, must necessarily be concluded to be the same . . .

For Example, my Lord, let your Lordships Idea, to which you annex the Sign *Man*, be a rational Animal: Let another Mans Idea be a rational Animal of such a Shape; let a third Mans Idea be of an Animal of such a Size and Shape, leaving out Rationality; let a fourths be an Animal with a Body of such a Shape, and an immaterial Substance, with a Power of Reasoning: Let a fifth leave out of his Idea, an immaterial Substance. 'Tis plain every one of these will call his a *Man*, as well as your Lordship; and yet 'tis as plain that *Man*, as standing for all these distinct, complex Ideas, cannot be supposed to have the same internal Constitution, *i.e.* the same *real Essence*. The Truth is, every distinct, abstract Idea, with a Name to it, makes a real, distinct Kind, whatever the *real Essence* (which we know not of any of them) be . . .

And therefore I grant it true, what your Lordship says in the next Words, *And let the nominal Essences differ never so much, the real, common Essence or Nature of the several Kinds, are not at all alter'd by them,* i.e. That our Thoughts or Ideas cannot alter the real Constitutions that are in Things that exist, there is nothing more certain. But yet 'tis true, That the change of Ideas to which we annex them, can and does alter the signification of their Names, and thereby alter the Kinds, which by these Names we rank and sort them into . . .

Your Lordship here ending your four Inferences, and all your Discourse about *Nature*; you come, in the next Place, to treat of *Person*, concerning which your Lordship discourseth thus:

2. *Let us now come to the Idea of a Person. For although the common Nature in Mankind be the same, yet we see a difference in the several Individuals, from one another: So that* Peter, *and* James *and* John, *are all of the same kind; yet* Peter *is not* James, *and* James *is not* John. *But what is this Distinction founded upon? They may be distinguished from each other by our Senses as to difference of Features, distance of Place, &c. but that is not all: for supposing there were no such external Difference between them, as several Individuals in the same Nature. And here lies the true common Idea of a Person, which arises from that manner of Subsistence which is in one Individual, and is not communicable to another. An individual, intelligent Substance, is rather supposed to the making of a Person, than*

*the proper Definition of it; for a Person relates to something,
which doth distinguish it from another intelligent Substance
in the same Nature; and therefore the Foundation of it lies in
the peculiar manner of Subsistence, which agrees to one, and
to none else of the Kind; and this is it which is called
Personality.*

And then your Lordship asks, *But how do our simple Ideas
help us out in this Matter? Can we learn from them the
difference of Nature and Person?*

If *Nature* and *Person* are taken for Two real Beings, that
do or can exist any where, without any relation to these two
Names, I must confess I do not see how *simple* Ideas, or any
Thing else, *can help us out in this Matter*; nor can we from
simple Ideas, or any Thing else that I know, *learn the
difference* between them, nor what they are.

The Reason why I speak thus, is, because your Lordship,
in your fore-cited Words, says, *Here lies the true Idea of a
Person*; and in the foregoing Discourse speak of *Nature*, as if
it were some steady, established Being, to which one certain
precise Idea necessarily belongs to make it a *true Idea*;
whereas, my Lord, *in the way of Ideas*, I begin at the other
end, and think that the word *Person* in itself signifies nothing;
and so no Idea belonging to it, nothing can be said to be the
true Idea of it. But as soon as the common use of any
Language has appropriated to it any Idea, then that is the
true Idea of a Person, and so of *Nature*; but because the
propriety of Language, *i.e.* the precise Idea that every Word
stands for, is not always exactly known, but is often disputed,
there is no other way for him that uses a Word which is in
Dispute, but to define what he signifies by it; and then the
Dispute can be no longer verbal, but must necessarily be
about the Idea which he tells us he puts it for.

22   From
EDWARD STILLINGFLEET
The Bishop of Worcester's Answer
to Mr Locke's Second Letter
(1698)

... in this Debate, I shall proceed upon these *Principles of Reason*, which have been receiv'd among Mankind; and from them I hope to make it appear, that the Difference of *Nature* and *Person* is not imaginary and fictitious, but grounded upon the real Nature of things.

The *Principles of Reason*, which I go upon are these;

1. That Nothing hath no Properties.

2. That all Properties being only Modes or Accidents must have a real Subject to subsist in.

3. That Properties essentially different, must subsist in different Essences.

4. That where there is an Agreement in essential Properties and a Difference in Individual, there must be both an Identity and Diversity in several Respects.

Now upon these *Principles* I build my Assertion, that there is one real and common Nature or Essence in Mankind, and a Difference of Persons in the several Individuals. For, that there are such essential Properties in Mankind which are not in Brutes, I suppose you will not deny. Now these essential Properties must subsist somewhere; For Nothing can have no Properties, and these Properties cannot subsist (where Individuals are multiplied) in any one Individual: For that is to exclude all the rest from the essential Properties which belong to them; and if they have them in common, there must be some common Subject wherein they subsist, and that can be nothing but the common Essence of Mankind. For the Essence of Brutes or Plants have them not; and therefore these Essences must be really different from one another ...

You tell me, *that it is more than you know, that the Nature of a Man is equal in* Peter, James *and* John. I am sorry for it.

For I thought you had *Ideas of particular Substances*. But *they may be Drills*[1] *or Horses for any thing you know*. I am again sorry, that you know particular Men no better; but that for aught you know, they may be *Drills or Horses*.

But you know a Horse that was called Peter, *and you do not know but the Master of the same Team might call other of his Horses*, James *and* John. Suppose all this. And could you not in the *Way of Ideas* distinguish them from those of your Acquaintance who had the same Names? I confess, this tempts me to think that *Ideists* (as you call them) have a particular *Turn* of their understandings about these Matters. For I cannot but think, that those who were not *very rational Men*, might understand the Difference between *Men* and *Horses*; without being told, that although Horses might be called by their *Names*; yet that these were real Men, and *their Constitution and Nature was conformable to that Idea, which the general Name Man stands for. But this is no more than to say, that he that has the Nature of a Man is a Man, or what has the Nature of a Drill is a Drill*; *and what has the Nature of a Horse is a Horse; whether it be called* Peter, *or not called* Peter. If this were really the Discourse of your Friends in private Conversation, you have been very obliging to them to publish it to the World: For Mankind are not so stupid, as not to know a *Man* from a *Horse* or a *Drill*, but only by the *Specifick Name of Man*. You may have a *Horse* called *Peter* if you please, and another *James*, and a third *John*; but for all that, there is no one that hath the Understanding of a Man, but will be able without your *Specifick Names* to tell the Difference of your *Horse Peter* from your *Man Peter*; and call them by what Names you please the Difference will not depend upon them, but upon the Essential Properties which belong to them; and so it will be owned by all that have not this *New turn of their Understandings*. But I plainly see, that a new Notion when it hath got deep into a Man's Head doth give a strange *Turn* to his Understanding; so that he cannot see that, which every one else can, that hath not the same

Tincture upon his Mind. And I remember an Observation of yours, *How dangerous it is to a Man's Reason to fix his Fancy long upon one sort of Thoughts.*[2] These *Ideas* are a very odd sort of *Spectacles* to our Understandings, if they make them see and understand less, than People of very ordinary Capacities do. For even the Man *who had the Horse with the Name* Peter, and *might have others by the Names of* James *and* John, would not a little wonder at a grave Philosopher that should seriously say to him; You see, Friend, that your Horses have the Names of *Men*, how do you know but that they are Men? *Know*, saith the Country-man, I hope you are wiser than to ask me such a Question? Or what do you take me for, if I cannot tell the Difference of Men from Horses whatever Names they have. Do not tell me of your *Specifick Names, and Conformity to your Ideas*, I know well enough the Difference between my *Horse Peter* and my *Man Peter* without such Gibberish. My Man *Peter* and I can sit and chop Logick together, about our Country Affairs, and he can Write and Read, and he is a very sharp Fellow at a Bargain; but my *Horse Peter* can do none of these things, and I never could find any thing like *Reason* in him, and do you think I do not know the Difference between *a Man* and *a Beast?* I pursue this no farther lest the Country-man should be too rude to the Gentleman, with whom you had this *Learned Conversation*, about the Difference of *Men*, and *Horses*, and *Drills* . . .

You say, *That the Nature of Man in* Peter *is the Nature of a Man, if* Peter *be supposed to be a Man, but if it be the Name of a Horse, your Knowledge vanishes*. Cannot you, *for your Life*, know the Difference between a *Man* and a *Horse*, by their Essential Properties, whatever their *Names* be? If so, there is a greater *turn of Mens Understandings*, than I imagined. But again say you, *Let it be impossible to give that Name to a Horse* (who ever said or thought so?) *yet you cannot understand these Words, the common Nature of a Man is in* Peter; *for whatsoever is in* Peter *exists in* Peter; *and whatever exists in* Peter *is particular: but the common Nature of Man is the general Nature of Man, or else you understand not what is meant by Common Nature; and it confounds your Understanding to make a General a Particular.*

To this I answer, That the Common Nature of Man may be taken two ways. *In the way of Ideas, and in the way of Reason. In your way of Ideas* it is not at all to be wondered at, that you cannot understand such *a Common Nature*, as I spake of, which subsists in several Persons, because you say, *You can have no Ideas of Real Substances but such as are Particular*; all others are only *Abstract Ideas*, and made only by the Act of the Mind. But I say, That in the *Way of Reason* you may come to a better understanding of this Matter. Which is by considering the Nature of Beings, and the Causes of the Differences amongst the several kinds of them. I had told you before, in my Answer to your first Letter, that we are to consider Beings as God hath ordered them in their several Sorts and Ranks, and that he hath distinguished them by Essential Properties from each other, as appears by Mankind, and Brutes, and Plants: And that although the Individuals of the several kinds agree in Essential Properties, yet there is a real Difference between them in several Accidents that belong to them, as to Time, Place, Qualities, Relations, &c. Now that wherein they agree *is the Common Nature*; and that wherein they differ, is the *Particular Subsistence*. And if this be so hard to be understood, why was it not answered here in the proper place for it? Is not that a Real Nature that is the Subject of Real Properties? Is not that Nature really in all those who have the same Essential Properties? And therefore the *Common Nature* of Man must *exist in Peter* because he is a Man, and so in *James* and *John*: and yet every one of these is so distinguished from the other, that we may justly say he hath a *Particular Subsistence* with that Common Nature. And this is *not making a General a Particular*; but distinguishing one from the other, which is a Distinction so easie and necessary, that I cannot but wonder at those who say, that *for their Lives* they cannot find it out.

I had said, 'For the Nature of Man as in *Peter*, is distinct from that same Nature, as it is in *James* and *John*, otherwise they would be but One Person as well as One Nature.' And what Reply is made to this? *You cannot understand what this is a Proof of.* It is plain that I meant it of a *Particular Subsistence*; and if you cannot *for your Life* understand such easie things, how can I *for my Life* help it? Read the Words over again which are before them, and join them together . . .

And now I come at last to the *Idea of a Person.* And here I am glad to find *something you do understand*: Which is great News. *This*, say you, *I understand very well, that supposing* Peter, James *and* John *to be all three Men, and Man being a Name for one Kind of Animals, they are all of the same Kind.* Do you mean that they have the same common Essence, or have only the same common Name? If you mean the former, there must be a common Nature; if only the latter, that cannot make them of the *same Kind.* For *Kind* signifies nothing but a meer Name without it. If it be asked you, whether *Men* and *Drills* be of the same Kind or not? Could you give no other Answer, but that the *Specifick Name Man* stands for one sort, and the *Specifick Name Drill* for the other; and therefore they are not of the same Kind? Are those Names arbitrary, or are they founded on real and distinct Properties? If they be arbitrary, they have no other Difference, but what a Dictionary gives them. If they are founded on real and distinct Properties, then there must be a real Difference of Kinds founded in Nature; which is as much as I desire. But to go on. *You understand too very well, that* Peter *is not* James, *and* James *is not* John, *but that there is a Difference in these Individuals. You understand also, that they may be distinguished from each other by our Senses, as to different Features and Distance of Place*, &c. But what follows, you say, *You do not understand*, viz. *that supposing there were no such external Difference, yet there is a Difference between them as Individuals of the same Nature.*

For all that this comes to, as far as you can understand, is that the Ground of the Distinction between several Individuals in the same common Nature is that they are several Individuals in the same common Nature. You understand, it seems, that they are *several Individuals, that* Peter *is not* James, *and* James *is not* John; and the Question is, what this Distinction is founded upon? Whether upon our observing the Difference of Features, Distance of Place, &c. or on some antecedent Ground? I affirm, that there is a Ground of the Distinction of Individuals antecedent to such accidental Differences as are liable to our Observations by our Senses.

And the Ground I go upon is this, that the true Reason of Identity in Man is the vital Union of Soul and Body: And since every Man hath a different Soul united to different Particles of Matter, there must be a real Distinction between them, without any respect to what is accidental to them. For, if *Peter* have a Soul and Body different from *James*, and *James* from John, they must have different *Principles* of *Individuation*, without any respect to Features or Place, &c.

Gulliver's patriotism: Satire versus panegyric

Satire and panegyric, normally opposites in terms of intention, tone and execution, are often travelling companions in Swift's satire. He praises by apparent blame and blames by overloaded praise. Gulliver's patriotism is a case in point. The essentially subversive nature of satire uses patriotism as the front for an increasing exhibition of Gulliver's crass complacency and smug insularity. The early details of Gulliver's biography suggest that Swift was not so much attacking a particular class as the sense of fixed security and happy adjustment perhaps best exemplified by the middle ranks of the middle classes (the suggestion of a parody on Robinson Crusoe's paternal advice at the beginning of Defoe's novel, a paean of middle-class values, is probable). So Gulliver is the middle son of a middle-class parentage of modest means, educated at a Cambridge College noted for its Puritanism and described by one commentator as 'the symbol par excellence of a middle-class education'.[1] Through Gulliver Swift attacks chauvinism and recommends self-criticism. Gulliver's sojourn in foreign lands does not lead to greater self-awareness but to an eventual collapse of his national identity. In the second chapter of his second voyage he freely admits that his patriotism leads to partial distortion:

I have always born that laudable Partiality to my own Country which *Dionysius Halicarnassensis* with so much justice recommends to an Historian. I would hide the Frailties and Deformities of my Political Mother, and place her Virtues and Beauties in the most advantageous Light. This was my sincere Endeavour in those many Discourses I had with that Monarch [the King of Brobdingnag], although it unfortunately failed of success.

Under the searching cross-examination of the King Gulliver is indeed forced to retract his idealist's sketch of 'our own excellent Constitution, deservedly the Wonder and Envy of the whole World', because the unfortunate mention of 'a Minister of State' leads to an admission of radical corruption. Throughout Gulliver's lengthy series of similar interviews 'the most august Assembly in Europe' is reduced (in Glubbdubdrib) to a 'Knot of Pedlars, Pickpockets, Highwaymen and Bullies'. Gulliver's mathematics reveals the previously unacknowledged fact that England pays vast sums in surplus taxes; that its democracy yet needs a standing army in peace-time; that its recent history is a holocaust of wars, slaughters, executions and treacheries. In short, Gulliver's 'most admirable Panegyrick upon [his] Country' (the King's words) is stage-managed by Swift into its very opposite. The King concludes, in an even-tempered broadside:

... by what I have gathered from your own Relation, and the Answers I have with much Pains wringed and extorted from you, I cannot but conclude the Bulk of your Natives, to be the most pernicious Race of little odious Vermin that Nature ever suffered to crawl upon the Surface of the Earth.

For patriotic Englishmen there were at least two counter arguments for their self-defence: to attack Swift as an anarchist, or to re-state the grounds for national pride. Some contemporary responses noted with disgust the subversive critique of England's political and social structures in *Gulliver's Travels*. An anonymous *Letter from a Clergyman to his Friend* (1726) asked:

What can be viler in the Intention? What may be worse in the Consequence, than an Attempt to interrupt the Harmony and good Understanding between His Majesty and His Subjects, and to create a Dislike in the People to those in the Administration; especially to endeavour at this in such a Juncture as the present? What could in all Probability be the Issue of bringing such Matters to bear, but the throwing ourselves and all *Europe* into a Flame? Ruining our Credit, destroying our Trade, beggaring of private Families, setting us a cutting one another's Throats; by which we should become an easy Prey to the common Enemy, who would at once subvert our Constitution, the happiest, the best in the World; destroy our Church Establishment; and subject us to all the Cruelty and sufferings the unbounded Lust of Tyrants, and the insatiable Avarice of Priests could load us with . . .

The next great Attack . . . is not less than upon a *British* Parliament; this August Assembly, the Wisest, the Noblest, the most Awful in the World, he treats with Words of the utmost Scurrility, with *Billingsgate* terms of the lowest Sort; this Body of the best Gentlemen in the Kingdom he calls Pedlars, Pickpockets, Highwaymen and Bullies; Words never spoke of a British Parliament before, and 'twould be a National Reproach they should now pass unpunished: This is beyond all Bounds; who that are *English* Men can with Temper think of such an Insult upon the Body of their Representatives; the Centre of the National Power; the great Preserver of our Laws, Religion, and Liberties, and of all that as Men and Christians we ought to hold dear and valuable.[2]

This was a typical response from those who resented Swift's levelling satire at a time when English pride in English institutions seemed mandatory and when chauvinism was a respectable fashion.[3]

It is impossible to indicate all the norms by which *Gulliver's Travels* was attacked as subversive, but the following extract goes some way to illustrate the grass-roots of English public life at the time in respect of the 'official' social and political assumptions. Sir Daniel Dolins's *Third Charge to the Grand-Jury of the County of Middlesex*, published three weeks before the *Travels* (October 1726), is a kind of guide to the values and beliefs of responsible English magistrates operating in the community at large. Here is English pride in the superiority of their constitutional organisation; the sensible derived Lockeanism; the belief in liberty without licentiousness; the loyalty towards a limited monarchy, to revelation, to the laws of the land; a strict attitude towards the political recognition of dissenting minorities; the jealous right to an elected parliament and a strenuous defence of the Protestant succession. These may in general terms be called the politics of the consensus in Swift's time, and he of course shared them. It is indeed on the basis of such norms that Gulliver's gradual revelation of corruption and his ultimate volte-face away from human society rests: it is made essentially satirical in the first place and ridiculous in the ultimate.

Taken together, Dolins' *Charge* and Swift's *Gulliver's Travels* illustrate two manifestations of moral reforming. The former is obviously concerned with the bureaucratic machinery for law enforcement and depends on a political structure (the Administration) for its implementation: the latter is free of such restraints and accordingly shows how the real delinquents may in fact be the occupants of high political office (e.g. Flimnap–Walpole). In this way Swift's satire operates *on* and not from *within* his contemporary society. Though *Gulliver's Travels* was received as a specific satire on the state of England at the time, Swift's intention was to make it at least European in its reference. To the French translator of the *Travels*, he wrote:

If the volumes of Gulliver were designed only for the British Isles, that traveler ought to pass for a very contemptible writer. The same vices and the same follies reign everywhere; at least in the civilised countries of Europe: and the author who writes only for one city, one province, one kingdom, or even one age, does not deserve to be read, let alone translated.[4]

Swift's moral satire cannot be tied to the Hanoverians nor to the administration of Walpole exclusively; the paradox is that his satire is unshackled and supremely inventive only when he deals with a particular, known, and contemporary target. Gulliver's fashionable patriotism played into Swift's hands: there was no better way of converting the traveller's tale into a national satire, and he was guaranteed of success in his aim to 'vex' the world and not merely divert it.

1 E. A. Block, 'Lemuel Gulliver: middle-class Englishman,' *Modern Language Notes*, LXVIII (1953), 474–6.

2 This anonymous pamphlet has been reprinted in the *Augustan Reprint Series*, No. 143.

3 John Macky's *A Journey Through England* (1714: five editions by 1734) stated: 'Every English gentleman of condition ought to go abroad, to see the miseries of the enslaved part of the world, in order to give him a better taste and value for the constitution of his own country' (vol. I, p. vi).

4 *Correspondence*, III, 225–7, in French, to the Abbé Desfontaines, July 1727.

23 From
SIR DANIEL DOLINS
The Third Charge ... to the Grand-Jury ... of the County of Middlesex
(1726)

... In my last Charge, I made an Essay to represent somewhat of the Excellency of our Constitution, and Frame of Government, of the Wisdom, Justice and Goodness of our Laws, by an Enumeration of several Particulars, wherein they appeared to be so, and by Guarding against some Objections that might stand in the Way, or obstruct an immediate ready Assent to those Propositions; I appealed likewise for the Truth of them to the Senses and Experience of every True *Briton*, and to the happy Effects which we all of us in our several Stations and Conditions of Life, see and taste, feel and find, as produced by them, being vigorously and prudently put in Execution. Such an Appeal cannot, I perswade my self, be rejected or denied by such as have any just Value, or pleasing Relish, of true, amiable, delightful Liberty, without Licentiousness; by such as have any due Regard for a Legally settled, secure Enjoyment, and free Use of Life, Property, and Estate, with all our other invaluable Blessings, Rights, and

Privileges, Civil and Religious; These we evidently enjoy in so full and ample a manner, as would require a great Strength and Extent of Thought, a vast Variety of Lively and Beautiful Expressions, and a large Space of Time to set them forth in any tolerable Degree, equal to their Nature, their Worth, and Perfection. Thro' the Goodness of Divine Providence, and the tender Care and Concern of our most Gracious Soveraign King GEORGE: Thro' the wise and watchful Counsels of our Nobles, and the steady, vigorous, and seasonable Resolutions and Laws of our whole Legislative Body: And, lastly, thro' the prudent, gentle, easy Methods, and unwearied Diligence and Application of our Great Ministers of State, in the Execution of Justice, and Administration of our Publick Affairs at Home and Abroad, with so much Secrecy, so much Dispatch, and so great Success and Reputation to our King and Country: I say, by these happy Means united, and blessed by Heaven, we still enjoy Abundance of Liberty, Peace, and Prosperity; a flourishing extensive Trade Abroad, and within our selves a plentiful Stock and Treasure, not only of the Necessaries, but of the Accommodations, the Conveniences, the Delights, nay, Luxuriances of Life; certainly that Person must be either unaccountably ignorant, and a studied Stranger to our present State and Condition, or wonderfully obstinate and perverse, who shall go about to deny all this. And can any doubt whether they proceed as proper Effects from our Happy Constitution, and just Good Laws, kept in their due Force and Vigour, and impartially and prudently administred and executed by a most wise and merciful Prince, by a most able, vigilant, and indefatigable Ministry, authorized and appointed by him?

The secure and peaceful Enjoyment of Life, Liberty, and Property, the mighty boasted Blessings and Privileges of every *Briton*, are not in our Days the Matter of vain-glorious Boasting alone, or only in Name, Shew, and Appearance, but belong to us in Truth and Reality. Life, the greatest Blessing of this World, both in it self, and as it is the Foundation and

Pre-requisite of all the other Blessings we can enjoy here below, is guarded and defended by the strongest Munition of Laws made forcible and powerful by the severest Penalties, to be inflicted on those that shall be guilty of the Violation of them, and by Punishments of a lower Nature for those that shall attempt to commit Murder, tho' the Mischiefs they do fall short of that Offence. We are in no Danger to have our Lives fall a Sacrifice to the Cruelty, Resentment, or Revenge, of the Greatest, no more than of the Least. We have nothing to fear from the Arbitrary Nod, or Command of any Superior, willing or ordering us, without Cause or Reason, or upon Surmise and Probable Evidence only, to be dispatched out of Being. And our Equals and Inferiours have our Lives at least as little, or less, in their Power, and at their Disposal; and should their Malice, or any other inordinate Passion, prompt or prevail on them to commit such a Wickedness upon us, their own Lives must be the Victim to attone for their Villany, and make some Satisfaction, tho' not an adequate one, to the Publick . . .

. . . The next Darling Favourite Blessing, and Privilege, we justly glory in as *Englishman*, GENTLEMEN, is Liberty; not such a Liberty as belongs to Savages, without any Law or Government; which, considering the violent and fierce Appetites, Passions, and Desires of Mankind, in his present distempered degenerate State and Condition, must almost inevitably be attended with Rapines, Murders, Robberies, Thefts, Assaults, Batteries, and all those other Disorders and Violences, which good Government and Laws are designed to prevent. Good restraining Laws, tho' they cannot fully and perfectly secure us from such Evils and Mischiefs, yet evidently, beyond all Denial, they must and do lessen their Numbers, and Frequency of Commission, abate, and mitigate their Degrees, and leave us easy and comfortable in the Possession and Use of what we have. But if these Fences and Ramparts of Law were once broken down, we could hardly quietly, and with Satisfaction enjoy them, even for a very short Space of Time. Such a Liberty being supposed equal in all the Individuals; as their Desires will often be insatiable, unmeasurable, and set upon the same Object, or Thing, which one, or a few only can enjoy, must unavoidably create Animosities, Confusion, and every evil Work: Mankind, therefore, have generally very wisely agreed to part with this Kind of Liberty, so troublesome, and mischievous, and to exchange it for one more limited by some Laws of Government of one Kind or other, as vastly more beneficial to the Species and Individuals . . .

. . . the Liberty therefore which we are to desire and covet, and which is only worth the having and keeping, is a Rational Liberty; that is, a Power to act conformable to the Dictates of Reason, and the Laws of God and the Nation, evidently tending to promote the Happiness of Particulars, and of the Body Politick of which we are Members; and therefore must share in the Happiness or Misery, the Health or Sickness of the Body: There are, as I said, several Sorts of Branches of true Liberty: One very considerable, if not the most advantageous Kind, is a Liberty of Thought, or the free Enjoyment, Use, and Exercise of our Understandings, Judgments, and Consciences: These are Powers and Capacities we received from our great Creator, and to Him we are accountable for their Use and Improvement; these are to be guided, directed, and governed, by the Laws of Nature and Reason; of Revelation, and the known Laws of the Land, not contradictory or inconsistent with the former . . .

. . . Time fails me at present to enlarge any further on this Matter, or so much as to name and mention a large Number yet behind, of considerable Rights, Privileges, and Blessings, which we of this prosperous Isle derive from our present Establishment and Government, under the Administration of His Majesty, and His Ministers, in the Highest Stations. They, with the Representative Body of the Nation in Parliament, are the High, Noble, and Honourable Guardians, of all these immense and inexhaustible Treasures of

Happiness, which we are blest withal. It is well for us the Legislative Power, and the Executive Power, are in Hands so faithful, so prudent, so diligent and industrious, so intensely bent on promoting the universal Good and Welfare of the whole Community . . .

NOTES

I

Satire on dissent and enthusiasm

HENRY MORE
Enthusiasmus Triumphatus: or
A Brief Discourse of the Nature, Causes
Kinds, and Cure of Enthusiasm
(1656)

Henry More (1614–1687), Cambridge Platonist; rejected the Calvinism of his parents and his society to embrace Anglicanism. More's otherworldliness was reflected in his sequestered life, spent almost entirely at Cambridge, in his refusal of all preferments (including the offer of two bishoprics and the mastership of his college), and his theology. Cambridge Platonism may be defined as a movement away from the materialism and unspiritual secularism of Hobbes (and of Descartes, who influenced them) towards a more inward morality, with a tolerant and rationalistic attitude towards both natural and revealed religion. They stand between the Puritans and High Anglicans, and flourished at Cambridge between 1633 and 1688, and the group was led by Benjamin Whichcote. Ralph Cudworth (author of *The True Intellectual System of the Universe*, 1678), More, John Smith and Nicholas Culverwel all reacted against their Puritan education and claimed that morality was essentially a matter of reason, not of a Hobbesian will. Their tolerance invited the label 'latitude men', since they denied that ritual, dogma and church government were essentials in Christianity. More himself was much interested in the occult science of Van Helmont and Greatrakes, and sympathised with Joseph Glanvill's belief in witchcraft and apparitions.

More's tract is taken from *A Collection of Several Philosophical Writings of Dr Henry More* (1662), second edition.
1   Pomponius Mela, the earliest Latin geographer. More alludes to his *De Chorographia* (A.D. 37–41), a survey of the inhabited world.
2   As More goes on to explain, his objection to this word is based on its ambiguity, in that it is applied in Greek to animate and inanimate,

divine and human subjects, combining the senses 'sacred' and 'mighty'.

3 Cf. the sect of tailor-worshippers in section II of *Tale of a Tub* and also the learned Aeolists in section VIII. The comedy in both More and Swift resides in the permutations on the sense of wind (inspiration, afflatus, vapours, flatulence) as containing within it the purely physical grounds of intellectual or emotional states.

4 Aeolipia: a pneumatic instrument, illustrating the force with which vapour generated by heat in a closed vessel rushes out by a narrow aperture.

5 Aristotle, *Problems*, II, xxii–xxxviii: see the Loeb Classical Library translation by W. S. Hett (Heinemann, London, 1957), pp. 157–69.

6 *Humour* was originally a fluid of the body. In medieval medicine there were four cardinal humours: blood, phlegm, choler, and melancholy. The mixture of these determined the 'complexion' or 'temperament' both physically and mentally. Thus a choleric man was quick to anger, yellow-complexioned, thin, hairy, proud, and revengeful. A sanguine man was youthful, sociable, etc., and a melancholic man was characterised by his solitude and misanthropy. This theory of humours is turned into a theory of *vapours* in section IX of *A Tale*. See further, R. Klibansky, Erwin Panofsky and F. Saxl, *Saturn and Melancholy: Studies in the History of Natural Philosophy, Religion and Art* (Nelson, London, 1964).

7 Simon Magus, magician (first century A.D.): See Acts, 8. 9–24. Sometimes regarded as an early type of Faust figure. For Swift's catalogue of fanatics, see *A Tale*, pp. 283–9, and for further discussion, R. A. Knox, *Enthusiasm* (note 3 below).

8 Menander was a Syrian pseudo-Messiah, a Samaritan gnostic. See Johannes Weiss, *The History of Primitive Christianity*, 2 vols. (Macmillan, London, 1937), II, pp. 756–66.

JOHN EDWARDS
The Preacher
(1705–7)

John Edwards (1637–1716), Calvinistic divine, was said by his admirers to have been 'the Paul, the Augustine, the Bradwardine, the Calvin of his age'. Edwards is chiefly known for his *Socinians' Creed*, which intended to controvert Locke's *Reasonableness of Christianity*.

The text of *The Preacher* used here is the London edition of 1709; extracts from pp. 45–101.

1 See Cicero's *De Divinatione*, I, xviii, II, xvii, pp. 223–7, 263 in the Loeb Classical Library translation by W. A. Falconer (Heinemann, London, 1964).

2 St Mechtild of Magdeburg (1210–c. 1280), medieval German mystic; Gertrude the Great (1256–c. 1302), German mystic whose cult was extended to the Catholic church in 1738; Dame Julian(a) of Norwich (c. 1342 – after 1413), English mystic, who described sixteen revelations in *Revelations of Divine Love*; Bridget of Sweden (c. 1303–1373), Dominican tertiary whose mystical visions began at the age of seven; Teresa of Avila (1515–1582), Carmelite reformer and mystic. See further, F. L. Cross, ed., *The Oxford Dictionary of the Christian Church*, corrected edition (Oxford, University Press, 1966).

3 Nicholas Storch (d. 1530), Anabaptist, who taught that a ministerial and sacramental church was superfluous because all Christians were under the direct influence of the Holy Spirit. Thomas Munzer (c. 1490–1525), German Anabaptist and radical reformer, executed after the Peasant's Revolt, 1525. Kaspar Schwenkfeld (1490–1561), German lay theologian, eventually expelled from the Lutheran church. See further, R. A. Knox, *Enthusiasm: A Chapter in the History of Religion* (Clarendon Press, Oxford, 1950), pp. 126–38.

4 John of Leyden (i.e. Jan Beukelszoon, 1509–1536), militant Anabaptist and supporter of polygamy and community of goods; David George (1501–1556), Dutch Anabaptist fanatic.

5 Henry Nicholas (c. 1502–1580), founder of the Anabaptist section of 'Familists' in 1539/40 in Amsterdam, although the movement was active in England. The 'Family of Love' amalgamated with the Quakers at the end of the seventeenth century. The term 'Quaker' in part refers to the spiritual tremblings experienced at their religious meetings.

6 Miguel de Molinos (1628–1696) was a Spanish priest and a proponent of extreme Quietism, which stated that perfection lay in passivity and the suppression of human effort, thereby allowing full power to divine promptings.

7 In *De Divinatione* Cicero defines this as presaging or foreknowing by 'frenzy' or 'inspiration' and has Quintus approve of it: 'true prophecies are made during frenzy' (I, xxxi: pp. 297–8 of the Loeb translation by W. A. Falconer): but Cicero later disapproves of this method (XLIX–LVII; pp. 485–505).

8 St Epiphanus (c. 315–403), Bishop of Salamis, author of *Panarion*, a refutation of all the heresies known to him at the time.

9 Montanus (Montanism): a second century enthusiastic and prophetic sect.

10 St Ignatius Loyola (1491 or 1495–1556), founder of the Jesuits, or Society of Jesus, in 1534.

II
Ancients and Moderns

SIR WILLIAM TEMPLE
*An Essay upon the Ancient
and Modern Learning*
(1690)

Sir William Temple (1628–1699) achieved fame and respect as a skilful diplomat for Charles II. He concluded the Triple Alliance (betrayed by Charles) between England, Holland and Sweden against France's designs on Spain. In 1661 he was a member of the Irish parliament and actively encouraged the marriage of the Prince of Orange to Princess Mary, an event of vast importance for the conduct and outcome of the Glorious Revolution of 1688–9. He eventually retired, frustrated and embittered by politics, to Sheen, and later to Moor Park, where Swift became his secretary, literary executor and pupil. Swift met Esther Johnson at Temple's home. For Temple's profound influence on Swift see the account by Ehrenpreis, *Swift*, I, 91–108: the *Battle of the Books* is in part a generous testimony of Swift's loyalty to the elder statesman. The text of Temple's *Essay* is taken from the third edition of Temple's *Miscellanea: the Second Part* (1692); the text of Temple's *Defence of the Essay* is taken from *Miscellanea: the Third Part*, published by Swift in 1701.

1 Thomas Burnet's *Sacred Theorie of the Earth*, a speculative work of geology within a theological framework, was translated from Latin in 1684. Part one describes Paradise and the Deluge; the second part appeared in 1689. Fontenelle's *Pluralité des Mondes*, a whimsical dialogue popularising Cartesian notions of 'natural philosophy . . . in a gay and pleasing Dress', was designed to be read as a 'Romance or Novel'. Its principal authority was Bishop Wilkins' *The Discovery of a World in the Moon* (1638). The theory of vortices upon which both works rested was refuted by Newton's *Principia Mathematica* (1687). Temple went on to read Fontenelle's *Digression sur les Anciens et les Modernes*, contained in *Poèsies Pastorales* (1688). In Swift's *Battle* Fontenelle is linked with Perrault, author of *Parallèles des Anciens et des Modernes* (1688–9).

2 The Alexandrian library was founded by Ptolemy I and enlarged by Ptolemy II and III. In the first century A.D. it was said to contain 700,000 books. Alexandria was one of the chief centres of the Hellenistic world.

3 Nicolas Copernicus (1473–1543), the father of modern astronomy; rejected the generally accepted Ptolemaic system (earth as centre of universe), and demonstrated the earth revolved around the sun.

196

William Harvey (1586–1657), discovered the circulation of the blood; leader of the Modern Dragoons in *The Battle of the Books*.

4   Job XI. 12. On each birthday Swift read the opening of the Book of Job, which includes the lines 'Let the day perish wherein I was born, And the night in which it was said, There is a man child conceived.'

5   Of the less familiar references: Plato's Academy, the school established on the outskirts of Athens near a grove sacred to the hero Academus, about 385 B.C., and which lasted until A.D. 529; Aristotle founded a school (Lycaeum) near a grove sacred to Apollo Lyceius and established a library there, supported by his ex-pupil Alexander the Great; Zeno's Stoa, a philosophical school was founded in about 300 B.C. and lasted until at least A.D. 260; Epicurus (342–271 B.C.), Athenian philosopher, whose Athenian garden gave its name to the school, who taught his atomist theory of physics; Hippocrates (469–399 B.C.), the most famous Greek physician, whose name survives in the code of medical ethics known as the Hippocratic oath; Archimedes (c. 287–212 B.C.), mathematician, popularly known for his invention of the water-screw.

6   Enrico Davila (1576–1631), Italian historian, author of a history of the civil wars in France (1630), translated into English in 1647/8. Famiamus Strada (1572–1649), Italian Jesuit, author of a history of the Belgian war (1632, 1647).

7   Johannes Sleidanus (1506–1556), historian of the German Reformation. Swift made copious extracts from his *Commentaries* on contemporary history while living with Sir William Temple at Moor Park.

8   Sir William Davenant's *Gondibert* (1650) is matched against Homer in *The Battle of the Books* and crushingly defeated.

9   This passage precipitated the Bentley–Boyle controversy over the Phalaris epistles: Bentley was to show in his *Dissertation* that they were in fact spurious, hence discrediting Temple's scholarship.

10 Fra Paolo Sarpi (1552–1623) was the historian of the Council of Trent, but in his *Defence of the Essay* Temple denies him the title of historian because he did not deal with 'great Actions and Revolutions'. Antonio de Guevara (1481–1545) was a moralist, preacher, chronicler and secretary to Charles V. Selden is probably included here as a legal historian. Macchiavelli's *Florentine Historie* appeared in English in 1595, the *Prince* in 1640. Temple's list is, clearly, limited to great prose writers, having stated already that 'the Consideration of Poetry ought to be a subject by itself'.

11 Roger de Rabutin, comte de Bussy wrote the *Histoire amoureuse des Gaules* (c. 1665).

SIR WILLIAM TEMPLE
A Defence of the Essay
Upon Ancient and Modern Learning
(posthumous publication 1701)

1 Compare the tone and content of this and subsequent paragraphs on modern inventions with the analogous list offered by the Academy of Lagado in Gulliver's third voyage.

2 See Ariosto's *Orlando Furioso*, Book 34.

3 'It is agreed therefore among such great uncertainties, that nothing is certain; with the exception of man nothing is more wretched or marvellous.' Cf. Pope's *Essay on Man*, II, 1–18. This sentiment, if not exact words,may be found frequently throughout Pliny's *Natural History*. See, for example, book VII, i, 5–8.

4 Ecclesiastes, I. 10.

5 Sciolist: a pretender to science.

WILLIAM WOTTON
Reflections upon Ancient
and Modern Learning
(1694)

Wotton (1666–1727) has achieved unflattering fame as one of Swift's satiric butts in *The Battle of the Books*. In his own right he was an able and precocious classical scholar. His *Reflections* states clearly and without contentiousness the aims and considerable achievements of the Moderns in the natural and physical sciences. Among his friends Wotton numbered Bentley and Newton. His last words on the controversy were in the *Defence* of his *Reflections* (1705). Text taken from the second edition of the *Reflections* (1697).

1 Democritus (c. 460–370 B.C.), physicist and philosopher (*On Cheerfulness* defines his moral ideal).

2 See Plato's *Timaeus*, translated by R. G. Bury (Loeb Classical Library, London and Cambridge, Mass., 1961), p. 193.

3 For Malpighius see note 10 below.

4 Arcangelo Piccolomini (1525–1586), Italian anatomist and physiologist, author of *Anatomicae praelectiones* (1586).

5 The latter part of this passage on the brain should be compared with Swift's *Mechanical Operation of the Spirit* (*Tale*, p. 277): 'For it is the Opinion of Choice *Virtuosi*, that the Brain is only a Crowd of

little Animals, but with Teeth and Claws extremely sharp . . .' and ff. It seems likely that Swift's literalising satire makes the brain as producer of 'animal spirits' into a substance itself made of spirited animals.

6 Galen (A.D. 129–199) began life as a gladiator-physician; philosopher, anatomist and physiologist, whose theoretical system was based on the humours. He was the principal authority in the medical schools of late antiquity and the Middle Ages, and his physiology prevailed until the time of Harvey. In the Renaissance he was exposed as an 'ape anatomist'.

7 Herophilus, a Greek physician of the third century B.C., made discoveries in anatomy based on dissection, and discovered the rhythm of the pulse; Eristratus, of the same period, developed Herophilus' researches into the nervous system; Asclepiades (d. 40 B.C.), physician, believing in diet rather than drugs for his therapeutic methods.

8 Nicolaus Steno (Nils Steensen, 1638–1686), Danish anatomist and theologian, author of a *Treatise on the Anatomy of the Brain* (1669); William Croune (1638–1684), physician and professor of rhetoric in Gresham College, author of *De ratione metus Musculorum* (1664).

9 Giovani Borelli (1608–1679) described muscular movement according to the laws of statics and dynamics in *De motu animalium* (1680–1): he was the most famous member of the first scientific academy, the Italian Accademia del Cimento (1657–67).

10 Wotton's list of international scientific worthies is designed as a European showcase of Modern scientific talents. Robert Boyle, one of the original members of the Invisible College, was a pioneer chemist as well as a propagandist for the Royal Society in his *Usefulnesse of Experimentall Naturall Philosophy* (1671); Isaac Barrow was considered as second only to Newton by his mathematical contemporaries; Huygens, the Dutch mathematician and astronomer, was the founder of the wave theory of light, and his theorems on centrifugal force in circular motion helped the formulation of Newton's law of gravitation. Marcello Malpighi's autobiography was published by the Royal Society in 1696, and he has been regarded as the founder of microscopic anatomy. His work on blood capillaries helped Anton Van Leeuwenhoeck to give the first accurate description of red blood corpuscles. Francis Willughby was an ornithologist. Thomas Willis did important work on the anatomy of the brain; he was professor of natural philosophy at Oxford in 1660.

11 Jacob Rohault's *Physics* was the standard textbook of the Cartesian system. Samuel Clarke translated it into Latin in 1697, incorporating Newton's theories as notes. Thereby Newtonianism entered the previously Cartesian Cambridge.

THOMAS SPRAT
The History of the Royal Society
(1667)

Thomas Sprat (1635–1713) was bishop of Rochester and Dean of Westminster as well as scientific historian. Probably out of a sense of loyalty to his alma mater Sprat attributed to Wadham College the distinction of fostering the birth of the Royal Society. But as early as 1645 groups of virtuosi were assembling in various places to discuss 'Natural Philosophy, and other parts of Humane Learning: and particularly of what hath been called the New Philosophy or Experimental Philosophy'. The subjects informally discussed at members' lodgings, at the tavern, at Gresham College, and later at Sir William Petty's London lodgings, included 'physic, anatomy, geometry, astronomy, navigation, statics, magnetics, chemistry, mechanics and natural experiments' (R. F. Jones, in the standard account, *Ancients and Moderns: A Study of the Rise of the Scientific Movement in Seventeenth-century England*, second edition (University of California Press, Berkeley and Los Angeles, 1965), pp. 176 and ff.). This was the 'philosophical' or to use Boyle's term 'invisible' college which continued to meet, though now less frequently, at Dr John Wilkins' lodgings in Wadham College.

Reference is made below to J. I. Cope and H. W. Jones (eds.), Thomas Sprat's *History of the Royal Society* (Washington University Press, St. Louis, 1958).

1   William Wotton, in *Reflections upon Ancient and Modern Learning* (1694) defines the *Chymist's Art* as consisting in 'making such Analyses of Bodies by Fire, or by other Agents, Chymically prepared, as may reduce them into more simple Substances, then those out of which they were before compounded' (quoted by Cope and Jones, *Notes*, p. 7).

2   See further Martha Ornstein, *The Role of Scientific Societies in the Seventeenth Century* (1913; University of Chicago Press, Chicago, 1938), 73–90.

3   The model for Sprat's *History* was Paul Pelisson-Fontanier's *Relation contenant l'histoire de l'Academie Françoise* (1653).

4   Schemes for reforming and stabilising the English language were fashionable at this time. See Swift's own scheme, *Prose*, IV, 5–21. Sprat goes on later to recommend the improvements to be made by the new science in the 'Manual trades' and says at one point: 'It was said of *Civil Government* by *Plato*, that then the world will be best rul'd, when either Philosophers shall be chosen *Kings*, or *Kings* shall have *Philosophical* minds. And I will affirm the like of *Philosophy*. It will then attain to perfection, when either the Mechanic *Laborers* shall have Philosophical *heads*; or the *Philosophers* shall have *Mechanical* hands' (p. 397, *op. cit.*).

MATTHEW TINDAL
Rights of the Christian Church Asserted
(1706)

Matthew Tindal (1657–1733) called himself a 'Christian deist' and inspired violent antagonism among the high church party. Along with Sacheverell's sermon the *Rights* was burnt by order of the House of Commons in 1710. Tindal's deism also earned him a place in Pope's *Dunciad*: 'Toland and Tindal, prompt at priests to jeer, / Yet silent bow'd to Christ's No kingdom here' (II, 399–40). His best known work demonstrated that Christianity was superfluous since reason alone could establish all the truths of natural religion: it was entitled *Christianity as old as the Creation* (1730).

The fuller title of the *Rights* is: *The Rights of the Christian Church Asserted, Against the Romish, and all other Priests who claim an Independent Power over it* ... (Part One). The text here is that of the second edition (1706). Swift possessed a copy of the third edition of 1707.

Swift's *Remarks* on Tindal's book may be found in *Prose Works*, II, 67–107. The following quotations are some of Swift's remarks provoked by reading Tindal's book, intermediate responses leading up to the *Argument Against Abolishing Christianity*.

1 'At his Rate of arguing (I think I do not misrepresent him, and I believe he will not deny the Consequence) a Man may profess Heathenism, Mahometanism, &c. and gain as many Proselytes as he can; and they may have their Assemblies, and the Magistrate ought to protect them, provided they do not disturb the State: And they may enjoy all Secular Preferments, be Lord Chancellors, Judges, &c. But there are some Opinions in several Religions, which, although they do not directly make Men rebel, yet lead to it. Instance some. Nay we might have Temples for Idols, &c. A thousand such Absurdities follow from his general notions, and ill-digested Schemes. And we see in the Old Testament, that Kings were reckoned good or ill, as they suffered or hindered Image-Worship and Idolatry, &c. which was limiting conscience.'

2 'This shews, that although they be *Turks*, *Jews*, or *Heathens*, it is so. But we are sure Christianity is the only true religion, &c. and therefore it should be the Magistrate's chief Care to propagate it; and that God should be worshipped in that Form, that those who are the Teachers think most proper, &c.'

3 William Laud (1573–1645), archbishop of Canterbury, attempted under Charles I to obtain 'unity of heart by the imposition of

compulsory uniformity of action' (*Dictionary of National Biography*). He was beheaded on account of his absolutist reforms. Hugh Peters (1598–1660) was a vigorous Cromwellian Independent preacher.

4 'That is his Modesty, it is his own Simile, and it rather fits a Man that does so and so, (meaning himself). Besides the comparison is foolish. So it is with Men as with Stags.'

Swift's parting comment on the *Rights* was prompted by Tindal's readiness to write another book: 'And must we have another Volume on this one Subject of Independency? Or is it to fright us? ... I pity the Readers, and the Clergy that must answer it, be it ever so insipid. Reflect on this sarcastic Conclusion, &c.'

HENRY SACHEVERELL
The Perils of False Brethren
(1709)

Henry Sacheverell (1674–1724), political preacher, outspoken propagandist for the High Church and Tory cause (though disliked by leading Tories), and fierce abuser of Whigs and dissenters (see his *Character of a Low Churchman*, 1701, and *On the Association of ... Moderate Churchmen with Whigs and Fanatics* 1702). The House of Commons declared Sacheverell's sermons *On the Communication of Sin* and *The Perils of False Brethren* 'malicious, scandalous, and seditious libels'. His trial became a political battle between the two parties. In 1713, after his three year period of suspension, he was presented with a rich living and died a wealthy man.

Text taken from *A Compleat History of the Whole Proceedings ... against Dr. Henry Sacheverell* (1710). For bibliography, see G. S. Holmes, *The Trial of Doctor Sacheverell* (1973), pp. 288–98.

1 1641 saw the Parliamentary rebellion against Charles I, the beginnings of the Civil Wars and rebellion in Ireland.

2 Deism was no single school of thought in the eighteenth century. It was a rationalistic attempt to define God's relationship with the world, which therefore minimised divine providence, revelation, and any supernatural scheme of salvation. On the continent Voltaire and Rousseau were its chief advocates. For an account, see Leslie Stephen, *History of English Thought in the XVIIIth. Century* (London, 1876); tritheism (belief in three Gods), denied the Christian Trinity as a unity of three substances; socinianism, the forerunner of modern Unitarianism, was also a rationalistic movement which saw Jesus as a man, and taught the separation of the church and state, and nonresistance. It influences the views of Newton and Locke.

3 Ahithophel was David's counsellor (2 Samuel, xv. 12), who abetted the rebellion of Absalom. The most famous application of this

biblical incident to recent contemporary politics was Dryden's *Absalom and Achitophel* (1681).

BENJAMIN HOADLY
A Sermon Preach'd before the King
(1717)

Benjamin Hoadly (1676–1761) was bishop in succession of Bangor, Hereford, Salisbury and Winchester. As leader of the extreme latitudinarians Hoadly was Sacheverell's rival and opponent of the high church party leader Atterbury (a friend of Swift). Hoadly firmly upheld the revolution principles (as Swift put it, he was 'a Champion for Resistance') and stood against the exponents of hereditary right and passive obedience. He was made Royal chaplain in 1715. The 'Bangorian' controversy produced about two hundred tracts and became a melting pot for all the issues in dispute between Whig and Tory, high and Low Church. His concern to minimise mystery and dogma in religion is shown in *A Plain Account of the Nature and End of the Lord's Supper* (1735). There are numerous contemptuous references to Hoadly in Swift's work.

A Sermon Preach'd before the King . . . on March 31, 1717 begins with the text from St John, XVIII, 36: 'Jesus answered, My Kingdom is not of this World.' Printed at the King's command, and denying that there was a visible Church of Christ, the sermon was a patent challenge to the High Churchmen. Text taken from the British Museum copy of the 1717 text.

WILLIAM WOLLASTON
The Religion of Nature Delineated
(1724)

William Wollaston (1660–1724) was a moral philosopher. He lived an uneventful life in seclusion and wrote on ecclesiastical and philological questions. But Wollaston seems to have impressed Queen Caroline, for she placed a bust of him alongside Newton, Locke and Samuel Clarke in her Richmond hermitage. *The Religion of Nature Delineated* was privately printed in 1722 and published in 1724. It sold ten thousand copies 'in a few years' and went through many editions (see *Dictionary of National Biography*). Swift owned a copy of the 1726 edition.

Present text taken from the 1725 edition.

1   animalculum: a microscopic animal, the germ of life. Wollaston used the word again in this work: 'If the semina, out of which animals are produced, are (as I doubt not) animalcula already formed.'
2   Cf. Swift's letter to Pope, *Correspondence*, III, 103: 'I have got Materials Towards a Treatis proving the falsity of that Definition *animal rationale*; and to show it should be only *rationis capax*.' The 'Treatis' was of course *Gulliver's Travels*.

HALIFAX
The Character of a Trimmer
(1688)

George Savile, Marquis of Halifax (1633–1695), statesman and essayist, friend of Sir William Temple and Dryden's Jotham '... of piercing wit and pregnant thought' in *Absalom and Achitophel*. At the court of Charles II he was created Viscount Halifax: the *Character of King Charles II* was printed in 1750. A prominent monarchist in the Exclusion Crisis of 1679–81, he spoke against Shaftesbury, and his contemporaries believed him to be personally responsible for the defeat of the Exclusion Bill. He strongly opposed the Catholic policies of James II, became William of Orange's adviser on English affairs and took a leading part in the transference of power from James to William III in 1688. Macaulay wrote: 'the revolution, as far as it can be said to bear the character of any single mind, assuredly bears the character of the large yet cautious mind of Halifax.'

The *Trimmer* was circulated in manuscript in 1684/5 and printed under the name of Halifax's uncle, Sir William Coventry, in 1688. No political group of Trimmers existed subsequent to this date. L'Estrange's definition of a trimmer (*Observator*, 3 December 1684) denotes 'a Comprehensive Christian', 'a man of Latitude, as well in Politiques as Divinity: An Advocate both for Liberty of Practice in the State, and for Liberty of Conscience in the Church'. Gilbert Burnet (*History of my Own Time*, 1723, 1734) described Halifax as a man who 'with relation to the publick ... went backwards and forwards, and changed sides so often that in conclusion no side trusted him'.

Text (modernised) taken from *The Life and Letters of Sir George Savile*, Bart., ed. H. C. Foxcroft, 2 vols. (1898).

1 The importance which Halifax attaches to the example of a virtuous prince is complemented by Swift's King of Brobdingnag and by the appeal to Queen Anne in *A Project for the Advancement of Religion and the Reformation of Manners* (1709), *Prose*, II, 41–63.

2 A Roman order of architecture, combining the features of the Ionic and Corinthian orders, sometimes known in the eighteenth century as the Heroic and Italian orders.

3 A swelling, especially of the abdomen.

4 Cf. Swift's remark in *The Sentiments of a Church of England Man*, *Prose*, II, 16: 'By the *Supreme Magistrate* is properly understood the Legislative Power, which in all Government must be absolute and unlimited.'

5   A sea-monster, the term used by Hobbes for the title of his political masterpiece (1651), and which there stands for the state or commonwealth, an 'artificial man'; hence the commonwealth as (a potentially unruly) organism.

6   A surgical device applied to the skin in order to draw off blood.

7   Swift noted another argument used at the Revolution (*Sentiments, Prose,* II, 17): 'Among other Theological Arguments made use of in those Times, in praise of Monarchy, and Justification of Absolute Obedience to a Prince, there seemed to be one of a singular Nature: It was urged, that *Heaven* was governed by a *Monarch,* who had none to control his Power, but was absolutely obeyed: Then it followed, That earthly Governments were the more perfect, the nearer they imitated the Government in Heaven. All which I look upon as the strongest Argument against *despotick* Power that ever was offered, since no Reason can possibly be assigned, why it is best for the World that God Almighty hath such a Power, which doth not directly prove that no Mortal Man should ever have the like.'

NICHOLAS LECHMERE
Speech at the Sacheverell trial
(1710)

Nicholas Lechmere (1675–1727) was solicitor-general from 1714 to 1718, attorney-general from 1718 to 1720 and a privy councillor. In 1710 he was one of the party managers appointed to conduct the trial of Sacheverell: in 1715 he was also involved in the trial of the rebel Scottish lords after the rising of 1715. He was raised to the peerage in 1721 by George I. In *The Examiner* No. 25, 1710–11, Swift suggested him as a possible champion of the freethinkers and deists. Lechmere assisted Steele in the composition of the Whig pamphlet *The Crisis,* to which Swift replied in *The Publick Spirit of the Whigs* (1714).

The text of Lechmere's speech is taken from the official record published by the House of Peers, *A Compleat History of the Whole Proceedings ... against Dr Henry Sacheverell* (1710). This extract should, of course, be read as referring to Sacheverell's sermon, reproduced in section III, item 8 above.

1   Cf. Anne's speech from the throne, May 1702: 'My own principles must always keep me entirely firm to the interests and religion of the Church of England, and will incline me to countenance those who have the truest zeal for her cause ...'

2   Edmund Grindal (1519?–1583), archbishop of Canterbury, employed by Edward VI and Elizabeth I as an Anglican apologist: a moderate Calvinist, with some sympathy for Puritans.

3   Convocation was the organ of the Church's self-government. Its lower House at this time was predominantly high-flying Tory and

therefore hostile to the Whig and moderate Tory upper house. Such tensions had made Convocation unworkable since 1701. It already stood prorogued until March 1706, therefore Anne's letter to Tenison of 25 February 1706 stated her intention to keep it prorogued until the end of the session, thus demonstrating royal supremacy: 'it has been our constant care and endeavour, as it shall ever be, to preserve the Constitution of the Church of England as by law established, and to discountenance all divisions and innovations whatsoever. In particular we are resolved to maintain our supremacy and the due subordination of Presbyters to Bishops...' See *The Letters of Queen Anne*, ed. B. C. Brown (1935), p. 182. For the circumstances which led to the letter being written, see G. V. Bennett, *White Kennett . . . Bishop of Peterborough* (S.P.C.K., London, 1957), pp. 66–7.

RAPIN
A Dissertation on . . . the Whigs and Tories
(1717)

Paul de Rapin-Thoyras (1661–1725), French Huguenot historian, came to England in 1686, and again in 1688 with William of Orange's expedition (an account of which is given in his *History of England*) and fought at the Battle of the Boyne. The first volumes of his History were published in French in 1723, the last two appeared in 1725. Nicholas Tindal (1687–1774), nephew of Matthew Tindal (q.v.) began to produce his translation in 1725 and completed the fifteen volumes in 1731. Tindal's translation of Rapin's *History* became the standard account until Hume's *History of Great Britain* (1754–62) and sold fifteen thousand volumes between 1725 and 1732. The *Dissertation on . . . the Whigs and Tories* appeared as an appendix to Rapin's *History*. The present text is taken from the second edition (1733), its full title being *A Dissertation on the Rise, Progress, Views, Strength, Interests, and Characters of the two Parties of the Whigs and Tories* (1717).

1   James Edward reached Scotland in December 1715 after the rising had failed. Rapin's *Dissertation* was finished in February 1715/16.
2   The Triennial Act of 1694 ensured frequent Parliaments.
3   Cf. Swift to Pope: 'I have often endeavoured to establish a Friendship among all Men of Genius, and would fain have it done. They are seldom above three or four Contemporaries and if they could be united would drive the world before them; I think it was so among the Poets in the time of Augustus, but Envy, and party and pride have hindred it among us' (*Correspondence*, II, 465).

BOLINGBROKE
A Dissertation upon Parties
(1733–4)

Henry St John, Viscount Bolingbroke (1678–1751), Secretary of State and Tory leader during Anne's reign. His career was closely bound up with that of Robert Harley, later Earl of Oxford. Both had been brought up under presbyterian influences. St John became secretary of state at war at the age of 26, when Harley succeeded Nottingham (1704); secretary of state in 1710 when Harley became chancellor of the exchequer. When Harley became a peer in 1711 St John was left to manage the House of Commons. Their serious cabinet clash of 1712 was an inevitable result of their conflicting personalities and Bolingbroke's scheming for power. Bolingbroke was regarded as chiefly responsible for the Treaty of Utrecht, — for which the triumphant Whigs hounded him by a committee of secrecy (1715). The episode of his negotiations with France and the conclusion of the War of the Spanish Succession forms the basis for a parallel episode in Gulliver's voyage to Lilliput. Bolingbroke was dismissed from office by the new king. Having taken up the Jacobite cause, he fled to France to avoid trial and became secretary of state to the Pretender. In 1723 he was pardoned and returned to England in 1725, to find that he was barred from all parliamentary office. Walpole had thus effectively created the extra-parliamentary opposition which centred on Bolingbroke for the next fifteen years, the chief organ of which was *The Craftsman*.

The *Dissertation upon Parties* was published in *The Craftsman* between 27 October 1733 and 28 December 1734; *On the Policy of the Athenians* appeared on 16, 23, and 30 September 1732. Texts (modernised) taken from *The Works of Lord Bolingbroke*, 4 vols. (Carey and Hart, Philadelphia, 1841).

BOLINGBROKE
On the Policy of the Athenians
(1732)

1 Pisistratus (560–527 B.C.), tyrant of Athens, a pliant survivor, like Walpole, who packed chief offices with his Athenian friends. Contemporary readers would pick this up as a parallel to the reign of James II, whose actions became synonymous with those of an arbitrary monarch. William III was, accordingly, the great deliverer.

2 Hippias (527–510 B.C.), tyrant of Athens, son of Pisistratus: a parallel with the Old Pretender, i.e. James Edward Stuart, 'James III' (1688–1766).

3 | It was a feature both of Walpole's rapid rise to power and of his long period of office that troublesome rivals and allies were speedily eliminated, by design, by chance or by fortuitous mortality. Before

the Bubble Crisis of 1720, which brought Walpole to supreme power, he had held the lucrative but comparatively minor office of paymaster. If Bolingbroke here is intending a close parallel, then the names Cimon, Aristides and Tolmidas could apply to the Whig allies Sunderland, Stanhope and Carteret. As first lord of the treasury Sunderland had managed the scheme for taking over the national debt by the South Sea Company. Its collapse in 1720 compelled him to retire, but his powerful challenge to Walpole's leadership was only ended by his death in 1722. Stanhope was secretary of state and architect of foreign policy while Walpole was leading the Whig opposition: admired by Bolingbroke, he died in 1721. Carteret, the only remaining rival to the supremacy of Walpole and Townshend, was removed from office as secreatary of state in 1723. He was appointed Lord-Lieutenant of Ireland and arrived there in the middle of the Wood's Ha'pence controversy. In April 1721 Walpole was appointed chancellor of the exchequer and first lord of the treasury. Others removed by Walpole included Pulteney, Chesterfield, and ultimately Bolingbroke himself.

4 Pericles (495–429 B.C.), brought Athenian democracy to its height. His career developed at a time when the popular vote began to figure as a vital political consideration for the career politician. The wars with Persia and other Greek States were ended in his reign. Bolingbroke intends some of these parallels to apply to Walpole's career.

5 One of the many soubriquets and pseudonyms bestowed on Walpole (Flimnap in *Gulliver's Travels*; Macheath, Bob Booty, etc. in *The Beggar's Opera*) was 'Skreen-Master-General' for his successful screening-defence of some of those involved in the South Sea scandal. Walpole undertook this defence largely to prevent any consequent Tory success. Bolingbroke may refer to the defence of Sunderland by Walpole and Pelham.

6 Bolingbroke and Swift frequently attacked the venality of Walpole's administration and the political power of money. Walpole's political distribution of offices to his friends, allies and relatives was notorious, and in 1730 a pensions bill was unsuccessfully introduced to curb Walpole's use of placemen by disabling persons in receipt of pensions from sitting in parliament. See also Basil Williams, *The Whig Supremacy, 1714–60* (Clarendon Press, Oxford, 1939), p. 195 for the number of placemen.

7 Areopagus, the Hill of Ares at Athens, to the west of the Acropolis. The oldest council in Athens, a powerful oligarchic body (cf. the Senate at Rome), whose members were appointed for life, with special powers to try cases of serious crimes. In a crisis it could assume dictatorial powers.

Walpole declined a peerage, preferring to remain at the seat of power in the House of Commons. He became Lord Orford only after his parliamentary defeat in 1742. |

8 The Commissioners of Public Accounts were used by the Tories in Anne's reign to attack Whig mismanagement of public money. Bolingbroke had been a Commissioner in 1702. As Secretary-at-War Walpole was successfully accused of corruption in 1712, expelled the House of Commons until 1713 and imprisoned in the Tower. Attempts were also made in 1725 to condemn Walpole for misuse of the Civil List and other public money. |

9 For Walpole's use of secret-service money in getting ministerial candidates returned in 1727, see J. H. Plumb, *Sir Robert Walpole: The King's Minister* (Cresset Press, London, 1960), pp. 176–78.

10 Walpole initiated the Sinking Fund in 1717 as a device to pay off the National Debt. In 1727 and again in 1733, with the consent of parliament, he appropriated large sums from the Fund in order to increase the king's Civil List and to avoid the unpopular measure of increasing the land tax (which would have lost him the support of the country landowners), both purposes for which the Fund was never intended. |

11 In 1727 Swift wrote to Sheridan: 'It is certain that Walpole is Peevish and Disconcerted, stoops to the vilest Offices of hiring Scoundrels to write *Billingsgate* of the lowest and most prostitute Kind, and has none but Beasts and Blockheads for his Pen-men, whom he pays in ready Guineas very liberally' (*Correspondence*, III, 207). Between 1732 and 1742 Walpole spent £50,000 on hiring penmen. Among his writers were Benjamin Hoadly, Defoe, Lord Hervey, Horace Walpole and Thomas Gordon. See Isaac Kramnick, *Bolingbroke and his Circle* (Harvard University Press, Cambridge, Mass., 1968), pp. 115–24. The first half of this sentence may be read as a compliment to the opposition Scriblerians (Swift, Pope, Gay, Arbuthnot), each of whom had produced their major works by this time.

V
The State of Ireland

SIR WILLIAM PETTY
A Treatise of Ireland
(1687)

Petty (1623–1687), even by the exacting standards of his contemporaries, would have been judged something of a polymath. Professor of anatomy at Oxford in 1650, professor of music at Gresham College, naval architect (his design for a double-bottomed boat amused Charles II and was ridiculed in Temple's *Essay upon the Ancient and Modern Learning*), he was also physician-general to the Parliamentary army in Ireland, and unofficial surveyor-general of Ireland in the Commonwealth period. At the Restoration he unsuccessfully attempted to realise his theoretical principles in an Irish statistical office.

Swift possessed the 1699 edition of Petty's *Political Arithmetic*. The *Treatise*, reproduced here from C. H. Hull's edition of *The Economic Writings of Sir William Petty*, 2 vols. (Cambridge, 1899), bears above the Syllabus the more descriptive title, *An Essay in Political Arithmetic concerning Ireland*.

1 See Swift's own ironic scheme, based on Petty's ideas for depopulating Ireland and converting it into a vast pasture for England's benefit, in *An Answer to the Craftsman*, *Prose*, XII, 173–8.

2 The Civil Survey was entrusted to a commission which was to ascertain the position and extent of the 'disaffected' estates in Ireland forfeited to the Commonwealth. Petty's task was to measure and map these estates. It was known as the 'Down' survey because the results were measured down on maps (see *Dictionary of National Biography*).

3 Ezekiel, XXXVII, 22: 'And I will make them one nation in the land upon the mountains of Israel, and one King shall be king to them all; and they shall be no more two nations, neither shall they be divided into two kingdoms any more at all.'

4 'Clarendon had been appointed Lord Lieutenant in Ireland, in September 1685. Tyrconnel became Commander-in-Chief and virtual viceroy in June 1686, and returned to the island as Lord Deputy to succeed Clarendon in February, 1687. His extreme Catholic policy in both positions alarmed the Protestants in Ireland and large numbers of them returned to England with Clarendon' (Hull, *Economic Writings*, II, 577). Swift was one of the many who left Ireland. For the difficulties suffered by Trinity College during this period, see Ehrenpreis, *Swift*, I, 65–71.

WILLIAM MOLYNEUX
The Case of Ireland
(1698

William Molyneux (1656–1698) humbly confessed that he could not understand Newton's *Principia*, although his own career was centred on experimental science. He took a most prominent part in the founding of the Dublin Philosophical Society (first formal meeting in 1683), becoming its first secretary. He translated Descartes' *Meditations* (1680), and was elected Fellow of the Royal Society in 1685. His *Dioptrica Nova*, written with the assistance of Flamsteed, became a standard work on optics. He corresponded with John Locke on the effects of English legislation on the Irish woollen and linen trade.

The preface to the *Case* bears the date 1697/8 and the work was published simultaneously in Dublin and London. Present text taken from the London edition of 1720.

1 For an account of Locke's obsession for the anonymity of this work, see John Locke, *Two Treatises of Government*, ed. Peter Laslett (Mentor, London, 1965), pp. 15–27.

2 Sir Edward Poynings was Lord Deputy of Ireland from 1494 to 1495. As Molyneux points out, the restrictive legislation associated with his office effected the subjugation of the Irish parliament to the English king and council. All draft legislation by the Irish parliament had to be submitted to and approved by the English government, and until 1782 the Irish parliament could only meet by licence of the English lord chancellor.

3 By 'we' Molyneux includes the English and Irish people, both equally bound by the parliament at Westminster. The patriarchal theory of government was widely held in the period. Swift in the *Contests and Dissensions* and Temple in *Upon the Original and Nature of Government* use it with reference to standing armies.

4 Richard Hooker's *The Laws of Ecclesiastical Policy* (1593): a famous anticipation of the theory of consent later elaborated by Locke.

5 Hugo Grotius (1583–1645), Dutch jurist, statesman, philologist, poet, theologian and historian. Swift owned a copy of his *Argumenti Theologici* (1652) and *De Veritate Religionis Christianae* (1640 edition). Samuel Puffendorf (1632–1694), German publicist and jurist best known for his pioneer work on international law, e.g. *Elementa Jurisprudentiae universalis* (1661).

6 Signed at Nantes by Henry IV in 1598, the Edict granted limited freedom of worship and some civil rights to Protestant Huguenots. It was revoked by Louis XIV in 1685. England's Toleration Act was passed in 1689: the Test was extended to Ireland in 1704 and Acts of Toleration (1719) extended toleration to Irish Protestant Dissenters.

7 A theory of government which Rapin thought was peculiarly English ('gouvernement Mixte': see section IV, item 13 above). It stated the equal importance of the three estates of the realm—king, nobles and commons—and saw the balance as kept by the king. For Swift's exposition of the natural and reasonable merits of a balanced constitution, see the *Contests and Dissensions* and the Brobdingnagian monarchy in Gulliver's second voyage: the Lilliputian 'mixed' government had been corrupted from its original state by a too powerful king and his advisors. The ideas of mixed

government and a balanced constitution were frequently cited in the works of Aristotle, Polybius and Cicero. For a discussion of this theory, see Z. S. Fink, *The Classical Republicans: An Essay in the Recovery of a Pattern of Thought in Sevententh Century England* (Northwestern University Studies in the Humanities, No. IX, Northwestern University Press, Evanston, Ill., 1945).

VI
Scientists and satire

STEPHEN HALES
Vegetable Staticks
(1726)

Stephen Hales (1677–1761) has been seen as second to Harvey for his work in animal physiology. Typical of his age, he was a versatile projector and most of his schemes had practical aims (e.g. the invention of artificial ventilators for prisons (including Newgate), ships, and granaries; schemes for fire prevention; for the preservation of meat and water on long voyages; schemes for winnowing corn. F.R.S. in 1718 and D.D. of Oxford in 1733, he was also one of the eight foreign members of the French Academy in 1753. Pope referred to him as 'plain Parson Hale': he was Pope's near neighbour and friend. But Hales' vivisection experiments distressed the dog-lover in Pope. In *Moral Essay* I, ll, 39–40. Pope alluded to Hales: 'Like following life thro' creatures you dissect, / You lose it in the moment you detect.' Joseph Spence exclaimed to Pope: 'What he cuts up rats?' and Pope replied 'Aye and dogs too! (and with what emphasis and concern he spoke it.) Indeed, he commits most of these barbarities with the thought of its being of use to men. But how do we know that we have the right to kill creatures that we are so little above as dogs, for our curiosity, or even for some use to us?' (see James M. Osborn, ed., *Observations, Anecdotes, and Characters of Books and Men*, Clarendon Press, Oxford, 1966, vol. I, p. 148).

The two volumes of *Statical Essays* were translated into French, German, Dutch and Italian. The first volume deals with plant physiology and was published in 1726/7 as: *Vegetable Staticks: Or An Account of some Statical Experiments on the Sap in Vegetables, Being an Essay towards a Natural History of Vegetation*. Also, a Specimen of An Attempt to Analyse the Air, By a great *Variety of Chymico-Statical Experiments; Which were read at several Meetings before the Royal Society*. Text from the first edition.

1   Aeolipiles: see note 3 in section I above, item 1.

THOMAS SALMON
The Theory of Musick
(1704)

Thomas Salmon (1648–1706), divine and writer on music, studied mathematics at Oxford. His publications included *An Essay to the Advancement of Musick, by casting away the perplexity of different Cliffs* [clefs] *and uniting all sorts of Musick in one universal character* (1672) and *A Proposal to perform Musick in Perfect and Mathematical Proportions* (1688). Contemporary response to this subject was lukewarm. Roger North stated: 'the mind likes and dislikes, upon principles no sagacity of sence can discerne'.

The text of Salmon's *Theory of Musicke* is taken from the *Philosophical Transactions of the Royal Society of London*, vol. 24 (1704–5).

1   Salmon is referring to Pythagoras, whose number theory was based on three observations: the discovery of numerical relationships of musical harmonies determining the principal intervals of the musical scale; the ratio 3 : 4 : 5 in right triangles: the fixed numerical relations of the movements of heavenly bodies. Certain significant numbers (or ratios) were interpreted symbolically: e.g. the number 1 (or monad) as the creative principle; number 2 (dyad) was identified with evil because it lacked the 'integrity' of the monad; and so on. Plato developed his cosmology in the *Timaeus* from Pythagoras. In *A Tale* (pp. 57–8) Swift pokes fun at the mystical interpretation of the numbers 3, 7, 9, in spite of the clear Christian significance of these numbers (the Trinity in particular), and for this he was attacked by William Wotton in his *Observations upon the Tale of a Tub* (1705). For further discussion of this important theoretical backround, see: Gretchen L. Finney, *Musical Backgrounds for English Literature, 1580–1650* (1962; reprinted Greenwood Press, Westport, Conn., 1976); John Hollander. *The Untuning of the Sky: Ideas of Music in English Poetry, 1500–1700* Princeton University Press, Princeton, N. J., 1961; and for Swift's period, chapter one of Douglas Brooks-Davies, *Number and Pattern in the Eighteenth-century Novel: Defoe, Fielding, Smollett and Sterne* (Routledge & Kegan Paul, London, 1973).

NATHANIEL ST ANDRE
An Extraordinary Effect of the Cholic
(1717)

Nathaniel St André (1680–1776), a notorious if skilful anatomist whose career nicely illustrates the companionship of credulity and science in the period. An unqualified practitioner, he first earned his living by fencing and as a dancing master. In 1723 he was appointed anatomist to the household of George I. Three years later he was totally persuaded by Mary Toft of Godalming that she had given birth to thirteen rabbits (in fact St André 'delivered' a couple himself), and rushed into print with *A Short Narrative of an Extraordinary Delivery of Rabbits* (1727). On confessing her fraud Mary Toft was committed to Bridewell for a time and St André's career was in ruins. Contemporary criticism was savage: Hogarth engraved his likeness as 'The Dancing-Master, or Praeternatural Anatomist', in 'Cunicularii, or the Wise Men of Godliman in consultation'. Previous to this he had been physician to Pope's friend Lord Peterborough and had actually treated Pope on one occasion (see *Correspondence of Alexander Pope*, II, 403: Bolingbroke to Swift, 1726). For a recent discussion of St André, see Marjorie Hope Nicolson and G. S. Rousseau, *'This Long Disease my Life': Alexander Pope and the Sciences* (Princeton University Press, Princeton, N. J., 1968).

Text taken from *Philosophical Transactions*, vol. XXX (1717).

1 peristaltick motion: the progressive movement of contraction and relaxation by which contents are forced down the intestine.
2 vasa lactea: lymphatic vessel which transmits chyle from the intestine.
3 miserere mei: literally, 'Take pity on me', the plea emitted by the victims of this intestinal pain, accompanied by vomiting.
4 chordapsus: a disease of the intestines.
5 Celsus (fl. A.D. 10–37), physician, author of the first scientific medical work in Latin, *De re medica*, and the first classical medical writer to be printed (in 1478).
6 omentum: a fold of the peritoneum connecting the stomach with other viscera (liver, spleen, etc.).
7 mesentery: peritoneal membrane which supports the small intestine.
8 bubonecele: hernia in the groin.
9 clyster: medicine injected into the rectum, and the syringe used.
10 jejunum: part of the small intestine.
11 ilium: lower part of the small intestine.
12 musculus scalenus: a triangular muscle.

JOHN LOCKE
A Letter to the Bishop of Worcester
(1697)

John Locke (1632–1704) was, to his contemporaries, second only to
Newton in intellectual stature. Educated at Westminster School and
Oxford, he mixed with the early founders of the Royal Society, including
Boyle, and was elected a Fellow of the Royal Society in 1668. Bachelor of
Medicine in 1674, he became personal physician and confidential
secretary to the Whig Earl of Shaftesbury (Dryden's false Achitophel)
from 1666 onwards. Locke was tainted by the suspicion of revolutionary
designs which fell on Shaftesbury's constant scheming to prevent the
Roman Catholic Duke of York from succeeding to the throne. He fled to
Holland in 1682 and in 1683 was deprived of his Oxford studentship by
Charles II. He returned to England at the Revolution in 1689 and rapidly
began to publish. The first letter on toleration (1689), the *Essay
Concerning Human Understanding* and the *Two Treatises of Government*
in 1690; *Some Thoughts Concerning Education* (1693); and *The
Reasonableness of Christianity* (1695). Only the *Essay* and the work on
education (written at the request of William Molyneux) were first printed
under his own name. The chronology of his controversy with Stillingfleet
on the doctrine of the Trinity dates from the *Essay* and Stillingfleet's
Discourse in Vindication of the Doctrine of the Trinity (1696). Locke
replied with *A Letter to the Bishop of Worcester* (January 1697), which
was answered by Stillingfleet in April. Locke published a second reply in
June and in 1698 Stillingfleet again went into print. Locke's final reply was
written in May 1698, but not published until 1699.

The text of Locke's *Letter to the Right Reverend Edward Lord Bishop
of Worcester* is from the first edition (1697).

The Locke–Stillingfleet controversy and its significance for Swift was
pointed out in an article by Rosalie B. Colie in the *History of Ideas
Newsletter*, II (1956), 58–62. (Its importance is out of all proportion to its
brevity.) Colie notes that Swift had easy access to all the works in this
controversy, because Archbishop Marsh acquired Stillingfleet's personal
library and installed it in Marsh's library in Dublin.

1   Bobaques: a burrowing squirrel found in Poland, i.e. an animal-name
     obscure enough not to possess information or associations
     concerning its nature.
2   Locke is offering Stillingfleet three names which have no a priori
     human connotations (unlike Peter, James and John). Swift's

analogous terms Yahoo and Houyhnhnm are similarly free of specifically human connotations.

EDWARD STILLINGFLEET
Answer to Mr Locke's Second Letter
(1698)

Edward Stillingfleet (1635–1699), bishop of Worcester and popular London preacher: Pepys described his sermons as 'plain, honest, good, grave'. Stillingfleet defended the divine authority of the Scriptures in *Origines Sacrae* (1662). He was on good terms with the nonconformists and in 1678 became Dean of St Paul's: he was nicknamed 'the beauty of holiness'. After his death his manuscripts (as opposed to his books) were bought by Robert Harley.

Text of *The Bishop of Worcester's Answer to Mr Locke's Second Letter; Wherein his Notion of Ideas is prov'd to be Inconsistent with it self, and with the Articles of the Christian Faith* from the first edition.

1 Drills: a West African species of baboon; the Swiftian element being the Yahoo. Johnson's *Dictionary* quotes Locke's usage: 'Shall the difference of hair be a mark of a different internal specifick constitution between a changeling and a *drill*, when they agree in shape and want of reason?' Cf. Gulliver's perplexing confrontation with the Yahoos in chapter two of the fourth voyage.

2 See Locke's *Essay Concerning Human Understanding*, Bk. II, ch. 11, 13.

SIR DANIEL DOLINS
The Third Charge . . . to the Grand-Jury
. . . of the County of Middlesex
(6 October 1726)

Introductory comments indicate that Dolins was chairman of the Middlesex magistrates and that this address was read at the General Quarter-Sessions, and published at the request of the Justices of the Peace for Middlesex county. The *Charge* (the last of three) demonstrates 'the Happiness of our Constitution under the auspicious Reign of his present Majesty, and . . . the Enjoyment of wise and prudent Laws'.

Text from the first, and only, printed edition. I owe my knowledge of this piece to the vigilance of Dr W. A. Speck.

Select bibliography

The standard reference bibliography for Swift's period is the *New Cambridge Bibliography of English Literature*, volume 2, 1660–1800, ed. George Watson (Cambridge University Press, 1971). See also J. E. Tobin, *Eighteenth-century Literature and its Cultural Background* (Fordham University Press, New York, 1939), and Stanley Pargellis and D. J. Medley, *Bibliography of British History: the Eighteenth Century* (Clarendon Press, Oxford, 1951). For Swift's work and its criticism see the following:

H. Teerink, ed., *A Bibliography of the Writings of Jonathan Swift* (1937), second edition revised and corrected by H. Teerink and Arthur H. Scouten (Philadelphia University Press, Philadelphia, 1963)

Louis Landa and J. E. Tobin, *Jonathan Swift: a List of Critical Studies Published from 1895 to 1945* (Cosmopolitan Science and Art Service, New York, 1945)

Milton Voigt, *Swift and the Twentieth Century* (Wayne State University Press, Detroit, 1964; contains an outline of modern reactions to Swift)

Claire Lamont, 'A checklist of critical and biographical writings on Jonathan Swift, 1945–65', in *Fair Liberty was All his Cry*, ed. A. Norman Jeffares (Macmillan, London, 1967)

The following suggestions are arranged in the order of topics discussed in this book:

Religion

Philip Harth, *Swift and Anglican Rationalism: the Religious Background of A Tale of a Tub* (Chicago University Press, Chicago, Ill., 1961)

R. A. Knox, *Enthusiasm: a Chapter in the History of Religion* (Clarendon Press, Oxford, 1950)

Ronald Paulson, *Theme and Structure in Swift's A Tale of a Tub* (Yale University Press, New Haven, Conn., 1960)

Ancients and Moderns

R. F. Jones, *Ancients and Moderns: a Study of the Rise of the Scientific Movement in Seventeenth-century England*, second edition (University of California Press, Berkeley and Los Angeles, 1965)

R. F. Jones, 'The background of the attack on science in the age of Pope', in *Pope and his Contemporaries*, ed. J. L. Clifford and Louis Landa (Oxford, Clarendon Press, 1949), 96–113

Church and State

Norman Sykes, *Church and State in England in the XVIIIth Century* (Cambridge University Press, 1934)

Geoffrey Holmes, *The Trial of Dr Sacheverell* (Methuen, London, 1973)

Geoffrey Holmes, ed., *Britain After the Glorious Revolution, 1689–1714* (Macmillan, London, 1969)

J. H. Plumb, *Sir Robert Walpole*, 2 vols. (Cresset Press, London, 1956, 1960)

Politics and parties

R. I. Cook, *Jonathan Swift as a Tory Pamphleteer* (Washington University Press, Seattle, 1967)

Geoffrey Holmes, *British Politics in the Age of Anne* (Macmillan, London, 1967)

Isaac Kramnick, *Bolingbroke and his Circle: the Politics of Nostalgia in the Age of Walpole* (Harvard University Press, Cambridge, Mass., 1968)

K. Feiling, *A History of the Tory Party, 1660–1714* (Oxford University Press, 1924)

Ireland

J. C. Beckett, *Protestant Dissent in Ireland, 1687–1780* (Faber & Faber, London, 1948)

O. W. Ferguson, *Jonathan Swift and Ireland* (Illinois University Press, Urbana, Ill., 1962)

Louis Landa, *Swift and the Church of Ireland* (Clarendon Press, Oxford, 1954)

Caroline Robbins, *The Eighteenth-century Commonwealthman* (Harvard University Press, Cambridge, Mass., 1961)

Science

K. Theodore Hoppen, *The Common Scientist in the Seventeenth Century: a History of the Dublin Philosophical Society, 1683–1708* (Routledge & Kegan Paul, London, 1970)

Marjorie M. Nicolson and Nora M. Mohler, 'The scientific background of Swift's *Voyage to Laputa*', *Annals of Science*, 2 (1937), 299–334

Marjorie Nicolson, *The Microscope and the English Imagination* (Smith College Studies in Modern Languages, Northampton, Mass., 1935)

Martha Ornstein, *The Role of Scientific Societies in the Seventeenth Century* (1913; University of Chicago Press, Chicago, Ill., 1938)

D. Stimson, *Scientists and Amateurs: a History of the Royal Society* (Henry Schuman, New York, 1948)

The nature of man

R. I. Aaron, *John Locke*, second edition (Clarendon Press, Oxford, 1955)

R. S. Crane, 'The Houyhnhnms, the Yahoos and the history of ideas', in *Reason and Imagination*, ed. J. A. Mazzeo (Routledge & Kegan Paul, London, 1962)

R. M. Frye, 'Swift's Yahoos and the Christian symbols for sin', *Journal of the History of Ideas*, XV (1954), 201–17.

Paul Fussell, *The Rhetorical World of Augustan Humanism: Ethics and Imagery from Swift to Burke* (Clarendon Press, Oxford, 1965)

D. G. James, *The Life of Reason: Hobbes, Locke, Bolingbroke* (Longmans, London, 1949)

Clive T. Probyn, ed., 'Swift and the human predicament', in *The Art of Jonathan Swift* (Vision Press, London, 1978), pp. 57–80.